THE UNMAKING OF SOVIET LIFE

CULTURE&SOCIETY
AFTER SOCIALISM
A SERIES EDITED BY
BRUCE GRANT&NANCY RIES

THE UNMAKING OF SOVIET LIFE

EVERYDAY ECONOMIES AFTER SOCIALISM

CAROLINE HUMPHREY

Cornell University Press Ithaca & London

First published 2002 by Cornell University Press
First printing, Cornell Paperbacks, 2002

Printed in the United States of America

Library of Congress Cataloging-in-Publication Data

Humphrey, Caroline.

The unmaking of Soviet life : everyday economies after socialism /
Caroline Humphrey.
    p. cm. — (Culture and society after socialism)
    Includes bibliographical references and index.
    ISBN 0-8014-3981-7 (cloth : alk. paper) — ISBN 0-8014-8773-0 (pbk.
: alk. paper)
    1. Russia (Federation)—Economic conditions—1991– . 2.
Post-communist—Russia (Federation) 3. Russia (Federation)—Social
conditions—1991– . 4. Mongolia—Economic conditions. 5.
Post-communism—Mongolia—Social conditions.   I. Title.
II. Series.
  HC340.12 .H86 2002
  330.947—dc21   2001005841

Cornell University Press strives to use environmentally responsible
suppliers and materials to the fullest extent possible in the
publishing of its books. Such materials include vegetable-based,
low-VOC inks and acid-free papers that are recycled, totally
chlorine-free, or partly composed of nonwood fibers. For further
information, visit our website at www.cornellpress.cornell.edu.

Cloth printing   10 9 8 7 6 5 4 3 2 1
Paperback printing   10 9 8 7 6 5 4 3 2 1

CONTENTS

ILLUSTRATIONS

Note: All photographs are by the author unless otherwise noted in legend.

FOREWORD
THE SHIFTING FIELDS
OF CULTURE AND SOCIETY
AFTER SOCIALISM

The formerly socialist world represents one of the fastest-growing and theoretically challenging areas in the humanities and social sciences. With perestroika and its legacies, the very contours of field studies after socialism are being fundamentally reshaped. In anthropology, for example, where fieldwork has always been the flagship, the former Soviet Union was all but closed to ethnographic research and regular scholarly exchanges from the early 1930s onward. The opening of borders in the 1990s brought a heady atmosphere of new possibilities: sustained conversations with specialists from across the socialist world, a return to more engaged field studies, and new access to archives. But the very drama of events also created a certain breathlessness, as the challenges of mapping such change overwhelmed more traditionally grounded historical and cultural analysis.

Over a decade later, we can begin to chart the topography of a diverse realm of new scholarship, built on the theoretical and methodological foundations of cross-disciplinary work. "Culture and Society after Socialism" looks to present the very best of this body of writing. Providing close-up perspectives on the lived experience of socialism and its aftermath, this series advances innovative work that fundamentally rethinks the cultural projects of socialist states and their outcomes. Through detailed readings of historical and cultural contexts, these works bridge the study of power systems and cosmologies, material practices and social meanings, political economies and the mythic forces that sustain them.

We see new work in and about the formerly socialist world as a vital opportunity to reconsider the analytical boundaries of area studies and their respective scholarly traditions. For example, whether Russia and its eastern European neighbors may one day be reclassified as "Western" seems less compelling than asking how communist cultural projects came to dialogue so provocatively with European enlightenment discourses of progress, sovereignty, and modernism and how that dialogue shifted and twisted during the Soviet era. Or, to move away from European frames, we might ponder the extent to which Slavic Studies can encourage greater intellectual porosity among the many world traditions under its banner. To speak of "North Asia" or "West Asia" seems almost oxymoronic under the confines of conventional areal divides, given the dominance of East and Southeast in Asian Studies. Yet millions of former Soviet citizens come from Asias North, West, and Central. By one logic, Uzbekistan may be "Central" to Asia, but not necessarily to Asian studies. By another logic, the country is too far west to be part of the "Middle East," somehow an entirely separate world area despite a well documented shared history driven by centuries of Islam and Silk Road trade.

Historically, most of us are trained to look for the "modern" at the threshold of Renaissance Europe. Yet, as Ernest Gellner (1981) and many others have pointed out, Islam's orthodox visions of egalitarianism, literacy, and transnational fellowship made it one of modernism's earliest harbingers. Where and when, then, does the modern begin? By inviting fresh perspectives that challenge these kinds of analytical and spatial boundaries, we gain a richer sense of socialism's pasts and futures. Might the postsocialist conditions of today be conceived, for example, as postcolonial? And if so, how might this reconfigure our now-conventional guides to the postcolonial condition? These are only a handful of questions that follow from mapping a world that has been always in flux.

Historically, socialist area studies have been expert at chronicling what Hegel called simply, "difference"—not the "blank pages" of everyday life but revolutions and state refracted through a focus on political and economic change. In the former Soviet Union, for example, this has led to tremendously rich coverage of 1917, the avant-garde experiments of the 1920s and 1930s, and the horrors of Stalinism and World War II. But scholars have had far less to say about the implied "blank pages" of post-Stalinist life in general or Brezhnev-era late socialism in particular. Was the *vremia zastoia,* or "time of stagnation"—the phrase so commonly associated with the late socialist era—really so stagnant after all? Only the briefest look at the shifts in popular culture of the 1960s and 1970s, the sexual and consumer revolutions of that era, ongoing environmental and social engineering, agro-industrial experiments, and nationalist movements suggest not. Yet scholarship is only beginning to come to grips with the increasingly available (and extremely diverse) records of that era.

Today, the prospects for new work richly informed by conversation, debate, and reading across national and disciplinary traditions are particularly clear. But this fact also raises the bar for breadth and depth of intellectual engagement: certainly the strongest work being done takes the intellectual traditions of the formerly socialist world quite seriously—not only as sources of empirical knowledge but as theoretical frames guiding innovative approaches to pressing issues.

The work of anthropologist Caroline Humphrey provides a sound beginning for our new series. Best known for her magisterial work, *Karl Marx Collective: Economy and Society in a Siberian Collective Farm* (1983, reprinted and updated as *Marx Went Away* in 1999), Humphrey has long been probing at the interstices of anthropological knowledge, structures of authority, economic practices, and everyday religious life in the former Soviet Union and abroad. Trained in social anthropology at Cambridge University, Humphrey made her first trip to eastern Siberia in 1967 and became one of only a handful of non-Soviet scholars to conduct even limited field studies in the former Soviet Union for two decades afterward. *Karl Marx Collective*, based on that first trip and a later visit in 1975, took what seemed to many scholars before her a stultifyingly massive, unreadable literature on Soviet economic theory and revealed therein a stunningly rich world of multiple and often competing realities, where enterprises relied on the very plasticity of socialist-era language to achieve often unrealizable goals. It was a tour de force, gleaned from remarkably creative use of variously constrained field researches and careful attention to long-available materials which had rarely been taken as seriously by others. In 1990, Humphrey was awarded anthropology's highest book award, the Staley Prize, in recognition of this work. A leader in the field of Inner Asia, she has done extensive fieldwork in Buriatia, Mongolia, central Russia, Nepal, India, and China. She is widely known outside Soviet studies for her many books and articles on ritual theory, shamanism, barter and exchange, nomadism, environmental conservation, and cultural politics.

In this volume, we bring together ten of Humphrey's essays that best indicate the deep study of what socialism meant to those who lived it and to those who wrestle today with its reincarnations. Each chapter demonstrates how everyday life in a variety of settings, from the villas of the new Russian rich to pilgrimage sites on the steppe outside Ulaanbaatar, is underwritten by deeply historicized local knowledge of both the presocialist and the socialist epochs. These are legacies that are everywhere being refashioned in myriad ways. Taking her trademark lead from the extensive writings of Russian, Buriat, and Mongolian colleagues, Caroline Humphrey reads the postsocialist world as a space of often agonizing, often hopeful reformation in a time of upheaval. These articles richly illustrate how much is at stake in laboring to understand what socialism meant to those who lived it, and where they look from here.

B. G. AND N. R.

NOTE ON TRANSLITERATION

The transliteration of Russian words follows the Library of Congress system. Soft signs and hard signs from the Russian language are recognized with one and two primes, respectively. General exceptions are made for accepted Western spellings such as Yeltsin, rather than El'tsyn, and Buriatia rather than Buriatiia.

The transliteration of Buriat and Mongolian words follows Cheremisov (1973) and that of Mongolian follows Haltod et al. (1982). An exception is made for *oboo* (sacred cairn) which is the usual spoken pronunciation of both Buriats and Mongols.

ABBREVIATIONS AND TERMS

ASSR
(Russian) Avtonomnaia Sovetskaia Sotsialisticheskaia Respublika
Autonomous Soviet Socialist Republic.
CIS
Commonwealth of Independent States.
DMP
Domestic Mode of Production.
GULAG
(Russian) Gosudarstvennoe Upravlenie Lagerei. State Directorate for
[Prison and Labor] Camps.
Khubi
(Buriat *khuv'*; Mongolian *xubi,* modern spelling *xuv'*).
Share or lot, held by labor, fate, or destiny.
Krysha
(Russian) literally, "roof"—widespread slang for protection services
offered by Russian mafia, police, or state authorities.
Oboo
(Buriat *ovoo;* Mongolian *obug-a,* modern spelling *ovoo*). Sacred cairn.
NEP
(Russian) Novaia Ekonomicheskaia Politika.
New Economic Policy (1921–1928).
SSR
(Russian) Sovetskaia Sotsialisticheskaia Respublika.
Soviet Socialist Republic.
Sotka
(Russian; gen. pl., *sotok*) A measurement of one hundred square meters.

RSFSR
  (Russian) Rossiiskaia Sovetskaia Federativnaia Sotsialisticheskaia
  Respublika. Russian Soviet Federated Socialist Republic.
Ulus
  (from Buriat *ulas;* Mongolian *uls,* people or state).
  Widely used to refer to a community or village.

INTRODUCTION

A decade has passed since the end of the communist regimes in Russia and Mongolia and the disintegration of the structures that gave meaning to so many people's lives. The collapse of Party rule, the ending of full employment, massive inflation after decades of stable prices, a labyrinth of new, widely disobeyed laws, and the chasm of unbelief opened after the rejection of the Soviet ideology all combined to cast people into a state of radical uncertainty. As the years passed, it became evident that the promised "transition" to prosperous market democracy was not going to happen in the near future, if at all. Accustomed institutions were disintegrating and decaying, and it seemed that only "wild" moneymaking and big-man politics were taking their place. Russians were used to inequality of status, but now suddenly miserable poverty came to exist alongside soaring, inexplicable wealth. The havoc, apparently, was interminable. Depression set in as ordinary people reviewed careers overturned and the tangle of obstacles that seemed to confront every glimmer of opportunity. Yet it is impossible for people to live without making some sense of the world around them. In fact, although people may see the above-mentioned processes as "happening to them," they themselves have been and are participants. This book is a chronicle of the dismantling of Soviet life that at the same time has brought about many new kinds of activity and new rationales. Its chapters were written as events were taking place, so they participate in the unfinished character of the times. But my hope is that we can perceive some emergent contours and thus be helped to think about how the myriad everyday actions of thinking people ultimately establish new forms of political economy.

The unmaking and making of relations, and the metamorphosis of those that have persisted, have been extraordinary. Yet the period has not had the character of a classic revolution, in the sense of an abrupt overturning of society led by a determined group from the top. Social changes have also come from inside and below. Some of them were also started "before," that is, they began under different conditions in Soviet times and later morphed into new phenomena in the postsocialist quasi-market situation, like the racketeering structures I describe in Chapter 5. Their complex incremental presence, underpinned by ordinary people's enduring abilities for reconstituting particular kinds of social relationships, has blocked many an initiative from Moscow. One thinks, for example, of the way rural collectives resisted the attempt in 1992–93 to set up private farming, or of how more recently new regional power blocs in the provinces have failed to fall in line with Vladimir Putin's policy of centralizing political control. It is precisely these obstinately resistant social forms—difficult-to-define, uneven, and transmuting as they are—that have persisted and become entrenched. Yet at the same time, their legitimacy, economic weight, and rationale for existence have altered profoundly. Perhaps the very intensity of this process in Russia can throw light on similar processes that may be less obvious in more stable situations in other countries.

In this introduction I explain the theoretical background to my approach to the anthropology of economic life, as this is only implicit in the chapters that follow. Anthropology's strength is its rootedness in the everyday, in its familiarity with the practices that ethnographers are able to observe and question. Anthropologists are unlike economists who, whatever their approach, need to define an abstract category of "the economic" and make predictive statements on this basis. At least since Geertz and the abandonment of functionalism, structuralism, neo-Marxism and all those other -isms that propose or deduce self-existent social categories, anthropologists have tended to conceive their objects in terms of meaning, that is, requiring interpretation. Since the reflexive turn of the 1980s, they have understood that such "objects" are both discovered and created, in other words that they are in some aspect an artifact of the anthropological process itself. Following the impact of Gramsci, Foucault, and others, anthropology has become increasingly aware of the dynamics of power in ordinary, sometimes unconceptualized and even unconscious relations, such as those regarding persons and the self. These are almost commonplaces of contemporary anthropology, but applying them to everyday economic activity, as this book does, yields something distinctive. Complex modern economies are normally understood in terms of broad, unclear categories, such as capitalism, "actually existing socialism," or globalization, which require explanations if observed facts do not fit the models. With an anthropological approach, on the other hand—at any rate, the one I take—one may start with the exception, as it were. To put this another way, one is enabled to take almost any event or action as significant in itself and representing no more than itself. But because the anthropologist "sees it" in all its dimensions of interpretability, createdness, and capacity for containing implicit power, this action can also be read for what it connotes about the world in which it exists.

A second distinctive feature of this approach as applied to economies is its requirement to conceptualize historical process. An economist normally sets out to determine what would happen if rational actors took decisions, "other things being equal" in a given situation, according to academically interesting models of behavior. The more abstract the resulting formula, and the more it can be held to apply over time and in various circumstances, the greater its explanatory power and success is held to be. Anthropologists, in contrast, work closer to the grain, aware of the actual flux of "objects" in time. Other things are never equal for them. Their very tools of the trade, or the ideas they come up with, whether this be Strathern's "dividual person" (1988), Appadurai's notions of "scapes" (1991), or Taussig's "mimesis" (1993), tend to be attempts to delineate some frame for understanding mutation and process.

The economy might seem to dissolve with such an approach, but the decisions, actions, relations, and institutions that make "it" up do not. On the contrary, they are held up to question by being subjected to a more rigorous (because more attentive) scrutiny. The task, as I see it, is to make a situation intelligible by means of general observations while revealing the spaces available to individuals to take particular decisions among a range of conceivable actions. This approach, which attempts to convey the sense that the actor has some freedom to think and speak, differs from one that would see him or her as "acting out" a Durkheimian system of meanings. True, to demonstrate a general point I have often used the method of providing specific cases to exemplify what might be said *characteristically* from within a given theorized position (for example, from "marginality," Tsing 1993). A case in point is my discussion of the narratives of the "dispossessed" in Chapter 2, which contrasts the mythic speech types characteristic of different subject positions I have delineated. But I hope also to convey the fact that what actors say or do is but one of the things they might have said or done, thus emphasizing the constitutive energy of the creative and responsive/responsible act. No doubt other approaches might be suitable if one defined the problem as one of "transition" to some specific new type of society. But how else to proceed if we are dealing with a time of uncertainty, when each action is both the unmaking of a previous way of life and a step toward a new, unknown one?

What kind of general characterizations can be made? Most books about postsocialist change take certain big notions for granted, such as the market or electoral democracy or the global economy, and one import of this book is certainly to say, "hold on a minute." An obvious reason to take pause is that these generally accepted ideas have run into the sands in Russia. "The market" is there, and yet somehow it does not operate as theory predicts, and the same is true of "electoral democracy" and other such categories developed to explain Euro-American actualities. Yet it would be a mistake to take the line that the standard concepts are fine in the abstract but they do not work in Russia, having simply run foul of something called "Russian culture." First, this would ignore the point made by several anthropologists (Zelizer 1997, Carrier 1997, Dilley 1992) that "the market" always has its being in one culture or another. Secondly, we are forced into the position of essentializing Russian culture, seeing it as an obstacle, as something preventing people from acting as "anyone" might, that is, according to the presumed default position of the universal market actor. To the extent that cultural dispositions influence how people behave, it would be absurd in my view to see them only as hindrances, rather than enabling. The task is to understand what they enable.

The havoc of the postcommunist period gives us an excuse to abandon certain accepted categories, not only assumptions about markets. but also the ubiquitous and hoary stereotypes of "Russian culture." For a start this book indicates that we have to take account of common responses across post-Soviet space, aligning Russians with non-Russian peoples such as the Buriats, Tyvans, and Mongolians. Some attitudes, such as those toward labor and property, seem to be very widespread among diverse peoples and could be described as "Soviet" rather than Russian (Anderson 2000, Grant 1995). So it is not an accident that the epithet "Soviet" has been replaced by a similarly all-inclusive idea. The term, *rossianin,* has reappeared—in the nineteenth century it meant "citizen of the Russian Empire"—to denote the post-Socialist status of a citizen, of any ethnicity, of the Russian Federation (Balzer 1999). At the same time, some excellent new ethnographies are beginning to appear that reveal the subtleties of what it is to be specifically a Russian (Pesmen 2000, Ries 1997). This book aims to convey something of the great range of cultural ways of being and doing in the post-Soviet world, from Moscow through Siberia to Mongolia. The reader will learn particularly about Buriatia in Eastern Siberia, the kinds of relatedness cultivated there and the part-Buddhist, part-shamanistic values of the Buriat people. We do not need to reify Russian culture, or any other culture, to accept that some combination of previous ways, beliefs, and habits of mind, many of which could be categorized as Soviet or post-Soviet, forms repertoires by means of which people can make sense of their activities. These meanings are important because, while they do not determine how people will act, they condition how an act is perceived. and hence the frame in which subsequent actions are undertaken. At the same time, these repertoires of the imagination enable people to construe whole social fields or emerging institutions.

Let me give an example, taken from the first essay in the book, to explain how local cultural interpretations not only condition action but can also provide pointers about the way people conceive general social configurations, enabling us as anthropologists to come up with ideas that can be tried out as explanations. In "Icebergs, Barter, and the Mafia," I describe how in Buriatia even as early as 1990 people were beginning to talk of local economies in terms of enclaves and fiefdoms, while they characterized outsider consumers as "army troops" coming in to clear out resources. Although the precise conditions of shortage and rationing of the late 1980s came to an end by 1991, this way of thinking has persisted and has been an important influence on subsequent local policies, such as the limitations on interdistrict movement of goods and the repressive measures meted out to nonlocal traders (see Chapter 4). It was the metaphor of the "fiefdom" used by ordinary people that gave me the insight that local political economies in general might indeed be coming to be run as "suzerainties." I am grateful to Katherine Verdery for taking up this idea and theorizing it comprehensively in her chapter "A Transition from Socialism to Feudalism? Thoughts on the Postsocialist State" (Verdery 1996, 204–228). The idiom of feudalism has continued to be resilient in Russia. In 2000, while doing research on bribery, I found that people were talking about the purchase of office as *dan'* (tribute) and the receivers of such payments as *malen'kie khoziaieva, malen'kie kniazi* (small masters, small princes). In 2001, the miserable condition of workers in collective farms was described to me as "serfdom" (*krepostnoe pravo*), referring to the fact that for most of the Soviet period, peasants did not have internal passports and could not leave the farm, while today they are tied to the village by poverty. As I was told by one Buriat economist, "The collective farmers under socialism were subject to administrative serfdom. Today they are subject to economic serfdom. Their plots are too small to produce a surplus, and even if they succeeded there is no public transport now and they cannot take produce to market on their backs. They have to rely on the collective farm to plough their land as they have no machines. That means they have no alternative but to bow to the farm leadership, to give their labor at any rate the boss will offer. The vast majority cannot even escape to the city—they don't have the money to pay to get there. What is that but serfdom?"

Of course, such a vision of hopeless entrapment does not represent the same relations as the feudal ties of the past. We are not in fact seeing that impossibility, a rerun of history (apart from a host of other differences, the legal-political status of "serf" does not exist today). But the point I am trying to make here is that such metaphors express something important about how people are thinking about the changing social world around them. They are grasping at an actuality they do not feel they fully understand, and yet by speaking metaphorically they enable us to see that the formations that are taking shape through their actions are part of worlds of the imagination and also ethically valued positively or negatively. This cannot but affect what happens in the future, since the ongoing reproduction of a relationship or an organization is influenced by what people *think it is.*

The chapters in this book were written at different times with various aims in mind, and I have grouped them here into three sections in order to convey something of their content. In Part One I show how, in different ways, people have struggled to create "localities" (their own worlds of value, following Appadurai 1991, 199; 1996) in the context of disintegrating Soviet institutions and wildly fluctuating prices. The general message here is that it continues to be impossible to disentangle the "economic" from the "political" in postsocialist Russia, and that, as in Soviet times, the political economy of the *kollektiv* (collective)—which can of course be defined at many levels from the household to society as a whole—implied not only enmeshing power struggles among those situated within but also a "moral economy" that reifies social boundaries and stigmatizes those cast outside (Kharkhordin 1999). In Chapter 1, I show how in the early 1990s familiar institutions, such as the collective farm, were subject to a process of economic attrition, causing the "clinging on" to ever scarcer resources, which at the same time implied the ejection of those considered expendable. Chapter 2 discusses some theories to analyze the different ways in which this process was envisioned and mythicized by those viewing the world from inside and those expelled. Meanwhile, in the sphere of consumption, the theme of Chapter 3, people even in the metropolitan city of Moscow around 1993 were concerned about delimiting "our" native products from the incoming "foreign" goods. Analyzing this situation enabled me to suggest that consumption is not only a matter of acquisition and personal identity signification but can also be a more socially general, localizing, and moralizing economic practice.

In Part Two, I analyze how the frontier spaces and gaps between local polities are exploited by new categories of actors and activities. Chapter 4 describes polities such as provincial republics, provinces, or cities as hierarchical acquisitive-cum-bargaining units, and it shows why the interstitial activity of mobile traders, who make profits from the existence of localized resources and demands, is regarded with suspicion and seen as creating "disorder." Regional sectors of the old Soviet state have morphed into entrepreneurial administrations that come down heavily on even minor challengers to their monopolistic system of control. At the same time, ordinary people have always sought to negotiate their own way through the anterooms of the state "castle," and Chapter 6 outlines one such strategy, describing the changing contours of bribery. The other chapter in this section discusses the cultural world of racketeers. These are people who use the threat of force to leech profits from any weakly protected resource, in so doing creating parallel relations of power within and beyond legitimate institutions. I argue here that a functional or rational-choice approach is insufficient to explain the particular ethos or cultural resources that racketeers employ to explain their activities to themselves and to obtain a hold over their clients.

Part Three takes up in various ways the question of how people constitute and imagine personhood in postsocialist social space. Chapter 7 examines issues of trust, theft, and personal responsibility in the context of a new shrine in Mongolia, where donations are left out in the open. In Chapter 8, I return to the social world of the collective farm and issues raised by the unity of the political and the economic in everyday life. How is personhood imagined in such a situation? Using Marshall Sahlins's idea of the "domestic mode of production" as a foil, I suggest that the person in this context appears as an actor in power relations that subsume the economic. I argue that the "exchange model" of social relations derived from Mauss cannot be used for all transactions and that in the Inner Asian cultural context other models, based on domination, obedience, and obligation may be more salient. The final two chapters of the book move to the urban scene. Chapter 9 describes the difficulties, subversions, and contestations surrounding the identity of the "New Russians," those who have made wealth in the new economy. Their villas, and their material culture more generally, are the medium through

which these battles are analyzed. The last chapter moves back to the predica-
ments of ordinary people and the new ways they are attempting to explain
fortune and, more particularly, misfortune. In many parts of Russia, including Buriatia, the scientific explanations of professionals have lost ground to
the "irrational" answers given by shamans and seers. Yet this phenomenon
should not be seen merely as an unfortunate aberration to be swept under
the carpet as a sad psychological reaction of no consequence. The chapter
shows how shamans are consciously creating new social relations between
the city dwellers and their half-forgotten kin in distant villages, and how the
value given to these magical-spiritual links is inextricably tied to the economic exchanges between the town and the countryside. Shamanic activity
thus revitalizes a sense of personhood in which the actor is made aware of
himself/herself as a channel (or joining part) between different yet complex
worlds, between rural poverty and the opportunities (political, monetary,
educational) of the city on one hand and between the absolute occult threat
of the country spirits and the misfortunes of urban life on the other. In the
"lived world" (Weiss 1996) of many post-Soviet people, the mundane and
the magical are intimately related.

I would like to end this introduction with some observations about specific
changes that have taken place since these chapters were written and with a few
more general thoughts about the emerging contours of postsocialist life.

Some quite minor changes show intriguing linkages between topics covered in different chapters here, while they also illustrate the theme of the
book as a whole, the unmaking of earlier ways of living and the putting together of new ones. For example, Chapter 4 describes how Chinese traders in
eastern Siberian cities, lacking both intimate understanding of local society
and their own traditions of aggression-protection, were the unfortunate
subjects of repeated raids by the police. I have heard recently that while this
is still true in Buriatia, in the city of Khabarovsk in eastern Siberia traders
have acquired "mafia" protection. This is a symptom of the consolidation in
Russian society of the "roof," the form of illicit protection (present already
in Soviet times) that burgeoned into virtually all spheres of post-Soviet life,
including government circles. For the Chinese traders the "roof" is provided
by Russian Koreans, who form a series of links between Korean racketeer-
protectors in the markets and Korean town officials. Now these Koreans had
themselves been persecuted earlier. They were farmers who had been removed en masse by Stalin from eastern Siberia to Central Asia. There they
came to flourish during the late Soviet decades (again as farmers and market

gardeners), but in the 1990s they were squeezed out of countries like Uzbeki-stan by national policies discriminating against people seen as outsiders. Themes discussed in Chapters 2, 4, and 5 thus combine here. Utterly adapted to life in Soviet contexts, having lost their language and hence not oriented to a return to Korea, some of these "Russian Koreans" moved to what was for them a new niche (the combination of racketeering, business, and city man-agement). This venture should not be seen merely as a "survival strategy" un-dertaken as a meaningless last resort. It is one attempt to make a whole new life, with all that that implies as regards identity and commitment. For the migration to eastern Siberia is imagined by the Koreans as a *return home,* as that is the land their grandparents were deported from.[1] This is an example of a very general phenomenon of the post-Soviet world, of how certain cate-gories of people are perceiving opportunities, moving out of their previous niches, and creating new social forms with their own rationales and inner tensions (see also Humphrey 2000). Already, the sum of such shifts is alter-ing the contours of the previously familiar social world.

Another example of this kind is what has happened with consumption, especially in major cities. If the rationing described in Chapter 1 is long gone, and the obsessive concern with "our" (as opposed to "foreign") products is now a relatively muted version of what I observed in 1993 (see Chapter 3), the use of material objects to denote status is alive and well. An interesting paper by Oushakine (2000) suggests that the consumption patterns of the wealthy have a particular character. They denote style by quantity, that is, by the ac-quisition of more of a limited range of status goods, as opposed to the branching out into a variety of items to signify difference from the *hoi polloi.* My study of the "New Russians" (Chapter 9) noted this feature, and indeed it uses almost exactly the same anecdote as Oushakine to characterize it. But what Oushakine adds is a perceptive analysis of such patterns (and the way they are interpreted by other young people who are not rich themselves) in terms of the inherited cultural logic of Soviet consumption habits. People, he writes, choose to understand "the taste of luxury" in terms of the "taste of necessity" (2000, 115). While the dominant Soviet pattern of consumption has been dismantled (in those days scarce, state-distributed goods were of necessity what people mostly consumed), the everyday practices associated with scarcity have persisted. Buy more if you can! But as several chapters in this book show, the old practices cannot but mean something different in the turbulent life of today. There is still scarcity, but this is no longer a matter of inadequate distribution. It is caused by poverty, by not being able to afford to buy what is available. The contours of desire and the symbolism of attainment must be different under these circumstances.

Collective farms, under whatever name, still exist in much of the Russian countryside, and most of them are in a ruinous economic state (Humphrey 1998). In the late 1990s, widespread de-monetization forced them to operate almost entirely by barter—itself a new twist on the old pattern of distributing goods between enterprises according to the plan. The new barter is conducted within the highly disadvantageous ("exploitative," "feudal," as Buriat farmers said) price limits set by the regional government (Humphrey 1998, 2000). Yet this very structure of barter is only seemingly a retrograde move. Perhaps it should be seen as a set of conditions for a radical transformation, for I am reliably informed that many farm directors are seeking to escape from it by creating an innovative economic experiment. They are setting up inter-enterprise cooperative networks with local manufacturers and suppliers of services.[2] This is also done by barter, but now on the farm's own initiative and on their own terms. A farm, for example, pays meat to an electricity substation for current, gives products to another local firm to provide oil and gas, sends its milk to the school to provide education, and so forth. This movement is likely to spread, as it enables farms to obtain the local value of their products, as opposed to the very low prices offered by the government as monopolistic purchaser. We may see the transformation of the Russian countryside as the collectives disintegrate and become smaller, more specialized members of wider regional "barter cooperatives" along with other businesses. What is innovative about this is not just that farmers are turning their backs on the government set-up and taking their own initiative, but also that—after decades of accepting prices decided somewhere "above"—they are perforce generating the real value of their own products in the locality and thereby creating a new kind of economic knowledge. If these experiments are successful, the whole in-turned, collective-minded, resource-guarding perspective described in the early chapters of this book may mutate into a different view of the world, one that values the mutuality with others enabled by the cooperative networks.

The "escape" from governments is also imagined as the creation of more equal and trusting relations in a world that is seen to be generally rapacious and threatening. The aggressiveness of everyday life has only increased since the chapters of this book were written. In fact, the image of the iceberg (using the English term) is still prevalent in Russia, suggesting that what we see is only the tip of something huge and dangerous hidden underneath.

Even more commonly, the idea that official institutions are pervaded with corruption is expressed by the word "shadow" (*tenevaia ekonomika,* the shadow economy). In addition to its sinister connotations, ordinary people have told me that they see "shadow" as referring to the inevitability of its presence—because nothing can exist without its shadow. In this way people are pointing to what is perhaps the most salient characteristic of emerging social relations in Russia, the participation in—but not necessarily the acceptance of—harsh practices of advantage and demonstrations of power. For this is what the "shadow" consists of, the unlegitimized intervention of threat into economic activity. In a recent book *Rynki vlasti* [Markets of Power] (2000), Simon Kordonskii has argued that the Soviet system was founded on practices of power bargaining that have persisted as the operational method of reproduction of the Russian social formation. Many ordinary people today imagine the new modes of authority rather differently, not as an ordered system but as the all-too-visible naked desire for power of certain individuals and the outcome of that—the erratic turmoil and pressure that takes place in the realm of "shadows." Especially in the provinces, where all the institutions and their bosses are well known, and where officials are widely held to be in league with one another, people (women especially) often have to submit to unreasonable demands or face being sacked or punished. The harshness of this world has only intensified since I began my work. As I was told sadly, "You know the saying that rule is carried out by the whip (*knut*) and the cake (*prianik*)? Well the cake part doesn't seem to work so well in Russia. No one believes in it. It's just a mirage." Yet people by no means mentally or practically accept these conditions. They protest and lament (Ries 1997). Countless acts of support and kindness in actuality counter the prevailing hostility and adversity. Indeed, anyone talking to a large number of people in Russia would understand that living through a process of cruel "unmaking" of an accustomed way of life at the same time sharpens the will to profit personally *and* sensitizes the moral faculty. I therefore maintain that one simple message of this book obtains: the everyday economies of Russia are a site of ethical choices, and from this some new, possibly more benign arrangements are bound to emerge.

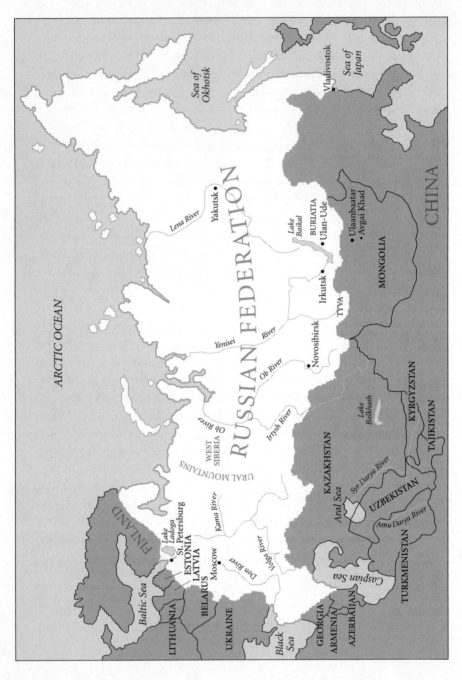

Russia, Mongolia, and the Former Soviet Union

PART I
THE POLITICS OF LOCALITY IN AN UNSTABLE STATE

INTRODUCTION TO PART I

The force and scope of the social upheavals centered in the Soviet bloc in the 1980s and 1990s transformed the geopolitical landscape with effects that continue to be felt globally. However, the very magnitude of these social, political, and economic transformations has often obscured the myriad, smaller-scale—but still enormous—dislocations that inhabitants of formerly Soviet territories have experienced. These dislocations are sometimes broadly and literally spatial, as for millions who suddenly found themselves keenly unwanted in new nation-states where many have lived for generations. Harder to grasp from outside the post-Soviet world are the many forms of social and symbolic dislocation produced by the upending and rupturing of state institutions of every kind.

Chapter 1, "'Icebergs,' Barter, and the Mafia in Provincial Russia" chronicles the unfolding of forms of resource protection that superficially resemble those of earlier Soviet eras but also diverge from these in key ways and portend the rise of the vast "protection regimes" to come. These regimes include the rackets of the familiar mafia organizations, but more significant for the people of Ulan-Ude, Tyva, and other provincial regions Humphrey describes are the development of almost feudal, self-protective "suzerainties" which tightly control access to every category of goods, whether it be cheese or carpets, sausage or apartments. Deploying complex systems of food cards, coupons, talons, and workplace provisioning to construct their regulatory "palisades" against incoming "foreigners," local bosses reconfigure themselves as patrons whose power increases as shortages grow. Originally published in 1991, at a key moment when the location of the powers of state became increasingly unclear, this chapter presciently anticipates much of what is to come in the way of enterprise transformation, the "potato economy," the expanding role of barter professionals, and the legal chaos of local law-making and "protection" as a broad social phenomenon. In fixing our gaze on all of these, "Icebergs" vividly foreshadows the spread of those very mechanisms that have proven durable barriers to the growth of free markets.

What happens to those who find themselves outside those protective barricades? How are social identities of inclusion and exclusion discursively produced and reified? These are questions engaged in Chapter 2, "Mythmaking, Narratives, and the Dispossessed." Taking as its starting point recognition of the enterprise as the "primary unit of Soviet society" (Clarke 1992)—the nexus of security, provisioning, identity, and locality for a Soviet citizen—Humphrey describes the terrible fate of those suddenly dispossessed, "people who have been deprived of property, work, and entitlements"—whether through voluntary or involuntary migration, unemployment, military demobilization, or other modes of dis/relocation. Spatially, socially, and symbolically interstitial within a system organized around the fixity of institutional emplacement, such categories of person are central to the mythicized defining and redefining of citizenship, status, security, and space. Interactions between the still-rooted and the dispossessed mark current disturbances of moral, temporal, and political order. Meanwhile, in the same historical moment, the mythos of possession and the nurturing/stifling surround of Soviet/post-Soviet social domains is ritually rejected by urban youth gangs even as they root themselves in those very domains.

From the late 1980s onward, trading and consumption became ever larger aspects of the construction of social space and symbolic value, but this enlargement took place within complexly nested domains of local and global, which themselves rested in a broad shadow of profound cynicism and suspicion. Chapter 3, "Creating a Culture of Disillusionment," gives new meaning to the notion of "consumer crises"—as Humphrey portrays the moral vertigo that accompanied any commodity transaction within a marketplace of constantly shifting signification and social relations. Where local public markets are seen by many as "huge fairs of disingenuousness" and the global market is widely envisioned as "the domain of the great deception," the personal and political cultures created through consumption are marked by disappointment, bewilderment, and fear. For many, retreat to the nonmarket realms of family, dacha, and subsistence production, and even nostalgia for the Soviet queue are not merely responses to poverty, but may also reflect a symbolic turn towards (mythicized?) moral clarity.

B. G. AND N. R.

CHAPTER 1
"ICEBERGS," BARTER, AND THE MAFIA IN PROVINCIAL RUSSIA

Late at night, I was driving through the streets of Ulan-Ude with a Buriat friend, and I saw a crowd of people huddled against the wall of a dark building, their shoulders turned against the wind.[1] I asked my friend what they were doing. "Ah, that is the queue for gold," he replied. "They stand there all night, and in the morning many more people come. Even though gold is so expensive, for the last two years everyone has been trying to get hold of it. They even buy and sell places in the queue."

A move to gold indicates a lack of trust in the value of the ruble. In Russia today this is combined, as everyone knows, with severe shortages of goods in the shops, general inflation and impossibly high prices in markets, production blockages in farms and factories, a chaotic legal situation, and the introduction of "rationing." But I believe that the social implications of the situation are less well known and understood, and it is these that I address in this chapter. One might imagine a parallel with the time after World War II, when many of these economic features were present. However, for reasons that will become clear below, the present situation should be seen as different even from that of Russia in the 1940s. Perhaps internal historical analogies can be drawn for some aspects of what is happening today, but they also are to be found further afield, and anthropology may be useful to elucidate them.

We can begin with a very brief outline of the situation in provincial Russia. The declaration of "sovereignty" and other forms of autonomy vis-à-vis the USSR, not just by the RSFSR but by regions within it, such as the Buriat ASSR, and districts within regions, such as the Aga Buriat Autonomous Okrug, means that there is widespread uncertainty about government and law at "higher" levels of the body politic. Consequently, organizations and enterprises in the regions, run in a personal way almost as local corporations, or what I call "suzerainties," by local bosses, have strengthened themselves and increased their social functions to protect their members. What are the relations between these organizations? It is not possible to rely on the law, or even to know what it is these days, while government, which used to regulate flows of goods and allocation of labor—including decrees by soviets and plan orders by ministries—has ceased to be universally or even generally obeyed. One could see this situation as the beginning of the reforms, the loosening of centralized authority and the devolution of power. But the social structures that are now toughening themselves are in contradiction with the goal of a free market, even with that of a regulated but all-USSR market. Symptoms of this are that economic relations between local "suzerainties" are increasingly conducted by distinctive methods (of which people in the West have little knowledge): by coupons and "orders," by means of direct barter, or via what is widely known as "the Mafia"—a heterogeneous collection of racketeer associations whose common feature is that they contain their own "protection."

Sometimes Russians use a metaphor to describe the suzerainties. They are known as "icebergs": of different sizes, perhaps melting a little at top and bottom, or maybe growing imperceptibly, floating and jostling one another in an unfriendly sea. Such images are all very well, but the real situation is so peculiar to the Soviet economy and so unfamiliar to readers from the West that we need detailed examples to understand what is happening.

Let us start with the case of carpets in Ulan-Ude, an example not of production but of distribution. In September 1990 the carpet shop on Ulitsa Pobedy was besieged, a seething mass of people from morning to night, though the shelves were empty. The "queue" had bureaucratized itself into a list of eight hundred names. The manager of the shop was in despair. He telephoned every morning to his suppliers and announced the paltry result (a few hundred square meters due from Mongolia sometime) to the customers, but "They don't believe me! They are there all day and become quite inhuman from the fruitless waiting. I need to protect my assistants from their insults." In fact, the manager had received some other carpets, but they had immediately been sent out "on order" to a collective farm. But it was not this that agitated the customers. They assumed that the manager could get carpets on the side, by barter. The manager said that, no, he had nothing to give in exchange. The same was true outside, in the town markets. A few desirable carpets were for sale, but the sellers wanted only certain scarce goods in exchange, and such things are, unfortunately, hardly produced in Buriatia.

Coupons and "Orders"

Western newspapers often inform their readers that the USSR has introduced rationing to cope with such situations. This may give the wrong impression. There is a distinction in principle between generalized rationing and limited "coupons." What is actually being used is the latter, a multifarious collection of food cards (*kartochki*), coupons (*talony*), orders (*zakazy*) and coupon orders, the two combined. This is an important factor that differentiates the situation at the start of the 1990s from that at the end of World War II. Then the centralized government was able to make an assessment of stocks and production flows in the country and assign goods to cities and regions by a single system of rationing. The system differentiated between social categories (soldiers, mothers, pensioners, etc.) but in principle it was universal for the whole country and population. Today (1991), no one knows what goods there are, and even if general rationing is introduced it will be impossible to establish universal norms. Entitlements to purchase are limited by a host of local factors. The coupons and orders enabling people to buy things are issued not centrally but by all sorts of regional organizations. Local government, that is, the soviets at various levels, seems to have sidestepped responsibility for the regulation of allocations as a whole.[2] The *talon* coupons and orders can be issued by the places where people work (the suzerainties or icebergs).

Long ago Mary Douglas (1967) explained the socio-political consequences of the use of coupons in her analysis of certain tribal economies in New Guinea. She contrasted three types of primitive economy, controlled, freely competitive, and mixed, and argued that the currencies found in the more controlled economies were more like coupons than money. "I would expect primitive coupon systems to emerge where there is some danger that the effective demand for scarce resources may so disturb the pattern of distribution as to threaten a given social order" (1967, 127). Both rationing and coupons (or licensing) are instruments of social policy, but whereas rationing is egalitarian in intent, coupons are not. The object of coupons or licensing is protective: to limit access to particular goods to certain groups of people. An important side effect of coupons is to create advantages, even sometimes monopolies, for those who issue them and those who receive them. "Both parties become bound in a patron-client relation sustained by the strong interests of each in the continuance of the system" (1967, 131).

It can be seen that coupons thus have social implications both within and between suzerainties. How does this work? In large metropolitan cities since

1 December 1990 all products are sold up to given "norms" only to people with residence permits. On the other hand, the food card[3] is the most prevalent form in the provinces. Such cards are for specific products that are scarce in a given town or region, and again they are issued only to people who have residence permits. This means that outsiders cannot buy such products at all. If a villager goes on a visit to Ulan-Ude for a month, he or she will have a hungry time of it without friends to provide food. As one Soviet economist has put it, "The *kartochki* only divide the market into 'appanage princedoms' and protect resources which have been 'beaten out' from 'aliens.'"[4]

"Orders," of which there are several types, are also common. A large factory, for example, may have its own grocery shop. In Moscow, local government insists that such shops be open to the general public at least one day a week, and perhaps to pensioners another day a week. The other five days are reserved for the factory. All shopping at the store is done "by order," that is, purchase of a limited bundle of products (the "order"—300 grams of cheese, 1/2 kilo of sausages, 3 tins of fish, and so forth), which the shop changes from time to time according to its supplies. Another prevalent form is for shops selling scarce goods, such as shoes and boots, to take a consignment directly "by order" to an office or factory where they are sold to employees by coupons which have been distributed beforehand. Just as common is a system whereby departments of an organization such as an institute of the Academy of Sciences fetch in their own orders and distribute them. The "orders" are advertised, and people queue to put their names on the list. When the set time is up, the department sends people down to the shop to collect the goods, and they are brought back to the institute and distributed. These orders are more or less "powerful" depending on the social weight of the organization concerned (academics rank rather low). The shops may give better or worse quality goods or fulfill only one hundred out of three hundred orders on the list, for example. I know one family that lives almost entirely on the "order" of its one privileged member, a long-time Party member and a veteran of World War II.

Talon coupons are similar to food cards, but even more limited in their use. They enable certain categories of people (workers at a factory, members of a collective farm, war veterans of a town, mothers of many children, etc.) to buy specific products. They are extremely heterogeneous. Sometimes coupons are limited to a specific shop, sometimes not. Sometimes they are allocated per head of family, sometimes by the number of adult workers.

They may be distributed randomly (drawn out of an urn), or they may be allocated to people who have worked especially well. Coupons may be given out by various organizations, from local Soviets to workplaces.

The situation is clearly unfair, as it gives people unequal access to resources. Not only are the "norms" different in the major cities, but in the provinces meat, for example, may be available by two different systems in neighboring towns, in one by *talon* coupons and in other only by orders made at the workplace. In the deep countryside people often have access to none of these systems and therefore have to provide their own subsistence. A woman working as a secretary at a state farm, for example, has an exhausting day as she rushes to combine her job with milking her cattle, tending her pigs, and so forth. To give an example, in 1988 in the Kalmyk ASSR 4,214 tons of meat were distributed through state outlets by coupons and orders. Of this, 70 percent was sold in the capital city of Elista, but Elista does not contain anything like 70 percent of the population. A meat coupon in the capital therefore "weighed" considerably more than in the country towns, and farmers were not given coupons at all.[5] But despite their unfairness these systems are widely popular as most people think they have something to gain from them.

Inside the organization there are many possibilities for deploying patronage, and they extend to hangers-on. In Kalmykia orders for meat were also made by workplaces. The construction group Kalmykstroi, for example, sent its order to the butcher shop, only for it to be discovered more or less by chance that the director of the group had personally added 110 names to the list. Since many people may get left off these lists for one reason or another (e.g., their official residence is in another town, they do not work, or they have part-time or unofficial employment), one could interpret the director's action as charitable, but it is also clear that the boss (*khoziain*—"owner," "master") only stood to gain by his increased patronage.

The coupon systems naturally have social effects at the receiving end, too. An example is the allocation of vodka coupons in regions such as Tyva, which are still subject to the "dry law" against alcoholism. Here coupons are allocated by committees within workplaces, and I was assured in 1989 that they take it upon themselves to judge whether someone is "suitable" to receive a monthly coupon. Drunkards and "unsuitable" people are refused, and they must prove themselves before their workmates to get back on the list.

The coupon system itself, however, is beyond the law. You can be prosecuted in some regions for illegal distilling, but not for issuing coupons. In

Yakutia a large cartel printed thousands of counterfeit vodka coupons. When this was discovered, several hundred people were arrested. But they were released because no law could be found under which to prosecute them. They had not sold the coupons and benefited financially; all they had done was to issue their own license to get drunk (depriving other people of vodka). As an observer commented, "In the present system the consumer is protected by precisely nothing."[6]

The result is that people are increasingly dependent on the services offered by their workplaces, especially in the countryside. It is not always realized in the West quite how all-embracing these may be. Again the situation is utterly heterogeneous. No matter if the old Victory Collective Farm has renamed itself the Victory Agrarian Industrial Firm, one must look closely at the individual farm to see what the reality is. When I returned in 1990 to the Karl Marx Collective Farm in Barguzin, where I had first done fieldwork in the 1960s, I found that it was now rather successful, having undergone a period in the doldrums in the 1970s, but was organizationally almost entirely

1. *Closed club at Karl Marx Collective Farm, Selenga, Buriatia, 1996. The farm has since built itself another club, but the old one stands as a mute memorial to Soviet times.*

2. *Rusting farm machinery in the Buriat countryside, 1996.*

unchanged. As in the old days, what I called the "manipulable resources" (the surplus product over the amount supplied to the state under the plan order) were used to provide services for the members as the chairman saw fit. In this case he had decided on cultural investment; a magnificent club had been provided, an ethnographic museum built, an integrated Buriat educational program was under way in the schools, and a sports stadium was under construction. Gorbachev's agricultural reforms were resolutely ignored. Although one or two young men managed to wrangle out low-quality leasehold fields, the chairman was adamant that classic collectivized farming was the only realistic alternative. Indeed, he, like most farm chairmen I met, saw individual farming as a threat; it would claim his best workers, who would put their energies into their own profits rather than those of the collective farm.

At the Bodongut State Farm, however, also in Buriatia, the chairman had gone over to the leasehold system entirely, even before it became government policy. The farm was divided into twenty-two leasehold brigades. Darmaev's brigade, for example, in 1990 sold produce worth 90,300 rubles to the state via the farm. During the year, the four families in the brigade lived on an advance worth 15 percent of their estimated income. Payment for any farm machinery used, for fodder, and for amortization, housing, and repairs was deducted from the 90,300 rubles at the end of the year. The rest of the income belonged to the families, to dispose as they wished. For this system to be profitable to the farm, the accounting office had laboriously to work out two new internal sets of prices. Taking into account the prices paid to the farm by the state for deliveries of the plan order, the farm had to set the prices it would pay to the leaseholders for each item and the prices it would charge them for machinery, fodder, and other goods. The result in this case was a brilliant success. The farm made such a profit that it was able to provide thousands of rubles to its workers for loans to build houses and acquire private livestock; to pay each year 300 rubles to mother-heroines, 200 rubles to families with many children, 130 rubles to war invalids, and 100 rubles to veterans; to provide paid maternity leave for three years per each child born; to hire a farm postman, club worker, and kindergarten staff; and to build a medical center, a general store, and an abattoir and meat-packing shop.[7]

What these two otherwise different farms have in common is the decisive power of their chairmen. This seems to have grown since my earlier visits, with a corresponding weakening in the authority of the Communist Party (not that there are any other political parties in Buriatia as yet). Both men had translated their economic authority into politics; the chairman of the Karl Marx (the same man who had presided in 1967) was also executive head of the local soviet, and the chairman of Bodongut was an elected deputy to the Soviet of the Buriat ASSR. But even in lesser and unsuccessful farms, the ordinary members are dependent on the "suzerain" in spheres that Western people would think of as having nothing to do with their work. Most housing, for example, is allocated by the workplace; and even if someone wishes to build a house, the loan necessary to do so can be obtained only from the employing organization directly or via its recommendation. One's standing with the boss is of direct consequence.

Farms and other enterprises have become economic subsystems with a noticeable degree of autonomy. There are peculiar internal arrangements designed to conserve and internally circulate their own resources. For example, I went into one farm general store and saw, prominently displayed against a rack of "ordinary" (actually fully adequate by British standards) coats, a few glossy furs and shiny Japanese anoraks. They had notices pinned to them; they were only for sale to people who had sold 300 kilos of potatoes or 50 kilos of meat to the farm. But the Bodongut State Farm went much further.

It printed its own money. All internal transactions in the farm were paid in this money, which was converted into rubles only at the end of the year when the farm itself was paid by the state. The initial reason for this internal money was that no one would give the farm a loan to pay its first-year advances to the lessee brigades, but it continued to be used because, as the chairman said, it prevented people and rubles seeping out of the farm during the working year.

A Soviet legal specialist has summed up the situation:

> Empty shop counters, as history tells us, are the initial syndrome of social discontent. Towns, oblasts (administrative divisions), and republics are fencing themselves off with palisades of rationing in defense against "migratory demand," they are bringing in nothing more or less than "buying tickets." The scale and consequences of this mutual alienation are unpredictable. A large number of people support such methods, and mass consciousness brands those who penetrate into "foreign" enclaves of the rationed market through a prism of confrontational mythology as *pokupanty* (a pun, combining the idea of those who buy up too much, *pokupat'*, with occupying forces, *okkupanty*—C.H.) or *pliushevnyi desant* (plush landing forces). In almost every region such epithets are widespread. The market is divided up, and aggressive particularism is growing. (Vengerov 1990: 58)

Turning to the relations between these defensive suzerainties we should note (1) that their "manipulable resources" are frequently goods and labor rather than money, (2) that the law gives little protection to informal contracts, (3) that commercial banks are virtually nonexistent in the USSR, (4) that controls are still exercised over farm markets, and (5) that regions have unequal access to scarce resources. These conditions give rise to barter and the operations of what all Soviet citizens call the "Mafia." As governmental decrees become less effective, the sheer number of informal contracts has risen, and these in particular are neither serviced by banks nor protected by the law.

The desperate attempts of the old system of decrees to maintain control is illustrated in relation to one autumn's potato harvest in Buriatia. Heavy rains during the late summer made the fields waterlogged and delayed the harvest. As usual in such situations, the ASSR government declared a situation of emergency and ordered all institutions such as institutes and schools to send labor to the fields. What was unusual in this year was that the government increased the rates of pay, lowered the work norms, and ordered farms to pay the helpers on time. But this was not sufficient to make enough people come out. Meanwhile city dwellers needed potatoes. The result was that many people made their own arrangements with the farms, harvesting in return for a direct payment in potatoes. Many farms were in such disarray that they turned a blind eye to people simply helping themselves in the fields.

Factories and farms have always, if they are at all successful, ended the year with some manipulable resources in products. In the past the state plan order was supposed to mop up all such assets, but now that enterprises are all officially based on self-accounting (*khozrashchet*) it is official policy to allow them to dispose of their surplus as they see fit. In theory, this could be done through the medium of money. Similarly, individual citizens with disposable assets (potatoes they have harvested, a dacha they wish to exchange, etc.) could use money. But in practice they frequently do not, and one reason is the absence of both commercial banks and personal bank accounts.

In the USSR there are only a tiny number of banks offering services to individuals or institutions, and none in places like Buriatia, as far as I know. Sberbank SSR, Promstroibank SSR, Agroprombank SSR, and the other state banks still play a traditional role. This means that they do not trust customers who might wish to bank with them, indeed they restrict access by placing fearsome militiamen at their doors to examine identity documents. In effect they still operate virtually entirely on instructions from above. They are ordered to finance X or Y project, and they do so, without regard for its further viability (this is one reason why so many construction projects lie unfinished in the Soviet Union). State banks even liquidate the assets of enterprises, or move funds between the accounts of various customers with impunity.[8] Not surprisingly, there is a widespread desire to keep out of their grasp. Individuals can place their money in a savings bank, but this is not a bank account as we know it. There are no checkbooks and the idea of making loans available to people who ask for them on their own initiative is a novelty. Rather than see their money eaten away by inflation, people are increasingly turning to saving in commodities (for example, gold, as we have seen).

Barter

The result is that both enterprises and individuals turn to barter. This is not a new phenomenon, but it is growing. Soviet friends told me that around 60 percent of the Soviet economy is now transacted by means of barter. This must be an exaggeration, but it shows how the phenomenon is perceived, whatever its actual dimensions. In farms and factories, barter has always been essential to maintain production, not just to dispose of surpluses. As my previous work on barter in northeast Nepal showed (1985), simultaneous barter is the kind of contract which can best dispense with trust. It has no need for the *generalized* trust epitomized by confidence in the value of a national currency. The transactors see what is on offer, come to an agreement, swap their products, and can then walk away from the deal, never to meet again. However, such direct barter is extremely rare, especially in agricultural economies. This is because the various products are available at different times of year, and because, since agriculture is cyclical and needs for supplies recur, it makes sense to repeat exchanges with the same partners rather than seek new ones each year. Unlike simultaneous barter, delayed barter or repeated barter requires a high degree of trust and fair dealing. Only this can ensure that a return is made later for an item given today, or that both sides will wish to repeat the transaction in the next cycle. As a result, transactors tend to establish exchange networks with "known people." But these can never provide the fluid, all-pervasive links of a monetary system, since they are limited by these very personalized relations, by the lack of generalized trust and information. Barter, therefore, is not only a symptom of a disintegrated economy but also perpetuates it.

All barter, whether immediate or delayed, requires information about what is available where, when, and at what rates. In the Soviet Union this is provided not by central exchanges but by special individuals or departments within each enterprise. These "supply departments," as they are known, are staffed by highly valued people, *snabzhentsy* (suppliers) or *tolkachi* (pushers). Their task is to travel around the country getting information and making deals. Although the products transacted may be valued in rubles, no money changes hands. In the Aga Buriat Autonomous Okrug, for example, the eastern region is treeless steppe where sheep farms produce wool and meat; the western part is heavily wooded. Farms of the two regions have set up their own regular exchange relations whereby meat and wool are exchanged for timber and fodder.

The barter contracts are unregulated by the state, and exchange ratios vary from year to year. The effect of this in recent years in Aga has been to advantage the eastern farms; timber and fodder are relatively plentiful and in any case could be acquired from places other than western Aga. The relative value of meat and wool, however, has risen with the general disarray of Soviet farming. As one farm director told me smugly, his single state farm in the east was now worth more than all seven farms of the western region put together. Barter can be combined with the system of "orders" and this may result in further trading. For example, a farm may give a refrigerator factory spare building materials in exchange for some refrigerators "on order," and then trade the extra fridges for fodder with some neighbors.

Barter thus establishes little pools of trust and mutual help, though it does not necessarily save a transactor from relative decline engendered by the wider external economic situation. As in Nepal, it is clear that, try as they might to influence "their" exchange partners, the disadvantaged side is forced to agree or to try elsewhere with people who may be less well known and less reliable in making payment. The whole system is carried out in circumstances of utmost uncertainty about its legality. Let us note, in brief, what the general attitude to the law is in the provinces and then relate this to the specific circumstances of barter and other economic exchanges.

A lawyer from Buriatia has written the following:

> Why has it happened that we are building a state based on law (*pravovoe gosudarstvo*) with the help of ever-spreading legal nihilism, and they even try to persuade us that this is a natural process?
>
> Yes, many legal statutes of the country turned out to be imperfect in themselves, and furthermore they have simply ceased to correspond to new realities. Congresses and parliaments have set about creating new laws on top of the old ones. Their numbers rise with great rapidity. A large number of corrections to the Constitution have been made. But alas, this high tempo has not led to a correspondingly fast growth in legal consciousness. Rather, [it is] the reverse. The feverishness with which laws are set up and put away, and the absence of mechanisms for enacting them, has led to a reverse process. And should we be surprised?
>
> In countries with a developed parliamentary tradition, corrections to the Constitution take years to work out, but we are prepared to take them up almost by ear. The next step is quite logical—generally to ignore the law in favor of some "higher goal." Republics and regions (*raiony*) of the country are establishing their own acts in contradiction to the Constitution. And not just regions! Districts, even village soviets give out declarations of their sovereignty, with the obligatory paragraph: the laws of all higher organs of power will be effective in their territory only after local ratification. This means chaos.
>
> How can the ordinary person even find out which laws of higher organs contradict one another? It is much simpler to declare your sover-

eignty and decide which laws you will apply and which not. It is not by accident that Rolan Bykov recently said to Gorbachev that one presidential decree is lacking, a decree that could provide the fundament of unity for all republics—on the sovereignty of the individual.

But would such a decree help when our people do *not* even understand that chaos does not lead to freedom but to dictatorship, that a man cannot count himself free unless he knows that his house is protected from disaster, that he cannot be driven from his work because of what he looks like, that his right to elect and be elected is secure? We need a state that can guarantee these elementary human rights. A state is powerful when its subjects can not only insult it but can also observe its laws, and if they are imperfect can change them only by parliamentary means, being guided by that wise principle which preserves stability. "The law may be bad, but it is the Law." (Subbotin 1990, 2)

What the author is complaining about is that concern with freedom/sovereignty at the level of the state has resulted in a situation that effectively "legalizes" (or makes unprosecutable) hitherto criminal activities. Take "speculation," for example. Speculation involves buying something in one place, taking it to where there is greater demand, and selling it at a higher price. It has always been illegal (because no good productive labor adds value in the process) and today in theory still is. But what about barter, which could be seen as speculation doubled?

Most people have no objection to barter, but they do feel very strongly about the new cooperatives (small private firms) which are only a step away. Cooperatives, to look at things from the outside, could be a solution to many problems discussed here. But in provincial Russia they are widely disliked, mistrusted, and even feared. Partly this is because of their great financial gains; a 1990 article estimated that, whereas the state paid 5 billion rubles to farms for grains last year, the cooperative sector had an income of 40 billion.[9] The author's cry, "Yet we all eat bread!" explains a great deal. No one in the West expects bread producers to be very rich, even at subsidized state prices, yet in Russia different, age-old values prevail. The cooperatives in fact operate in those very areas of the economy where there is acute demand for high-value, scarce, and novel products—not bread but exotic cuisines, computer software, or fashions in clothing. Many are involved simply in moving such products around the country, in pure "speculation" in Soviet terms, or in the production of low-quality but glamorous goods which are then sold expensively. When this is done by an officially registered cooperative, it is not illegal but legitimate business. No wonder ordinary people are dismayed. From this it is another short step to Mafia-type operations. These have homed in even more specifically to areas of extreme demand and vulnerability, but the point is that these foci for threatening activity are multiplying with increased scarcity. So it is not just the expected areas of drugs and prostitution which see such operations, but also taxi networks (particularly in cities where there are foreigners with dollars, or where there is a scarcity of gasoline), video parlors, and home and vehicle repairs. There is even a specialist area of "queue management," which consists of taking money from people who do not have time to stand for days or weeks themselves.

In everything that has been said it is apparent that belonging to a "suzerainty" is almost a necessity, even if it results in dependency, even if some people can perceive the general social alienation involved. How else would one get "orders" or "coupons," let alone somewhere to live? In effect, this means having a steady job, and preferably an established position under a powerful and successful boss. Many people do not have such jobs. Pensioners, the disabled, dropouts without training or diplomas, demobbed soldiers, and refugees from areas of civil unrest may find themselves out in the cold. Ex-prisoners find it almost impossible to get good jobs. In many areas of the RSFSR this problem of dislocation has become aligned not just with social class but specifically with ethnic boundaries.

I would not say that this is invariably the case. Some non-Russian cultures encourage their own forms of integration, and this is a subject that should be further investigated by anthropologists. For example, the Buriats have strong ties to the land, hence stable and loyal populations in collective farms, and a tradition of literacy; and they thus include a numerous administrative/intellectual class well integrated into regional institutions. The Koreans, to take another example, have maintained their tradition of intensive vegetable cultivation and successfully engage themselves as temporary summer brigades all over the RSFSR, returning home during the winter to live on the proceeds.

But we find the reverse case in Tyva. Here young Tyvinians do not want to work on the farms and yet many of them have not adapted to the urban work ethic either. Rootless gangs of young men, with no jobs or only temporary employment, roam the towns, living any way they can. These days people do not dare wear valuable fur hats in Tyva for fear they will be snatched from their heads; muggings, knifings, and attacks on buses and cars are common. This anomie lies at the base of the Tyvinian "nationalist" riots that have caused hundreds of Russians to flee the province. In fact, there is no real

Tyvinian nationalist party or political agenda, though one may develop.[10] The situation is that many young Tyvinians simply resent the Russians: Russians, who are better trained and more culturally attuned to industrial work, dominate the suzerainties and have access to better facilities, especially accommodations, and it is mainly Tyvinians who find themselves left outside.[11] Furthermore, Tyvinians, among whom worship of sacred mountains, rivers, trees, and springs is virtually universal, hate the Russians for their careless attitude toward the environment. The result in regions of mixed population is numerous, sporadic, disorganized uprisings and armed attacks on Russians, which extend to Russified Tyvinians. For example, gangs may stop someone in the street with a simple question: unless the answer is given in fluent Tyvinian, the person is knifed or even shot. In provincial Russia, hunting guns are found everywhere, and these days they are frequently stolen and taken to the cities. The stated reason for concerted attacks is often economic, especially the smuggling of vodka, and there have been serious economic results. As already noted, Tyva is subject to the "dry law," while neighboring regions are not. Throughout Tyva, construction projects, entirely staffed by well-paid Russians, allow the smuggling in of vodka together with building supplies. So violent have been the attacks on the workers and truckers by resentful Tyvinians that many Russians have lost their lives. Factories and mines staffed by Russians have had to close after workers fled in panic. In reprisal, the neighboring, and much richer, Russian regions have halted all capital investment in Tyva. Poor Tyva has hardly any paved roads, few bridges, and much of the rural population lives in yurts.[12]

Russians also attack native peoples for directly economic motives. In all the forested regions of Siberia there are logging enterprises (*lespromkhoz*). They are entirely manned by Russians and have begun to be much disliked by native peoples, as the swathes of desolation become more and more apparent. This was so at the Barguzin Karl Marx Collective Farm, which had objected many times to the activities of the nearby Jubilee *lespromkhoz*, though without result. I was told about a more serious example: the Udegei are hunters living in the Amur River region, for whom destruction of the forest is the destruction of their subsistence and way of life. With the new political conditions, their protests apparently met with some positive response from the local authorities. The reaction of the Russians in the logging village to this threat that their enterprise might have to close was to cut off the supply of electricity to the Udegei village. Such disputes are everywhere and are bound to increase, since there is as yet no effective law in the

RSFSR to establish rights to land for any individual or group apart from "the state."

One result of all this "aggressive particularism" is that "protection" of various kinds is emerging all through society. This is not the night watchmen of old, but new organizations and rackets, staffed, it seems, often by the very dislocated people who have lost their footholds in the suzerainties. The old underworld is prominent, but so are former soldiers and even ex-members of the KGB. I have little evidence on quite how this works, but it seems probable that the local bosses are the main employers of the more legitimate forms of protection. I was told that the chairman of the first farm where I did fieldwork in 1967 (also called Karl Marx Collective, but in a different region from the one mentioned earlier) had been shot by angry workers. The precise reasons are not known, but it is easy to see that the immense power of such bosses over ordinary lives might give rise to occasional, or even not so occasional, acts of violence, especially when the hazy and exciting idea of "democracy" is around.

We are witnessing the falling apart of civil society in Russia. The conditions I have outlined give rise to local defensiveness in economic, social, and political spheres. In my view, many of the ethnic movements of small minorities in Russia are primarily defensive in character. Their aim is to preserve or resurrect different cultures, not to impose on the Russians. But every barrier raised—or, to put this in the language used in Russia itself, these "palisades" surrounding "icebergs" or "appanage princedoms," this view of outsiders as locustlike "occupying forces" buying up everything in sight—is also a barrier against the ultimate goal of the economic reforms, at least as envisioned by metropolitan liberals. It is difficult to see how a free market, even a relatively free market, can be attained through the hedges of coupons, orders, and local barter systems which are now beginning to form a veritable maze. Let us hope that the example of Tyva will not be reproduced elsewhere and that these economic barriers will not also bring to naught the generous gestures between social groups in other areas of life that are still prevalent in provincial Russia.

CHAPTER 2
MYTHMAKING, NARRATIVES, AND THE DISPOSSESSED IN RUSSIA

This chapter addresses what I believe to be an essential but neglected process in the current dynamics of the Russian political economy.[1] This is the production of the "dispossessed," and I use this term in a double sense. The dispossessed are people who have been deprived of property, work, and entitlements, but we can also understand them as people who are themselves no longer possessed. That is, they are no longer inside the quasi-feudal corporations, the collective "domains," which confer a social status on their members and which in practice are still the key units disposing of property and people in Russia.

The dispossessed include: refugees coming into Russia from the successor states of the CIS; the unemployed; economic migrants; demobilized soldiers, abandoned pensioners, invalids, and single-parent families; vagrants and the homeless (*BOMZhY*);[2] and people living in various illegal ways, such as contract laborers without residence permits in large cities (*limitchiki*). Grouping these disparate types into one category is not simply an idea of mine. In February 1992, by presidential decree, the Russian government set up a single bureau, the Federal Migration Service (FMS), to deal with all these groups. "Migration," that is, movement and interstitiality, was thus defined as the problem to be solved.

The current "transition" being attempted in Russia is heavily ideologized or mythicized, no less so than the revolutionary transition to socialism. We should not, however, see mythicization simply as false consciousness, as masking some grim, but different, "reality." As many studies of discourse have pointed out, the use of linguistic tropes is integral to the struggle for the definition of reality (Appadurai 1981; Herzfeld 1985). Thus the events and decisions that create the dispossessed are not just plainly and simply the inevitable fallout of the collapse of socialism; if they are thought about and objectified at all, they are also deeds in fields of semiological battle, where myth-making faces its enemies, prosaic recitals and narrative accounts.

In counterposing mythicization to narrative in this way, I wish to lend my voice to those who have challenged the Lévi-Straussian reification of "myth" as a universal, object-centered category. I use the word "myth" here in the sense of decontextualized (Bauman and Briggs 1990) or objectified current images that effect a transformation of history into timeless nature (Barthes 1957), but I am interested not so much in definitions as in mythmaking as part of socio-political activity. There are particular Soviet and post-Soviet practices of mythicization, which differ significantly from comparable prac-tices in Western Europe. I suggest that, in their mutual interactions, people still inside the domains tend to use an ahistorical, non-narrative kind of mythmaking as a gesture of repudiation of alienness and change, while the dispossessed, who need to establish their identity if they are to be noticed at all, perforce create narratives that are historicized in a lived temporality. These interactions, of course, do not preclude the use of other types of dis-course in different contexts, such as the often spurious links made with an-cient cultures to legitimate a sense of identity, essentially a discourse ad-dressed within the group. To provide the grounds for an argument as to why interactions between the settled and the dispossessed take such mythic forms, I start with a preamble about the political conditions for such myth-making in Russia.

Who are the dispossessed in Russia? In some sense, the creation of dispos-sessed categories of people has been a global, or at least an all-European, phenomenon in current decades. It is depressingly familiar to all of us, who have become, to use a medical analogy, "unemployment-positive." But the character of the Russian experience is specific, because it rests on signifi-cantly different operative concepts of political economy from those used in Western Europe and on a particular Soviet construction of what elsewhere might be called "colonial" relations with other classes and cultures. The "dis-possessed" in Russia are created by the specifically post-Soviet political do-mains of which they are no longer a part.

Let me start by giving three examples of the creation of the dispossessed.[3] During 1992, one of Yeltsin's decrees on privatization filtered down through republican and district administrations to the collective farms (*kolkhozy*) of the Barguzin valley in the Buriat Republic of the Russian Federation. Early in 1993, five collectives held meetings of their members. One decided to re-ject the edict altogether, and another three agreed to set up a tiny handful of people as private farmers on collective land. The Uliun collective, however, decided to go the whole hog, disband itself, and become completely "privatized." Within six months they had got together again and turned themselves back into a collective farm. But in so doing they got rid of two hundred laborers, who were simply not included in the reconstituted collective. Overnight these people turned into the dispossessed. They were neither "kolkhozniks" nor "unemployed," which would entitle them to benefits, since the farm had not issued them with official redundancy papers.[4] During 1993 the collective used them for the harvest and sometimes handed them odd jobs, but the rest of the time they were forced to subsist on their tiny plots and few animals, or on handouts from relatives or by thieving.

A look at systems of pay in the state and the industrial sectors near Moscow provides my second example. In February 1993, state employees such as teachers or doctors were relatively secure, but they earned only 12,000 or 13,000 rubles a month.[5] Factory workers were better off; they earned 30,000 to 40,000 rubles (an adequate wage at the time), but could go for months without either work or pay as factories closed down temporarily for lack of orders and supplies. Meanwhile, banks and private companies paid even a

3. Economic differentiation in the postsocialist collective, Buriatia, 1996: the wealthy build themselves comfortable log houses.

4. *Economic differentiation in the postsocialist collective, Buriatia, 1996: the poor and dispossessed are reduced to living in huts.*

simple clerk around 100,000 rubles a month. The "dispossessed," however, were deprived of any security, financial or otherwise. Temporary contract workers were not counted as "inside" the organization. Often on tiny wages (6,000 rubles), they had no entitlement to job security, insurance, sick pay, housing, or other benefits. Worst off were the out-workers at home (*nadomnye rabotniki*), such as seamstresses, whose minute earnings hardly covered the cost of the machines, electricity, and rent they had to pay for themselves. "You would have to work twenty-four hours a day to make enough not to die of hunger," one person said to me. These sudden gulfs in pay and security destroyed old relations of easy equality, tearing apart lifelong friendships and breaking marriages.

The most radically dispossessed, however, are the migrants and refugees, my third example. No one knows the true dimensions of migratory processes in Russia, and there is no law in place to define these people's rights. As Brubaker (1992) has written, "The collapse of centralized authority has 'internationalized' what was previously counted as internal migration. This has transformed yesterday's internal migrants, secure in their Soviet citizenship, into today's international migrants of contested legitimacy and uncertain membership." According to the Federal Migration Service, there were at the end of 1993 around 2 million such "international" refugees, most of them Russians returning to the homeland from the Baltic, Central Asian, and Caucasian states.[6] But at the same time, there are uncountable numbers of migrants within Russia, such as people fleeing from intolerable conditions in the polar regions or people squeezed out of jobs and seeking their luck wherever they can. As there is no operating law on migrants, the FMS has resorted to what it calls "sublegal" methods to sift out what it sees as deserving cases among the myriad categories; on these it bestows its tiny resources.[7] The great majority of migrants have never heard of the FMS, or else they correctly reckon that it can be of no help to them, and all these people are left to fend for themselves in the exhausting practicalities of Russian society.

To understand this, we need to think about how being a member of a Russian work collective differs from "having a job" in Western Europe. As Simon Clarke (1992) has observed,

> The Soviet enterprise is almost as different from the capitalist enterprise as was a feudal estate from a capitalist farm. Like the feudal estate, the Soviet enterprise is not simply an economic institution but is the primary unit of Soviet society, and the ultimate base of social and political power. The basis of the Soviet enterprise was not capital, but the productive activity of the labor collective. The public measure of its success was not its profit, but the size of its labor force and the numbers of tons they produced, the houses it had built, the number of places for children in its kindergartens and in summer camps, the sporting, medical, and cultural facilities it provided, the number of pensioners it supported. . . . This was not just rhetoric, it was an ideological expression of the social relations of production and forms of surplus appropriation on which the Soviet system was based.

Such a system was based on an exchange, between the workers who were persuaded to produce something and hand it over to the state and the managers who agreed to redistribute state benefits of every kind of the workers (Humphrey 1983; Verdery 1991).[8]

The dispossessed person is outside such a "primary unit of society." This is a serious and terrible deprivation, since even those "inside" are living at the level of mere subsistence in most rural areas. To be specific, the rejected workers of Uliun are (in the autumn of 1993) no longer entitled to receive the crucial monthly distribution of free flour (instead they must pay for flour);

they no longer receive firewood for the winter or fodder for their animals, and they cannot use the collective's tractors or other equipment nor its supply of petrol. Unlike members of the *kolkhoz* they do not receive vouchers entitling them to obtain goods from the collective's shops on credit; again they must buy such goods. Although no one is proposing to drive them out, their entitlement to the crucial means of life, a house, a cow, and a plot of land, is now cast into legal obscurity. As for the rest, access to medical services and education increasingly involves a certain amount of payment, while the facilities of the work unit such as kindergartens, social club, library, sporting facilities, vacations at resorts, and so forth are in disarray; if they still exist, such services are at best kindly allowed to the dispossessed because they are still around the place.

Even so, with all this material deprivation, the most terrible thing for many people is that "their papers are no longer in order." In Russia, entitlements in general have long been represented by possession of numerous interrelated documents, and I briefly discuss these now.

A Russian friend once quoted to me a saying he attributed to Dostoevsky, "A human being consists of three things: a body, a soul, and a passport." Dostoevsky, if he ever said this, was presumably being ironic, but I can vouch for the sincerity with which ordinary people feel it to be true. I was traveling in China with a Russian friend whose passport, money, and other documents were stolen. He minded about the money, but he was aghast at the loss of the documents, fearing being not admitted back into Russia ever again, or alternatively being deported by China and then punished with prison by the Russian authorities. During the weeks when he did not dare approach the Russian consulate in China, he sighed many times, "*Bez bumazhki ty bukashka, a s bumazhkoi—chelovek*" ("Without papers you are a tiny bug, but with papers you are a person"). The papers a fully integrated Russian person should have include: birth certificate, internal Russian passport, *trudovaia knizhka* (booklet documenting the work record and giving entitlement to a pension), *propiska* (permission to reside at a given place), and *order na dom* (certificate of proprietary rights on a dwelling). These are tied to one another in a circular way: without a job you cannot get a *propiska*, without a *propiska* you cannot get a job, without a passport you cannot get a *propiska*, without a *propiska* you cannot get an *order na dom*, and so forth. The dispossessed, we can now see, come in many categories, signaled by deprivation of one or another document; but what is important is that a loss of one official status threatens the unraveling of the whole edifice, that is, descent into the wilderness of having no entitlements at all.

One highly significant power of the work collective is that it can set someone up as a full citizen by itself supplying certain documents and by requesting the local administration (government department) to issue the others. Because of the de facto political nature of the collective institution, I prefer the term "domain" to the more conventional "enterprise." Whatever we call them, these institutions have weakened, but they remain necessary to ordinary people in the years since perestroika, especially in the countryside. With the collapse of Soviet power they are now virtually independent of state production plans.[9] To simplify outrageously, we can say that in the majority of cases "privatization" of various types has left intact the previous social relations of production. The difference is that a far greater proportion of the product now remains in the hands of the managers as opposed to the state, and they use it in a desperate attempt to barter or buy essential items (such as clothes or food) to redistribute to their members. Many enterprises exist at a constant loss, on the basis of loans. None of the Barguzin farms, for example, has been able to pay its workers money wages for the past six months. Instead they are paid in products or the farm's own vouchers which they can exchange only for goods at the collectives' shops. The very basis of subsistence is the plot, the cow, and the pig; and as for the rest, people are tied more closely than ever before to the collective, since they hardly have money with which to make exchanges outside.

Katherine Verdery (1996) has called the current parceling of sovereignty a transition from socialism to feudalism. In an influential analysis Burawoy and Krotov (1993) see Russia as a social formation in transition to a kind of "merchant capitalism," in which commercial relations act in such a way as to preserve the old monopolistic "indigenous" regimes of production. Simon Clarke (1992) sees the enterprise today as a "state within a state," an institution that is not just a place of work but a way of life. He asks: given the failure of capital to penetrate into the sphere of production, are we not rather seeing the reconstitution of the old Soviet system from below, with the enterprises as the main building blocks? All these images of a backward shift in time echo statements made by Russians themselves, a point to which I return later.

It is essential for us to grasp the cultural concepts held of the Russian polity if we are to understand what it means to be ejected from one. The writers mentioned above are right to stress collectivity and the fact that recent political changes have enabled workers to use elections to get rid of unpopular managers or to use the press to rail against illegitimate privatization. But they underestimate the fact that enterprises or domains are both conceptually and in practice still politically centralized, continuing the exhaustive invasion of the economic by the political seen by Gellner (1994) as definitive of socialism. Agricultural domains are called *khoziaistvo,* a term deriving from *khoziain,* the proprietor or master. This is no mere curiosity but a sense firmly attached to the institution in daily usage.[10] The term *khoziain* was used at each hierarchical level of the Soviet system, such that the directors of enterprises, and the Party bosses of districts and provinces were all called "proprietors," and at the apex of the system Stalin in his time was called *nash khoziain* ("our master"). It is true that the word *khoziain* in this political sense is now often used with a sense of irony, but this is not the case with the parallel term *vlast'* (power). *Vlast'* is not only used as an abstract noun. In the plural (*vlasti*) it refers to "the authorities," and with the epithet Soviet (*sovetskaia vlast'*) it refers to the Soviet regime. This vocabulary was developed during the Soviet period, and despite contradictory tendencies in Marxist and Bolshevik theory, it served to strengthen an earlier and important strand of Russian thought. According to this idea, socio-political order is brought about by the exercise of centralized and personified power, not by law, the observance of principles, or the existence of civil society. Crucially, this idea is also represented in the term for the state (*gosudarstvo*), deriving from *gosudar'* (the sovereign). I am arguing here that the cultural concepts of the "domain" (*khoziaistvo*) and the state (*gosudarstvo*) encode in themselves from the beginning the reification of political entities in which a central personification of power creates order.[11]

Let me give an example of how this way of thinking emerges in everyday speech. Earlier this year a sympathetic Russian was asking a Tajik refugee wandering in Siberia when he would go home. "I suppose you'll go back," he said, "when power in your place has strengthened itself again?" What he implied by this was, "Will you go back when order has returned to Tajikistan?"

The nightmare of chaos, in this way thinking, is counteracted by the exercise of power.[12] This is different from the strand of Western European thought which conceives of the state in reified form as "that which has always existed," as Herzfeld (1986) pointed out in his analysis of the etymology of the term "state" from the Latin *stato.* The reification of state as the ultimate eternal verity, deriving its legitimacy from its foundation in "nature," results in a different configuration of mythic images from that found in Russia, where "naturalization" passes through the prism of the personality of the master, who is honed and dedicated to power such that he becomes one of the naturally existing powers. Of course, opposition to such attitudes also has a long history in Russia.[13] But the very simple point I wish to make here is that many people seek order not *in* themselves but *for* themselves, that is, from powers (*vlasti*) conceived as above; and therefore if the local polity does not provide order, they seek it from higher levels, culminating in the symbolic reification of an ultimate power. Thus the Tajik refugee replied that he would go home, "When there is the Soviet Union again. We don't want our own [Tajik] power!"

Related to this search for power is the existence in Russia of a form of political discourse from below that has completely different connotations in western Europe, the petition (*zaiavlenie*). The term *zaiavlenie* means "announcement" or "declaration" and is essentially the putting of oneself into the public arena, where naturalized power (power made public) will decide.

In the local domains members petition for thousands of matters of importance to existence, like dismissing and accepting members, allocating houses, giving permission to go away on a visit, making recommendations for higher education, or finding a cow to support an aged aunt, and the decisions are taken personally by the director.

The stifling combination of quasi-autocracy and deadening powerlessness created a deep ambivalence; there was a sort of nausea and exhaustion inside, but at the same time a dread of being outside. We can see from the memories of ex-convicts like Marchenko (1989) that in the Brezhnev period the system was so totalizing that some level of inclusion was absolutely necessary and was the first concern on release from camp (at least get a *propiska*, at least get a share of a bed). People were thus trapped in place. This reinforced the Russian country people's sense of rootedness, which persisted despite the great peasant migrations of the turn of the century (Figes 1989) or the forced dislocations of the Stalin period, and it colored any group of incomers (say, Ukrainians living in Siberia) with the "jovial" taint of being outsiders for several generations (Marchenko 1989).

Many people nevertheless wanted out of the suffocating mesh of benevolence and cruelty, and the Gorbachev years of perestroika suddenly made this possible. In all Russian cities and towns, the Komsomol gave way to rebellious youth gangs, which we may see as historically antecedent to, but in most ways different from the current waves of the dispossessed. It is worth considering the gangs at some length, since this enables us to point to significant contrasts with the political discourse of the dispossessed. To take the example of Ulan-Ude, the capital of the Buriat Republic in Siberia: numbers of young people running away from the countryside appeared in the city at the end of the 1980s. They were immediately confronted with city gangs, which were composed of Russians and Buriats together, defending their territory. The country girls called themselves Sultanki and formed a women-only band based on a hangout at an open-air dance floor near the station. They wore a particular uniform of long swinging skirts, heavy sweaters, a bobbed haircut, and multicolored makeup. They drank, fought, smoked dope, and laughed loudly. Outraged citizens ended by calling the police, and the Sultanki were removed from the scene after a year or two, but the gangs of country boys, called Golovar,[14] still exist. The city youth perceive the Golovar as bumpkins, but rich, with their gold watches, gold teeth, and Chinese sports clothing.

Meanwhile, the city youths formed themselves into mutually hostile gangs that covered the entire city. In late 1993 they included virtually all adolescents, since the initial recruiting was done in schools. The names of gangs included Aziia, Amerika, Hunghudze,[15] Chiangkaishe,[16] Generaly, Shanghai, and Bratva ("Brothers").[17] Some of the large gangs have subdivisions (Shanghai 1, Shanghai 2, and so forth) and Amerika divided its streets into "states"—Nebraska, Virginia, Alaska, and so forth. Each gang had its own war cry, such as "Uuch!" "Asso Assa!" or "Shik-Shik!" These were written on house walls to delimit a given territory within which the gang jealously "preserved order" (Khaludorova 1995). The gang included people of any nationality, because the principle of organization was territorial. All of them were hierarchical: they had a leader, called the *nachal'nik* (leader) or *boss,* usually someone legitimated by having served time in prison; then there were "seniors" (*starshaki*) and "middle people" (*sredniaki*), and at the bottom was the *shpana,* a term that means rabble "who wear messy clothes." In the Gorbachev period, now regarded as a heroic era, the gangs sang songs, hung out, and fought momentous battles.[18] By the mid-1990s the gangs had begun to engage in competitive trading, and physical fighting became a little less common. Active membership seems to die out when people are in their mid-twenties, but the ties of identity and comradeship last well beyond that time.[19]

It is impossible not to see here, I think, a mimicry, played on the city streets, of the adult world of the domains. This is a mythicized enactment of the "true nature" of the Russian world. Its rural-urban confrontation and its mapping of all city space into domains is just as totalizing. The anarchic, a-Soviet self image of the gangs can be seen in their emblematic names: Chinese bandits, anticommunists, and American states. Although the gangs are apolitical, in the sense of not having any agenda, the ironic idiom they have created is a theatre of "oriental" military power domains: the Sultanki, the Generaly, and Russian terms used, such as *nachalnik* (leader) or *golovar* (headman), are mocking counters to the foundering post-Soviet culture of the state.

If there is anything the provincial town gang organization denies it is the possibility of interstitiality and migration.[20] This is the central difference from the situation of the dispossessed. The gangs' mythicized street domains emerge from an actual rootedness, from the fact that most of their members live at home or in hostels belonging to colleges and enterprises, that is, they are tied at some level to the institutions they despise. Of course, some individuals may be both members of gangs and "dispossessed," but the mythic construction of a totalized space like Gangland is not something available to the vast majority of the dispossessed, since they have had their roots cut from under them and are dispersed, mostly leaderless, transient, out of touch, and unsure of themselves.

I argue that the gangs and the people who see themselves as settled in effect engage in somewhat similar kinds of mythmaking in relation to the "outside," an authoritative labeling based on shared assumptions. These differ from the representations of the dispossessed, who live in shattered worlds where nothing can be presumed to be shared and where the main task is to be recognized and heard at all. Of course, we can no longer agree with a Lévi-Straussian categorization of "societies" by the presence/absence of "myth" defined in a universalistic way (Herzfeld 1987, 44; Bauman and Briggs 1990, 59–61): in any community people have an enormous range of discursive and semiotic possibilities at their disposal. But what does limit this is the political situations or real engagement in interaction. People can throw a heartfelt rhetorical message into the empty air, as we shall see, but it may not be listened to, or it may be willfully misunderstood. It is hardly ever the case that people are so naive as to be unaware of this. Therefore in practice people in given situations find themselves engaging more in certain types of discourse, not only because of the political position they find themselves in, but because it is these types of discourse that elicit, or lock into, responses. I call these, for the sake of brevity, powerful discourses. It is therefore important, from the ethical point of view, not only to look at the relationship between socio-linguistic features of genres, such as verbal explicitness, and types of political interaction, such as consent, resistance, or accommodation (Herzfeld 1986; Gal 1989, 361), but also to think about the context and effectiveness of a given genre: which one will get the people anywhere? Mythicization can be very powerful in this respect, but not invariably so, and this relates to the different techniques of mythmaking evident in particular interactions.

How can the authoritative labeling type of mythicization used by the people from inside the domains be characterized? It is a striking fact that one prominent objectified form of discourse in modern complex societies that the literature calls "myth" does not have a narrative character. This feature of Roland Barthes's mythologies (1957, 1979), for example, of the new Citroen, the Eiffel Tower, or Garbo's face appears again and again in the ethnographic analyses of texts of exclusion. One could cite Susan Gal's study of the rhetoric of "Bartok" in Hungary (1991), Phyllis Chock's analysis of the myth of "illegal aliens" in congressional testimony (1991), or Bruce Grant's myth of "Siberia" in Russian culture (1993), to name a few. "Myth" appears in these texts as a loosely organized amalgam of significance, essentially synchronic in character. Some interesting studies have contextualized and historicized such mythic constellations of features, analyzing their development over time and in particular situations, and tracing their changing symbolic significance (Gal 1991; Khapeva and Kopossov 1992).

Although I do not intend to focus on the object quality of such myths here, something more can be said about such contemporary myths if we consider their rhetorical features. I refer to an argument made by Barthes in his seminal paper "The Rhetoric of the Image" (1985 [1982]). Barthes was analyzing a photographic advertisement for an Italian pasta sauce, which presented the "mythic" image of an abundance of peppers and tomatoes tumbling from a shopping bag, together with the name of the firm, Panzani. He points out that this image has two aspects—a symbolic constellation, connoting values such as "plenty," "Italianness," "still life," or "homemade"[21]—and the literal, nonsymbolic, denotative image, which consists of red and yellow vegetables, the bag, the table, the kitchen floor, and so forth. Most important, he writes, is to understand that the inventory of symbolic connotators, the "mythic" aspect, is constituted as a set of discontinuous or erratic features. They do not fill the entire lexicon and are thus "caught" in the continuous literal scene, which is not theirs and which in effect naturalizes them. He concludes, with characteristic hyperbole, "The discontinuous world of symbols plunges into the narrative of the denoted scenes as into a lustral bath of innocence" (1985, 40). Barthes thus enables us to see that there is a relation between the synchronic constellation of symbolic features ("myth") and narrativity. In the advertisement, the strong, erratic, and "reified" signs are actualized by means of the syntagmatic "flow" of the literal image.

If we use this analysis, it can be seen that certain, relatively sealed-off mythic images—like insults, graffiti, or racist posters—suppress latent narrativity or effect a closure of narrativity. Other forms of discourse, in contrast, draw out the narrative potential, in stories tied to actual or imagined events. Here the mythic elements are no longer clustered in a synchronic amalgamation, but emerge here and there as significant moments in a plot—that is, they are subordinated to concepts of time and chronology. However, it is crucial that such forms of discourse be recognized as what Terence Turner (1991) calls "operational structures," that is, not as inert, preconstituted objects but as operations whose tropes vary as they are involved in interaction, "where the meaning appears in the doing."

It is evident that the relation between mythic or symbolic tropes and narrativity will be different in oral and visual/physical/gestural forms of signification. Such differences are pertinent to my theme, although I cannot attempt anything like a full analysis of them here. Both gangs and the dispossessed make mythicized image signs to the citizenry. We can understand that the signs of the gangs (weird dress, war cries, graffiti, raucous laughter) are a powerful form of discourse since they elicit fury as a response. But the equivalent signs of the migrants are disregarded or misread. The difference is that the gangs are part of a citywide community of understanding, whereas the migrant dispossessed are not. They have another strategy, which is to draw out the prosaic narrative aspect of their accounts, thus building up a cumulative picture of who they really are, in the hope that they will be recognized and that this will influence their fate. We hear an endlessness in the narratives of the dispossessed, in their stories that keep starting up again each time they experience another disappointment or another rebuff. Perhaps the narratives of the dispossessed only end when they are no longer dispossessed.

I propose to illustrate these points by considering further the interaction between the Tajik refugee mentioned earlier, his Russian interlocutor, Sergei Panarin, and the citizenry of Ulan-Ude (where the conversation took place). The Tajik told Panarin the following history: he was the head of a group of related families, some thirty-five–forty people, whose fine courtyard in Dushanbe was burned down by the "Karategin" (southern Tajiks) in November 1992. The fire spread so fast that only one of the refugees was able to save his passport and other documents. The group decided to flee, because "there was nothing to eat in Dushanbe," they had lost their homes and documents, and they were afraid of the further depredation of the Karategin. They fled in search of security. First they went to Bishkek in Kyrgyzia. There, it seems, the station was full of other "outsiders," possibly refugees from Abkhazia. The Tajik said, "But could they really have been refugees?—all with their gold teeth like Gypsies?" The "powers" (*vlasti*), he continued, couldn't cope with Tajiks as well, so the group moved on to Russia, to the town of Barnaul in the Altai. Here they were at first welcomed and given jobs, but for some reason which he did not choose to explain, they were sacked and soon they moved on to Novosibirsk. Here, right in the railway station, they came across another crowd of Tajik refugees, who threw themselves on the new arrivals saying, "Why have you come? It was bad enough here without you too," and so the group traveled on to Irkutsk. In Irkutsk station exactly the same thing happened, so the band went on, ending up in July 1993 in Ulan-Ude. They now (November 1993) live in the railway station, by begging (Panarin 1996).[22]

At each stopping place on their journey, the Tajiks had addressed a petition to "the most powerful authorities." At Ulan-Ude, too, they were awaiting the arrival from Omsk of a particularly respected relative, someone who could both speak and write Russian fluently, and he was to make an appeal the Supreme Soviet of the Buriat Republic for permission to stay officially on Buriat territory. But abandoned at the station, the Tajiks' best hope would be to persuade some domain lower in the hierarchy to take them in and help them. Now the Tajiks, in their view, make their identity absolutely clear: the men make a point of wearing colored national skullcaps, the women wear striped Tajik national dresses, and they all when begging hang cardboard signs round their necks saying, "Help the refugees." Nevertheless, Panarin found that everyone else he talked with in Ulan-Ude (young, old, Russians, Buriats, Germans, and so forth) was convinced by their own myth: the Tajik refugees were Gypsies. "Those people begging, with their colored rags, their gold teeth, and all those children, of course they are Gypsies." Panarin explained to the citizens that the refugees were speaking Tajik, that the skullcap was Central Asian national dress, and so forth. The citizens responded, "Well then, they must be Tajik Gypsies." It should be explained that the townspeople rarely come across Tajiks, and Gypsies are not that common either; but the fact is, the citizens hardly looked at the refugees. The townsfolk said that the cardboard signs were typical tricks, and of course those people are dirty and beg and live at the station, because "that is the Gypsy way of life" (Panarin 1996). There is a Russian saying, "A Gypsy—the more hungry he is, the more cheerful."

Here we see how mythicized images typologize but in the hands of the dispossessed can fail. The synchronic image signs made by the Tajiks to indicate "Tajikness" were radically misread, because the literal "flow" that was simply visible—raggedness, lots of children, begging, and so forth—was so immediate, and so easily available for another symbolic interpretation (Gypsies). The Tajiks' mythic presentation of themselves was overwhelmed by a "myth" imposed from outside, one they had no intention of creating and which was forced on them.

In this situation, the cultural identity of being a Tajik could only be conveyed by creating a more powerful discourse, that is, the history of their origin and flight in words; and in fact, when Panarin recounted their narrative, explaining the wanderings of the band through Siberia, all of his citizen respondents without exception accepted that the people at the station were Tajik refugees, switched their attitude, and in many cases began to help them in practical ways. But without Panarin's intervention, perhaps nothing of the Tajiks' story would have been heard, a point to which I return later.

Of course, the initial view of the citizens from "inside," the almost willful mythic misrecognition of the Tajiks as Gypsies, was a way of rejecting people seen as alien. We must remember that it was not just Russians who took this attitude but also Buriats, Jews, and Germans in Ulan-Ude. Even the Tajik refugees themselves had labeled fellow-suffering Abkhazians in this way. Perhaps Szynkiewicz (1990) is right to argue that such rejection stems not so much from particular national chauvinisms as from a huge, general indifference. This is the pervasive residue of the Soviet tendency to ignore difference in the subject peoples for the sake of commonality, that is, to encompass other people and assume they are the same or "benignly overlook" their differences. As a result, in the post-Soviet era differences may be evident, but they are incomprehensible as history. Part of the explanation for this attitude lies in Soviet teleological evolutionism (the mythic advance towards Communism) and, at the folk level, the construction of the past as a succession of eras of personalized power. But its essential ground of the recourse to myth-labels and the rejection of narrativity in respect of the excluded is the sameness and systemic evolutionary timelessness attributed to the "primary units of society." The past events (history) of the domains were always systematically occluded so as to present the seeds of what exists now as having always been there all through the Soviet period (Humphrey 1983), just as the present was seen as tending to the glorious future.

As Garros (1992, 994–995) observes, in the early 1990s there was no future that did not at the same time appear to be a return to the past (a return to capitalism, the church, and so forth). "History then," she writes, "has no more sense, or at least another sense. How then can it be narrated, aided by what temporality?" Even if glasnost has enabled people to investigate the blank pages, it has not (not yet) provided an answer to the questions, "Who are we? What kind of society have we created?" And even if, now, the domains are positively differentiating themselves, what this means, to quote Garros, is that knowledge has been broken apart and chopped up. It appears as various versions of the past, or as an incomplete mosaic of fortuitous happenings, both of which fail convincingly to explain the essential question of social identity in the present. "Historical facts may have become accessible, but it has not been possible to reappropriate history. What characterizes the mass of publications is an absence, the impossibility of reconstituting a chronology" (Garros 1992, 995). As a result, some years after glasnost we find among ordinary Russians a pervasive rejection of senseless historical facts, a rejection of "all these revelations," all this "rummaging in our tombs." This dilemma strips narration of the Soviet past of legitimate explanatory power in interaction. Of course, the historiographic crisis of the early 1990s may be gradually resolved, particularly with regard to the Russians' own history, but as it is, the uncertainty and atemporality with regard to the self-identity of those "inside" cannot but be related to their impatience with the disturbing cultural differences now revealed among other former Soviet peoples.

Thus the colored caps and striped dresses of the Tajiks were a riddle no one even wanted to unravel, unlike the signs of the familiar gangs, which were immediately understood as provocations. "Gypsies" in Russia are not the subject of quite such strong paranoia as seems to be the case in Eastern Europe (Verdery 1996, 97–99), but the term connotes alienness, mythic romance, and threatening greed. The Gypsies are the very epitome of the people who do not belong "inside" but have their own mysterious interstitial existence. So although many of them are clearly both migratory and needy, the Gypsies remain outside the remit of the Federal Migration Bureau. Russian villagers call Gypsies black and suppose them to have "black powers" (Lemon, 1996). The Gypsy epithet thus joins other characteristically post-Soviet forms of myth-making that imagine alienness by reference to types of power. This relates to the fact that from "inside" the past is seen not chronologically but through a succession of regimes, uncertainly related in time. An example is the insulting term for the Congress of People's Deputies used by some of their enemies,

Stepnoe Aziatstvo ("the rule of the Asian steppe"), with its connotations of bar-
barism, antirationality, passivity, and so forth, reappearing from an unspeci-
fied past. For the villagers of the domains, those other people who had previously been hazily regarded as distant members of the Soviet Union, "younger
brothers," and so forth, but now appeared on the doorstep making no bones
about their foreignness, could be readily assigned to such mythic generalized
categories of the alien; for example, in Ivanovo province Russian peasants talk
of the "the blacks" (*chernye*), which includes Georgians, Tatars, and Gypsies.

The Tajik refugees themselves, as we have noted, were not immune to such
a type of mythic categorization of others. But for them this was no more than
incidental. The creation of powerful narratives to which the citizens of Ulan-
Ude would listen was more important, because it would enable them to construct a new life, in effect conferring on them a historical sense of their own
identity. This is not a Barthesian constellation of symbolic labels given plausi-
bility by literal images. On the contrary, by living through the events of dis-
possession the refugees are forced to cast their previous domains into an irreversible and chronologically connected past. The journey, with its movements
and its encounters, enables space to pin down time, producing a historical
temporality which enables them to say, "We, the people you see before you,
are the people who experienced this, and this, and this." Identity in these narratives thus appears as cumulative, changeable, and unprecedented, not typo-
logical. However, this discourse is mythicized too, as can be seen from the narrative of Liudmila Troiankina, a Russian refugee, also from Tajikistan, when she
was talking with myself and Sergei Panarin in Moscow.

Troiankina recounted how the Russians had prevented the destruction of
Dushanbe in 1991 by organizing a volunteer force during the riots; how when
Tajik became the national language the Russians were forced to acknowledge
what their own culture really was; how the collapse of the beloved "Center"
(that is, the union government in Moscow), which paid for nearly all their
jobs, made them see they were now abandoned and on their own. She described saying goodbye to Tajik friends, recounted how her group had then
been cheated by a construction firm offering housing near Voronezh, and
how they had then been offered radioactive land for settlement at the Gagarin
airport. She told how she had acquired the official status of "refugee," which
in her growing political realism she now calls a "papal indulgence."

Confrontation with today's terrible practicalities in Russia made Troiankina
muse on what the Russians of Tajikistan had been and on the historical fate
of Russians in general:

You know, Caroline, I am so lucky. I escaped early and so managed to exchange my flat in Dushanbe for somewhere to live. I had a wonderful, central, spacious apartment in the center of town, and at first I couldn't accept giving it up, but now I see how lucky I am. I exchanged it for a room in a communal apartment here in Moscow, where there are five other families apart from us. Now the cities won't take Russian refugees: my friend is in Tambov province, in a wretched hut in the depths, fifteen people in two rooms; oh, they live poorly. My friend—she knows it painfully. Out in the sticks some collective farm, or whatever they call them these days, will give us jobs. But soon we realized, we couldn't do them. It's not that we won't. Everyone is blaming us for not wanting to go to the villages, but it's not that, it's that we can't. Our ancestors came [to Tajikistan] with the Revolution, as teachers and doctors; they were missionaries of culture; they tried to give all they could to that people; for three or four generations they lived in the town and now they are not adapted to work on the land. For someone over forty, how can he start afresh? He has to shift dung, to struggle for fertilizer and concentrated feed, do you know what that is, Caroline? Oh heavens, may God give him even five years with such a life!

"And again," Troiankina continued,

my cousin was an architect in Dushanbe. Now she is living in Kaluga province, in some distant, distant village; she hasn't got a job, she just tends her vegetable plot. And she can't send her daughter to school. It's twenty kilometers, too far to walk, and they haven't allocated her a horse yet. . . . Such a great wave of people has come to Russia, and they've been so territorially dispersed that maybe all their talents and potential will die out; it's like water disappearing in sand. Yes. There is a continuous dissipation of culture in Russia. It might have seemed that we could have learned from the past—the Revolution, 1937, the present economic chaos—and what has happened, this is Russians being wasted, who have nowhere else to go but Russia. If we do not take this chance now, then that will be it. Finished. It will be "drunken Russia," and I say this with pain because we Tajik Russians were a non-drinking people.

Mythic elements appear in this narrative. They were framed in our conversation as somehow superhuman events, and their form and speech style had "decontextualized" aspects (the rehearsal, reiteration, and patterning of tragedy). In conversation Troiankina felt her way towards orienting our response. She first talked of the Dushanbe riots as a "pogrom," and her evocations of the heroic volunteer troop of 1991, or the Russians as "missionaries of culture," were replete with mythicized revolutionary romanticism. But in the actual situation of our conversation these symbolic images weakened rather than strengthened the case. No one apart from other Russians from Tajikistan could have shared quite these symbols and they were therefore powerless in dialogue. Panarin looked wary and then began to dispute exactly these points—what was pogromlike about it? And weren't those "missionaries of culture" oppressive to the Tajiks? By contrast, he listened attentively and with respect to the plain narrative of what had actually happened; he smiled at the trope of the papal indulgence.

Nor is it the case that the dispossessed have abandoned the collection of legitimating documents and the genre of the petition. Troiankina had signed a letter addressed to Yeltsin, Popov, and Rutskoi, which says, "We place responsibility for our fate and that of our children on the government and President of Russia." But about such documents and petitions she said, "I know it is useless. I don't blame them; they cannot help us. The powers (*vlasti*) have become powerless (*bez sil*)."

I told Troiankina I would send her a copy of my article if she'd be interested to see it. She concluded, as we must conclude with her, "I would not just be interested. I would hope this would help find some way out for us, those hundreds of people who signed all those useless petitions. If they only could feel that someone, somewhere knows about this. Not much is needed, just that someone knows, because otherwise we are completely abandoned people."

Perhaps it would be going too far to suggest that the narratives of the dispossessed are liberations from the repressive power of labeling myth. Such mythic images require a shared cultural context to be understood, but then they have a relative incontestability: they are given luster by the accompanying images of "reality," not challenged by them. It is therefore difficult to counteract a mythic constellation with event-based narratives, as can be seen from the example of the Tajik refugees at the railway station. But these narratives are the outcome of the opening of the eyes of the tellers. I think we can say that they correspond to the structural interstitiality, the actual movements, and really felt time experienced by the dispossessed, and that anthropologists can take part in the dialogues that could make these narratives powerful forms of discourse.

CHAPTER 3
CREATING A CULTURE OF DISILLUSIONMENT
CONSUMPTION IN MOSCOW, A CHRONICLE OF CHANGING TIMES

The turn toward a market economy has brought a flow of goods from all over the world to Russia.[1] The items range from franchises for expensive cars and designer clothes, through cheaper manufactures from China and Turkey, to a mass of quickly run-up clothing, handicrafts, and southern fruits sold by traders from the former Soviet republics. By late 1993 basic foodstuffs were also pouring in. All these things are seen as *ne nashi* ("not ours," foreign).

One might have expected Muscovites, after decades of imposed homogeneity, to delight unambiguously in the possibility of using consumption for self-expression by means of exotic and global signs. Undoubtedly there is pent-up demand in Russia. Nevertheless, attitudes to consumption are complex, sometimes negative, and subject to rapid historical change. Soviet society had earlier created consumers, that is, people conscious of living through objects and images not of their own making. However, this consciousness was significantly different from that of late industrial market economies. In fact, a large section of the population continued to produce for subsistence in their own households,[2] but more important than this was the Soviet ideology, which insisted on the citizen's conscious identification with the activity of the state. Virtually all industrial and manufactured goods and most agricultural ones were produced by state enterprises and distributed throughout the Soviet Union according to state plans. This meant that, although the vast majority of products and images were consumed by people who had not created them, it was ideologically enjoined that people feel them nevertheless to be "ours." At some level people did make this identification, while simultaneously realizing this to be part of the gigantic deception (*obman*) of the Soviet regime. What we need to try to understand now is how people conceive of consumption when the category of state products is shrinking by the month and "foreign" goods are flooding in, even foods, which people literally consume in their own bodies.

This chapter supports the view that consumption is the key means of creating culture in the urbanized and industrialized societies of the modern world (Miller 1987). This view may be contrasted with the idea that some preexisting culture molds consumption, which thereby appears as an outcome of culture. The idea of a preexisting culture suggests something timeless and homogeneous, but it is evident that neither of these qualities is appropriate for our times. In Russia today attitudes toward consumption cross-cut the various ethnic "cultures" of a vast country. One may find more in common between the consumption cultures of youthful urbanized Russians and Buriats, say, than between different classes within the Russian population. This is not to deny ethnic diversity, but it is to challenge the idea that it can be the sole or even main explanation of consumption patterns. It would be interesting to explore whether the revival/reinvention of ethnic traditions is not in fact leading to parallel phenomena in "different" ethnic groups, somewhat like Wilks's "structures of common difference." However, the focus of this chapter is elsewhere. It is suggested here that certain immediately preceding economic practices and attitudes of the late Soviet period have driven current consumption in particular directions, and that the extreme compression of historical changes into a few years has polarized the population; this has occurred most notably by generation, separating those people whose attitudes were formed by the Soviet regime from those who came to adulthood after the advent of Gorbachev in the mid-1980s.

Perhaps it seems extravagant to write as if there were much choice when so many people struggle only to survive. It is true that the vast majority of Russians have very low incomes and quite simply cannot afford to buy foreign goods. Over 30 percent of the population of Russia has an income below the "threshold of survival," that is, they must use existing stocks, sales of property, or loans from kin and friends to stay alive (Valiuzhenich 1993). However, poverty alone cannot explain the present Russian attitudes toward consumption, since even the most desperate are conscious of other times and of themselves as "poor people" within the diversified world of the city.

If contemporary culture is being created by consumption, we need to ask what are the dynamic mechanisms that influence attitudes and affect actual choices. Friedman (1990) has made an important step in suggesting that we think about consumption attitudes not as intrinsically ethnic but as the specific product, in any given situation, of a series of historical global transformations. However, in the case of contemporary Russia a purely externalist analysis of economic and political development risks diverging from Russian understandings and producing an over-coherent analysis remote from the actual chaotic situation. Therefore, this chapter explores three quite different representations of the historical transformation out of Sovietness as seen from inside. The first two of these were suggested to me by reading Bukovskii's *Letters of a Russian Traveler* (1981), his images of "deception" and the "crisis of values." The third is the social and ethical image of the "New Russians," the perception that business and entrepreneurship have produced a totally new kind of person. In this chapter, rather than standard categories like price and demand, I use these historically formed value-laden perceptions as ways of getting at the factors influencing people to consume in the ways they do.

"We know that they [the Soviet Government] always want to deceive us, and because of this we seek deception in everything," wrote Bukovskii (1981, 43). He was writing about attitudes to the press, but it is clear that, just as the Soviet ideology was in fact an attempt at a totalizing hegemony, the sense of deception among ordinary people also extended into virtually every sphere of life. It seems that from the mid-1960s onward the fitful opening of Soviet society to the world outside, and glimpses of global technology and consumer goods, began to play a role in the internal relations of state and people.

> It is strange, but totalitarian regimes are very sensitive to social pressure, though they carefully hide this. These regimes are maintained by fear and the silent complicity of those who surround them. Each person should be absolutely powerless before the state, completely without rights and generally to blame. In this atmosphere the *word* (even spoken from abroad) comes to have a huge strength (it is not by chance that they executed poets among us). At the same time, both the powers and the people understood perfectly the illegality of the regime, its *illegitimacy*. In this hidden civil war the external world (*zagranitsa*) becomes the highest arbiter. Just as a gangster, who has become wealthy through fighting, attempts to be accepted by high society, arrays himself in a dinner jacket, and imitates the habits of the profit-making businessman, the Soviet regime thirsts to be accepted as an equal in world society. The exclamations about being the most just, the most happy, the most progressive, and absolutely the most socialist state have long disappeared into the shadows. "It's no worse among us," or "Do they have it any better?"—these are the subtexts of present Soviet propaganda. (Bukovskii 1981, 29)

If the illegitimate and deceiving regime itself came to mimic the West, this placed all emulation in an ambiguous light. What was "real," when everything produced by the quasi-hegemonic regime at the same time copied and denounced the outside world? Russians, habituated to cynicism, continued to search for the fraud of the even more powerful West, and this rendered people perpetually aware of a certain conditionality, removing any possibility of simply and directly accepting capitalist consumption patterns at face value.

Bukovskii describes an instant from his own life to illustrate the "crisis of values" as the Russian economy faced that of advanced capitalism. He had been freed from camp and reached the West:

> It is just the same as when I stood in the airport in Zurich over my bag of prison odds and ends—completely amazed that all my valuables, penknives, razors, and books, accumulated over the years by generations of convicts, were turning under my eyes into nothing. I myself had hidden them, I had sewn them into linings, and trembled over them at each frisking. And I even brought a condom to Zurich, what a blockhead. . . . You see, Soviet people spend a great part of their lives in endless cares, how to get hold of, how to obtain, how to dig out the most elementary things. What trickery, what resourcefulness is needed to do things that over here take only five minutes. And now all this experience, all your property, collapses in a single instant. (1981, 83)

If such a crushing realization brought bewilderment and dejection to each Soviet person, that time has passed now. Three or four years have gone by in which Muscovites have become accustomed to there being an array of glittering goods and to their vastly high prices in comparison with those of local manufactures. Nevertheless, the historical instant of the "crisis of values" has made its mark, so that all attempts to come to terms with the new economic circumstances, to make a life somehow with all these goods, take place in its shadow.

The Russians' exaggerated cynicism and despairing sense of loss of value emerged from within their own, radically different, economic experience. Furthermore, perhaps only a professional economist could separate out such an object as "the Soviet economy." For everyone inside, it was experienced as a *political economy*, that is, imbued at every point with policies and ideology. The habit of seeing all "economic" activity as also intrinsically laden with political-ideological value is particularly marked and conscious among former Soviet people (though it must apply in other kinds of economy too). One aspect of this was the glorification of production/labor and the condemnation of commonplace trading for profit, called "speculation" in Soviet parlance. The quasi-illegitimacy of the Soviet regime itself did not thereby make speculators a positive category. Nor have they become so today. Rather, the historical (and so far only partial) transformation of the economy has seemed to Russians to produce an original breed of business people, the "New Russians." New Russians are seen as a continuation of the speculators, but with the shocking difference that their activities are now approved by the government. These political-moral attitudes set the New Russians apart, and they have reacted with a boldfaced rejection of all such views. In the following section I give a description of the consumption situation in Moscow, and this is followed by a discussion of the role of the three perceptions introduced here in influencing consumption decisions.

An Ethnography of Consumption in Moscow, 1993

In the Soviet period, the people of Moscow bought basic goods mostly in state shops and, if they were relatively well off, in the few state-run markets, where vegetables and fruit were sold by collective farms and peasants at higher prices. Besides this, there was an extensive system of allocation of difficult-to-obtain goods through the workplace, sometimes paid for "by order" and sometimes distributed free as a bonus (Humphrey 1991). Meanwhile, of course, people sought every means—the black market, networks of acquaintances, barter and exchange magazines, patrons and back doors of all kinds (*blat*)—to get hold of other things they needed.

In Moscow in the spring of 1993, there were not only the state stores and official markets of old but also private and foreign shops, kiosks, street peddlers, informal markets, and huge weekly fairs, such as the arts and crafts fair at Izmailovo Park. However, all this did not make shopping in Moscow like shopping in London, Paris, or Rome. Somehow, the sovereignty of the Western shopper, enticed to wander and inspect, to titillate desire, to take pleasure in the whole process—that is, shopping promoted as a leisure activity—had not occurred and seemed indeed far from Russian reality.

In Soviet times, there used to be an underlying sense that for the most part goods were not really bought by choice but were allocated. This intensified during the first years of economic collapse (1989–91) before the freeing of prices. During those years there was an increase in workplace orders and state distributions to various needy and honored social groups, and rationing was introduced in many places for basic goods such as meat, flour, or butter. Thus, even though the Soviet consumer formally engaged in buying—went to a shop, decided what to purchase, and paid money for it—the ways people talked about this revealed that at some level they realized that they were at the receiving end of a state-planned system of distribution. People said that goods were there to buy because "they" (the authorities) had given them out. "What are they giving (*daiut*) in GUM today?" people would ask. In slang "they" threw out (*vybrosili*) or chucked out (*vykidyvali*) the goods to the people.[3] This was recognition that shops and markets were lower-priority parts of the same system as the specially distributed package of luxuries of officials and the nameless, closely curtained buildings that contained foreign currency stores. Voinovich (1985, 113) wrote ironically, "With socialism, as everyone knows, there can be no *uravnilovka* (egalitarianism, a pejorative term in late Soviet times—C.H). From each according to ability, to each according to rank. Even Marx said that. Or Lenin. Or maybe I dreamed it up myself, I can't remember when."

In working-class Moscow in the spring of 1993 the stark signs of the distributory era—"Bread," "Footwear," "Meat"—were still virtually the only labels a shop was likely to have. Most of them, private or not, did not bother with anything much in the way of window displays (though they were not as downright misleading as they used to be: in the old days, if you saw something in a shop window it was almost a guarantee that it could not be bought inside). Strangely, rather than private shops approximating some Western model, and state shops being forced by competition to emulate them, almost the reverse was the case. State stores remained unchanged, and private shops, which were often only state ones taken over by the collective of workers, were usually indistinguishable from them in any outward way. Only locals could tell if a given ruble grocery was in private hands (though the prices were higher). It is true that private and foreign shops selling in dollars were somewhat different, since hardly anyone could afford to buy at them;[4] but here, too, minimal effort was made to make the goods attractive. Decorated Italian sweaters jostled with Swedish fridges, lace underwear with salami, whisky, or videos. The idea was simple: these things are foreign; bring your dollars and pay up. Inside state shops for basic goods, in contrast, there were crowds, and the salespeople, as of yore, had precedence. The shoppers were subjected to the triple queuing system, as irritable shoulder-to-shoulder masses shuffled in three lines to order the goods, pay for them, and collect them.

In its way, the Soviet state shop was a microcosm of what Bukovskii called the "hidden civil war," and essentially this system continued into the spring of 1993. As befits the idea that the state managed this microcosm to its own Olympian benefit, the manager remained invisible in a separate room and the cashier's desk was often elevated on a stand, so buyers had to pass money up to someone sitting at shoulder height. This made it feel as though one was petitioning to be allowed to pay. The cashier might refuse to accept anything but the exact sum, or alternatively might throw down (literally) some sweets as change. The shoppers cursed or agitatedly counted through their packets of multifarious banknotes. In the ordering queue something of the distributive mentality remained, partly because prepackaging of goods in units a shopper might want to buy was still a rarity. So when buying butter or cheese, for example, the purchaser named a weight and the shop worker cut a certain amount off a huge block with a spatula and weighed it, often with a bored and careless look, so the buyer had to glare or remonstrate that it was too little, and then a bit more would be added, all with the facial expression, "This is as much as you deserve." Frequently shoppers were turned away if they had not brought their own wrapping paper. In the case of meat, people could reach the top of the queue only to find that the shop worker refused to give a good piece unless some scrawny, dried-up bits were taken too. So mistrustful of one another were the two sides that payment by check (were such things to exist) was unthinkable. In 1993, a few large stores introduced their own "credit cards," and some people were attracted by such a seemingly Western modernity. But not only did purchasers have to buy the cards by paying up to their "credit limit" in advance, they soon found that the goods in these stores were regularly more highly priced than outside. Shoppers were not really surprised to be disillusioned, and queuing continued, though during the year it changed its goals.

The queue, heaving involuntarily forward and looking with gimlet eyes at each transaction, could not be said to be supportive of the shopper at the head. An almost palpable vexation arose if someone "bought too much," and it was almost as bad if they "wasted time" by querying the weighing, or insisted on picking and choosing between good and rotten fruit, or made a mistake in their sums and arrived from the cashier's queue with a chit that did not exactly correspond with the price/weight of the items. Of course, queues varied: in neighborhood shops people often kept places for friends or jumped the queue by prior arrangement with the shop worker (this was grimly borne by those behind). In the fashionable Western franchises in central Moscow, it was more a case of each for himself and physical elbowing into a more advantageous position.

The Russian queue was not simply a social presence but was also a social principle, one that regulated social entitlements in time. It enshrined the social and psychological idea of consumption through state distribution. As Voinovich (1985, 42) wrote, and it is still true, "Queues are various. They can be for a few minutes, overnight, for several days. People stay in the queues for cars or apartments for years." Russians fleeing from Tajikistan report that the Dushanbe riots of 1991 were caused by the rumor that Armenian refugees had been allotted places at the head of the queue for apartments. The preservation of the queue for flats in the metropolis was the main reason given by the Russian Federal Migration Service for their support for the residence-permit system, despite its "undemocratic" nature and the fact that it served to exclude their clients (refugees) from all major cities (Baiduzhii 1993).

How did this change during 1993? On one hand, the system of consumption through the allocation of benefits if anything increased. On the other, the old Soviet-type queuing, where the availability of scare goods rather than price was what mattered, has to a great extent been replaced by the desperate search for cheap goods.

One reason why allocated benefits have increased relative to money wages is the newly introduced income tax (Hansen 1993, 92). Wage increases over government-regulated levels are subject to punitive taxes of up to 60 percent, a measure to control inflation. But social welfare benefits are exempt from taxation. Many state organizations and companies therefore choose to give workers raises in the form of vouchers or coupons, calling them something like "subsidy for food." A recent study of living conditions in a northern province of Russia (Hansen 1993) showed the benefits to be: free/subsidized transport (27 percent), vouchers for purchase of consumer durables (7 percent), humanitarian aid from Western countries (7 percent), free meal at the workplace (6 percent), food orders for families with many children (2 percent), food orders for invalids and veterans (15 percent), and food orders through the workplace (35 percent). This essentially continues an old practice of the Soviet state, but it is now supplemented by the distribution of imported goods which companies can obtain by purchase or barter for their own locally generated profits.

This system may take the edge off subsistence shopping for some employed people, but it leaves the unemployed and the dispossessed in a desperate situation. Furthermore, state wages do not keep pace with inflation, and many loss-making factories, though they do not dismiss their workers, close down for months on end without pay. During 1993 large numbers of state and collective farms were unable to pay wages for as much as six months. Russians divide their "money" into *nalichnye* (cash in hand) and *beznalichnye* (notional money owed). There is a terrible shortage of cash.[5] Thus the glittering goods are mostly things people are unable to buy, and the Soviet search for scarce goods has been replaced by combing the city for cheap basic products.

However, this is exactly what the market is not providing. There are many reasons, perhaps the main one being that state shops (and even privatized state shops) still to a great extent rely on their old suppliers, and these are the doddering collective farms and ramshackle factories which themselves have problems with supplies. Here, however, I focus on the activities of entrepreneurs, which are another major factor. Entrepreneurs in Russia, not surprisingly, started out by trading the most profitable goods, luxury items not found in the Soviet economy. This explains the historical appearance first of foreign liqueurs, "designer" jeans, expensive flashy jackets, and so forth, in the Russian marketplace. People rushed to buy them in 1990–92, but now they are beyond the pockets of ordinary workers. Only a few Western goods have penetrated everyday consumption, notably Mars bars and Snickers ("Karl Mars and Friedrich Snickers"). In 1993, entrepreneurs started to import American and European foods (Norwegian salami, American butter, and so forth), which have appeared in state and private shops. But the prices are still too high, and today, if you see a crowd of people, you know the queue is for cheap Russian produce—the very opposite of the situation a few years ago.[6]

A friend of mine "in business" said that if a certain item sells well, her reaction is not to get in more of the goods but to raise the price. Muscovite shoppers describe how you may hear that something (soap, tights, cassettes) is cheaper in one quarter of the city than another, but it never makes sense to trek over there to get it, because by the time you get there the price will have gone up. It is clear how pricing tricks work locally: there is a row of kiosks all selling the same items. One has a lower price for something. Thinking they have got a bargain people eagerly buy it. The kiosk holders are in league and divide up the profits. In fact, local Mafias ensure that prices are never truly lowered.

The purchaser thus encounters a different kind of anxiety from the queue: a threatening kind of lawlessness. The kiosks which cluster around railway stations and the entrances to the Metro sell a range of profitable goods: Western cigarettes, cans of drink, electronic equipment, Italian shoes, CDs, briefcases, tights, and obscure (but always the same) liqueurs. Near the kiosks sit the peddlers, with their trays of local cigarettes, ice cream, Mars bars, or apples. But roundabout, sometimes hidden, but often sitting openly alongside, are the minders. There is not a single old woman selling Marlboros and matches who does not have her allotted stretch of pavement and pay her protector for the right. One kiosk cannot lower prices or the owner would immediately be beaten up by the others or by the minders. If a customer spots a fraud and complains about it aloud, a number of leather-jacketed men are likely to appear instantaneously at his or her elbow. They do not hesitate to threaten or even beat ordinary women shoppers.

People shop at the kiosks with their threatening entourages even though they know they are being "cheated." They know a good proportion of the price is going to the minders and the higher-level Mafia, not to speak of the "good-for-nothing" young kiosk holders themselves. The goods are suspected of being counterfeit and defective. A kiosk worker I knew, a Russian dropout student, worked for Chinese merchants, and she realized she was hired to do the face-to-face selling because foreign traders are so resented. I heard people liken them to cockroaches. Where this differs from negative attitudes to ethnic groups as traders elsewhere in the world is the cynicism in every relationship down the line. All sides cheated one another: the owners underpaid the sellers, the purchasers tried to steal, the buyers were given defective goods, and the sellers hid some of the takings from the owner. Massive takings nevertheless ended up with the main Chinese trader (early 1990s), but my friend was almost sorry for him because, since banks took high taxes, he had to sit day and night by his trunk of rapidly devaluing money.[7]

As for the street peddlers, Muscovites know exactly how they operate. Often they are old people who have fallen on hard times, and almost all are women. They get to know the managers of large shops located in inconvenient places. Having paid a bribe, they are able to buy up quantities of the goods before other shoppers get access. They then take the goods (say, cans of beer or flowers) to strategic spots where people are in a hurry and are prepared to pay far more than the usual price.[8] Sometimes goods change hands through several traders before they reach the streets. A money-conscious Muscovite would not buy from these peddlers but would prefer to do without or to make the trek to the original shop and pay the lower price. Nevertheless, passersby, being certain the women must have been driven to it, are horrified at the plight of the elderly street-sellers, who stand meekly in rows, with their prowling minders nearby.

As the structure of the Soviet Union collapsed, two things happened: there was a phenomenal growth in the number and type of economic transactions, and the old system of laws became obsolete. New laws hurriedly passed have failed to keep pace with the economic life of the streets, and the growth of some kind of "protection" for transactions was inevitable. This has become so pervasive that the authorities, colluding with at least some parts of the Mafia, have so far only ventured to attack relatively powerless outsiders (traders from the erstwhile "younger brother" peoples of the Caucasus and Central Asia).

The following newspaper report is noteworthy because it links such anti-foreign drives with new consumer reactions. In October 1993 the mayor of Moscow, Iurii Luzhkov, justified the use of the state of emergency as a way of expelling from the city several thousand Armenian, Georgian, and Azerbaijani traders without residence permits.

> Mr. Luzhkov . . . said that after the state of emergency ended, he would probably introduce an entry visa regime to prevent those expelled from returning to Moscow. As for the markets, they might offer fewer "exotic fruits" in future, but "honest traders from Tambov, Lipetsk, Briansk, and other [Russian] towns will arrive with good products and will sell traditional Russian food."
>
> If Mr. Luzhkov carries out his threat, Muscovites will face a diet of potatoes, beetroot, cabbage, and pickled cabbage. But they don't care. Because some Caucasians are involved in crime, they blame them all and welcome the police action. "It's just a pity this state of emergency can't be permanent," said Vera Vladimirovna, a pensioner looking for something affordable on the few stalls left at the Chernomuzhkinskaia Market. (Womack 1993)

Sometimes at a market one can see heaps of unsold meat. It is not just that many people cannot afford it, a large number refrain from consuming altogether as far as possible. They prefer to save or invest, for reasons that will be explored below.

It is interesting to try to discover what people do actually buy. Some information is available from large-scale, all-Russian statistics, although it is not clear how these were gathered. In 1991–92 Russians spent between 30 and 40 percent of their incomes on food, 40–50 percent on nonfood manufactures, around 12–15 percent on services, and 8–10 percent on alcohol. In 1992–93 the amount spent on food rose to 40–50 percent, payments for manufactures and services declined, and alcohol remained the same (Struktura 1993). A probably more reliable survey in 1992 in the Kola Peninsula suggested that householders spent between 70 percent and 82 percent of their budget on food (Hansen 1993, 99).

I close this section with a description of the budget of a Moscow middle-class family with whom I stayed during March–April 1993. I wish to use this to make two points: first, to show how consumption even in the middle class was largely devoted to basic necessities; and second, to indicate the kind of bouleversement that people are living through, since only six months later, such a consumption pattern became impossible. The family in the spring of 1993 regarded itself as not particularly well-off, less so, for example, than that of an experienced factory worker. Their income for the month from March 15 to April 15 was 70,100 rubles.[9] In December 1992, a Russian economist from the Ministry of Labor estimated that the "threshold of survival" of such a family (three adults and a child) would be around 16,100 rubles a month, while the "poverty line" would stand at around 40,000 rubles a month (Valiuzhenich 1993).[10] Extrapolating this by the 70 percent price increase between then and March 16, 1993 (Goriacheva 1993), we can estimate that the family's income of 70,100 rubles was around the official "poverty line," though well above the survival rate. The family's food for the month cost 25,955 rubles; payment for services (including transport and one-time payments for school repair and a foreign passport) were 14,319; nonfood manufactures were 5,121; and alcohol was 550. The total spent was 45,695 rubles. Potatoes, bread, cabbage, pickled cabbage, and beetroot indeed figured prominently in the budget, though the family was also able to afford meat, fish, eggs, and cheese. Fearful of total economic collapse, the household also kept stockpiles of food like flour, tea, noodles, and sugar, and these were being gradually used up as such Russian goods became more and more difficult to obtain.[11]

We should note that the budget was provided by the wife and assumed to cover the whole family. This is a characteristic Russian assumption regarding the household, according to which it is the wife who has to make do.[12] In fact, the housewife's budget did not take into account certain expenditures of the husband and older daughter. I have estimated these to include around 8,600 rubles for cigarettes, 1,000 for vodka, some 1,000 for newspapers, and around 5,000 for dressmaking. The family's total expenditure would therefore have been at least 61,295 for the month. Any savings were put toward purchase of a dacha outside town.

Although the family did not spend their entire income, they felt hard-pressed. Steep inflation was perceptible even during the month. The house-wife, the main shopper, went to great efforts to find products that were good bargains. She was dependent on the fact that it was possible to buy good bread cheaply (bread is subsidized, and people buy it even several times a day from numerous local bakers). Very little was spent on clothing, and nothing on books, cinemas, or music. What is most noticeable about this budget is that, with the exception of one piece of imported butter, nothing in it was foreign. "American butter" was regretted and bought only because "our fatherland's butter" was sold out. The cigarettes were Russian, and so were a door lock and pair of child's skis. It was as though the global influx of goods to Moscow had never taken place.

Before discussing the thinking behind this kind of consumption, I should explain that its Russianness is no longer an option. Even the state and collectively owned shops are now full of imported products, and to the amazement of Muscovites these are packaged in convenient units and in such a way that they can be preserved longer. But people told me they would rather go without, or restrict their food to a few repetitive items, than buy foreign produce. However, they do not have much choice. The Caucasian and Central Asian traders with their fruits and kebabs continue to be kept out of Moscow. Unless you can grow produce yourself or have relatives on a farm, it is a case of imports or nothing, and these tightly packaged foods many Russians find "doubtful" and "likely to cause illness."

Deceit

From the 1920s onward, the Communist Party's propaganda sections put forward Soviet styles for people to emulate. These included styles of clothing, house interiors, food, and etiquettes of behavior that were designed to express the classless, health-conscious, labor-oriented direction that society should take. In the Khrushchev era (1950s–1960s), an important change took place. Rather than representing goals for the future, the propaganda images were presented as if they really existed. At first, these images were deceitful because they were utterly unattainable—all items represented either were absent from Soviet shops or so expensive as to be beyond ordinary people's most extravagant hopes. But later, as these very goods became available for the middle class, it became apparent that the range of products was so limited as to enforce an involuntary homogeneity on all consumption.

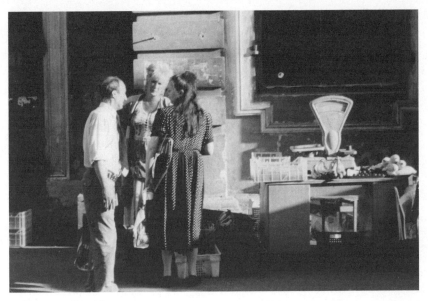

5. A street stall in Moscow, 1997.

Thus there was another aspect to the feeling of being involved in a gigantic deception. This derived from the growing sense during the 1970s–1980s of being removed, by being entombed in the Soviet Union, from another more real but curtained-off history, that is, from the history of the world. Soviet citizens were told that they were at the forefront in every sphere, they led the world, but disorienting glimpses on television, and above all foreigners themselves, seemed like evidence that this might not be so.

So propaganda images were widely seen as a deceit, even though they aroused consumer desire. Furthermore, as Verdery (1992) has perceptively observed, this desire was constituted as a "right," since material plenty was an essential measure of the advancement of the Soviet socialist system. Quoting a Romanian friend, Verdery wrote: "What everyone strives to do is to figure out how not to have frustration be too costly: not to want something so much that being denied it will devastate you. The test of character becomes managing to accept yet another denial without being undone by it." Verdery continues,

> Socialism intensified this experience . . . for the regimes themselves paradoxically abetted the emphasis on consumption. First, organized shortage made procuring something—anything—a major triumph. Sec-

ond, even as the regimes prevented people from consuming by not making goods available, they insisted that under socialism the standard of living would constantly improve. . . . Socialism . . . aroused desire without? focalizing it, and kept it alive by deprivation. That is, in socialism desire floated free in endless search of goods people saw as their right.

. . . The arousal and frustration on consumer desire and East Europeans' consequent resistance to their regimes led them to build their social identities specifically *through consuming*. Acquiring consumption goods and objects conferred an identity that set one off from socialism. To acquire objects became a way of constituting your selfhood against a regime you despised. (Verdery 1992, 25–26)

Russia under the Soviet regime was more pervasively subject to hegemonic propaganda than Eastern Europe, and this ensured that Western goods were not merely representative but constitutive of social identity (see, for example, Friedman 1990, 318). Ordinary people would hide things, such as tape recorders, of obviously Western provenance, since they were associated with resistance to the regime. The *soccer fans, hippies, punks, rockers,* and other counterculture groups in Moscow in the 1970s–1980s used English for their graffiti, wore approximations of Western fashions and hairstyles, and conceptualized their way of life by "English" terms: *flety* ("flats," or crash-pads), *grin* ("green," dollars), *askat'* ("to beg/ask"), and so forth (Bushnell 1990, 116–117). Just looking like a *khippi* was enough to provoke the authorities. Many were dispatched to short terms in the *kreiza* (loony bin) just for their appearance (Bushnell 1990, 115).

There is a crucial difference between Eastern European countries, discussed by Verdery, and Russia. In the former, the Soviet system was easily seen as alien, whereas in Russia it had to be acknowledged as "ours." Consequently the experience of deception was both internalized and globalized, as though that was the way things were in the world in general. So "the West," too, was read as some kind of mirage or trick. Both Bukovskii and Voinovich describe this reaction of the Soviet visitor first faced with the unimaginable plenty of the West, the "pointless" diversity, the objects "of whose use we know nothing, even old people can't remember them" (Bukovskii 1981, 82). Voinovich recounts how an elderly Russian came to visit his daughter who had emigrated to Germany; she took him into a shop. He looked around and frowned, "No," he said. "Take me to a real shop. This must be a special one for foreigners. Show me one for ordinary people" (Voinovich 1985, 44). Bukovskii (1981, 82) describes the same feeling of the visitor to the West: all these things must be for show (*na pokaz*), as in a Soviet shop window, and of course, no one will buy them. That is why there are no queues and such huge quantities of goods lie around unsold. Real goods must be procured with difficulty (*dobyvat'*), unearthed (*otkopit'*), or obtained on the side (*nalevo*), from under the counter, or from such crafty places as are known only to the dedicated.

A first reaction to "the West" was to buy everything in sight. A second was depression and inertia, "too good is also no good," and the feeling that it was impossible to find anything unique in these jungles of wealth. "I stood before a counter with twenty-four kinds of salad oil, and I couldn't choose one, I only got tired. What is oil, after all? One can live without it" (Bukovskii 1981, 83). It seems to me that these reactions are not irrelevant to the stages of the opening of Moscow to global goods in the early 1990s. Muscovites now are tired, having experienced the "deception" they were expecting. "Sophisticated Western equipment is not for us," people often say, suspecting it to contain some hidden drawback or delicate mechanism which will prevent it from functioning in Russian conditions. My Russian friend, whose budget is given above, had rushed to buy a magnificent German washing machine. It does not work. Nobody quite knows why, but not many efforts are devoted to finding out. "We should have realized," sighs my friend. Now the machine stands there, taking up a lot of space in the bathroom, and everything is washed in a "reliable but rough" Soviet contraption or by hand. Likewise, glossily packaged produce like salami is suspect. Why encase it in such brightness? People say, "At least with our Russian sausage we won't be eating all those chemicals."

This feeling that Western goods are in some way a sham, contaminated, or somehow inassimilable and unsuited for Russian life has transformed the politicization of consumption noted by Verdery for the late Soviet period. Now, for many people at least, Western goods are no longer a goal in themselves, and they have lost much glamour. Above all, using Western consumer goods no longer confers a defiant social identity against the regime. Rather, they are associated with the new businessmen created by the Yeltsin government's economic reforms. Their suspect nature is compounded by their contiguity with shady dealings and what is guessed to be an insubstantial, dangerously risky kind of existence. Hundreds of thousands of Muscovites have been turning in another direction; they are forgoing Western consumer goods for the sake of more down-to-earth values: plots of land, dachas, or, if they have country relatives to look after them, cows, chickens, and pigs.

Prices for vegetable plots and small farms have grown enormously, and in the more desirable, unpolluted environs of Moscow they are now always quoted in dollars. It is possible to build a dacha, plant a few trees there, and sell the whole thing a year later for a large profit. Thus both entrepreneurs and ordinary workers invest in land, but they do so for different reasons. Even in 1991 over 30 percent of Muscovites owned a dacha (Hansen 1993, 100), and since then the country cottage has become even more a part of city life. The produce of the plot is important to subsistence, but the dacha also has a symbolic value. It represents space, repose, "Russianness." The dacha may be no more than a hut, and the journey to get there may involve several wearisome and expensive trains and buses with a walk at the other end, but people say it is worth the effort, since in the country they can recreate a familiar, "age-old" security lacking in Moscow. All this requires effort, saving, self-denial, and forethought. Sudden huge drops and gains in income have torn apart relationships, but the situation has also welded together families in new, strained dependencies. Saving is a survival strategy, and there is almost a frenzy to produce safety against the unpredictability of chaos. This pulls people back from "the market" and turns them inward to networks of security. The dacha is one of these, and combining a city job and even a moderately productive plot is not something anyone can do on their own.

The Crisis of Values

Bukovskii's image, his small bag of prisoner's treasures confronted with the opulent plenty of Zurich Airport, is in one sense a contradiction of values that exists in any complex economy: the incalculable value created by a person and the socially measured values of industrial production indicated by their prices. But there is a difference between Russia and the West. As Alexander (1992, 91) has argued, in the West:

> Deep down inside, we all know that commodities and services have an appropriate price—a fair price—and should normally be traded at this price, although in special conditions prices may be lower. One reason for the robustness of this view is the continuing stress in advertisements on value for money, another is the observation that prices seldom fluctuate . . . and that the gradual increases are always justified in terms of increasing costs. "Firms not only behave that way but also condition their customers to expect them to behave that way." (Okun 1981, 153)

Admittedly Alexander goes on to suggest that the supposition on which this close relation between price and value rests—that firms will act relatively honestly by raising prices only when costs also rise—is "the most unrealistic assumption of modern economic theory" (1992, 91), but my point is that the assumption of there being such a relation has not existed in Russia since the 1930s.

The state fixed the prices for all goods at "arbitrary" rates, that is, with a whole variety of rationales (here for political reasons, there to make a profit, here to subsidize some necessary branch, there to buttress some ideological policy). The state also promoted essentialist-ideological values, designating items that were beyond price. The range of these was different from in the West and much wider. Land was the most central, but other natural objects such as timber, coal, oil, or building materials also became quasi-sacred "people's wealth." Ordinary people could, in fact, only gain access to them by fiat of the state. It was absolutely forbidden simply to cut down a tree in the forest. Other state-imposed values were "negative," for example, typewriters: however much a typewriter cost and however many were sitting in the shops, it was illegal to own one without permission (they were regarded, rightly, as powerful potential dangers to the regime). Since I wish to illustrate how the disjunction between price, ideological value, and what I call "value-in-life" was experienced by everyone, let us take the case of bread.

Bread had a symbolic value to Russian peasants before the Revolution; for example, it was offered, together with salt, to welcome visitors on behalf of the village community. In the Soviet period, bread was first and foremost simply the epitome of food. Bread was part of every meal. "Almost all of us, growing up in the conditions of Soviet reality, earlier or later in our lives experienced war or hunger, and we have got used to relating to bread as something almost sacred," wrote Voinovich (1985, 26). Now all through the Soviet period the state kept the price of bread extraordinarily low. For decades bakeries made the same sizes and shapes of loaves, and all of them kept the same prices, which were as axiomatic as the unchanging fare on the Moscow Metro. It was part of Soviet life that bread was ideologically beyond price: "How many angry lines have I read in poems and prose about people who have forgotten about the war and the blockage of Leningrad and fling bread into the rubbish chute in loaves. I think I have read considerably more verses about this than there can have been cases of its happening" (Voinovich 1985, 26). People were instructed to save every crust, to pick fallen pieces from the floor, to moisten dried-up bits with water, to remember that even mold contains beneficial penicillin.

However, Russians were past masters at dealing with sacrosanct values; some peasants used to feed bread to their pigs. In the end, bread had a value in life, just like anything else. It was the disjunction between price and value promoted by the Soviet state itself that provided scope for divergent values in life. An ordinary product like onions could have two quite different prices in neighboring provinces. Of course, people knew about this, and state agencies had to spend unknown resources in clamping down on the main lines of smuggling. In all this, prices, being unrelated to any kind of value, were just what they were, a mystery, but people got used to them. So when travelers came back and said that prices in the West were higher for some goods than in Russia, people refused to believe it. In the Gorbachev era, classes were introduced in schools to explain that price depends on the cost of production. "But look around you," people of that generation now say, "it's obviously not true."

Now that almost the whole consumer sector is under the control of various Mafias, it is unlike other economies where trust is difficult to establish. The age-old method of the bazaar, bargaining in public, is ruled out. We cannot be surprised at the bewilderment, anger, and mistrust of consumers. Even though prices in Russia are still significantly lower than in Western Europe (from where many of the goods come), a fact published in Russian newspapers, many people would rather not buy anything than put a ruble in the pockets of traders they consider must be cheating them. When a "fair price" can only be guessed at, and you cannot bargain, then you look at who is selling.[13]

The "New Russians"

The attitudes I have described above do not apply to the "New Russians," the business people, stockbrokers, commodity traders, Mafiosi, personal assistants, computer specialists, bankers, private hotel owners, masseurs or taxi drivers of the metropolis. They know the rules of the bribe and the payoff and are firmly attached to Western styles and to the accumulation of elite and luxury goods. One of the first things they do, if successful, is to travel abroad and then try to reproduce the signs of capitalist practices in Russia. So they have personal bank accounts and credit cards at Western banks, use email and faxes, and make arrangements to have their children taught in English. They have no interest in Russian nationalism and little respect for the state.[14] In Russia as a whole, they are a tiny proportion of the population, but many more yearn to join then, especially among young people.

It is not entirely clear why the New Russians are so bitterly disliked. One can hardly hear a good word said about them among factory workers, farmhands, government and service employees, or elderly people. One of the explanations must be the extraordinary success of the Soviet propaganda against "speculation."

Speculators are people who make a profit by buying and reselling goods without adding any value by means of their own labor. This became a crime in Soviet times, and especially in the provinces it remains a gray area today. For example, if you lived in Cheliabinsk, took a train to Moscow, queued up, and bought twenty bottles of shampoo, brought them back to Cheliabinsk, and sold them for more than the Moscow shop price, you could be punished with a prison sentence. Not only was this a crime, but people in general condemned it, and many would still do so today. This blanket, almost unthinking dislike is oblivious to the economic reality of "speculation," the fact that people in Cheliabinsk needed shampoo or that the trader was put to trouble, danger, and expense to get it.

Negative attitudes toward trading are not an intrinsic part of Russian peasant culture, though some writers maintain such a view (Nikol'skii 1993a). Historical evidence indicates that in the sixteenth to eighteenth centuries a greater proportion of Russians engaged in trade and manufacture for profit than in any other European country, and furthermore they "had a passion for it" (Pipes 1974, 192–193). After the Revolution, during the Civil War and into the 1920s, the peasantry successfully revived both barter and market trade, even though the new Soviet government was ideologically opposed to it (Figes 1989, 26).

The reaction that developed during the Soviet period rests, of course, on the Marxist teaching that true value is created by labor. It was reinforced after the late 1920s by the Soviet social organization which ensured that labor was all that Soviet people gave. There simply were no legitimate people in the Soviet Union whose activity was conceptualized as creating wealth in any other way. Even workers for state trade organizations received only wages for labor, and only the director knew (or cared) whether the firm was trading at a profit or not. An extensive vocabulary developed to obscure the very existence of "profit," because this idea was incompatible with the unique institution that in fact gathered it, the Soviet socialist state. All this is another way of saying that the great hidden "speculator" was the state itself, which would brook no competition.

It is interesting to consider this in relation to Parry's theory (1989, 84–85) on the hostility to commerce in Europe and Latin America. Parry suggests that ideological commitment to a traditional household economy oriented toward self-sufficiency was accompanied by mistrust of trade and money, which were seen as a dangerous drain on subsistence needs. In India, in contrast, the caste order was founded on the fundamentally different premises of a division of labor between castes. Not even the local community was seen as an ideally self-sufficient entity. In India, without an ideology of autarky, trade and commerce were not condemned. To explain Soviet Russia, we need to add to this theory the political element. The USSR actually involved an extremely complex division of labor, but this was disguised by the fact that the positive function of distribution was taken over by the "fatherly" state. Thus independent trade became subversive of its monopoly. For their part, ordinary people perceived traders as siphoning off the scarce goods that the state should distribute to them as their due. This explains why extravagant consumption by highly ranked officials and their families was seen as their right, even if one that was grasped in the teeth of popular envy. The reaction of the privileged was often defiant and crude: load on the jewels, the furs, and the perfumes, because *we are in power.*

It should not be forgotten, nevertheless, that in the 1950s, the 1960s, and even the early 1970s, there was also still an austere Soviet style, a declaration of respect for the old revolutionary ideals. There were professors who dressed in workmen's clothes, officials who indignantly refused to use foreign currency stores, people who had their false teeth made of gray proletarian metal. But such plainness withered away during the Brezhnev years, and people began to seek all possible methods of differentiating themselves from the mass by small signs.

The black market existed surreptitiously in every town. It was called *tolchok* or *tolkuchka* (from the word "crowd," "push," or "bustle"), and this expressed its mobile reality. In the old days it was fed largely from the depots of imported goods, where employees regularly stole whatever they could for distribution to traders. Closed down in one alleyway, the market would spring up in another. "Where's your *tolchok?*" strangers would ask, as they looked for the only institution in town that might make their visit profitable. In Soviet times almost all city people had some consumer goods that clearly had to have come from the black market—a Hungarian sweater here, a packet of Western cigarettes there. Such goods sharply divided opinion. Some would remark, with envy, "She dresses from the black market." Now, criticism of buying black market goods has disappeared, but dislike of those selling them remains strong.

The early years of perestroika suddenly liberated street markets from their back-alley existence. The largest ones sprang up in the focal point of the city:

on the Arbat in Moscow, in Revolutionary Square in Ulan-Ude, and right out-side the doors of Ikh Delguur in Ulaanbaatar (the only state department store in the city). In the last year or two, city authorities have tried to curb markets. Essentially, they are still thought of as "black markets" and they are still known as *tolchok*. Thus, for example, on November 3, 1992, the newspaper *Buriatiia* gave out a schizoid message. On the front page was a long article: "The Buriat Republic: The Way to the Market"; on the back page was another long article, about how to put into effect the mayor's decree closing all street markets.[15]

It is very difficult to discover what are the meanings of "the market" to Russians. The market as a rational system sits uneasily with earlier values. In the following newspaper clipping the market seems to represent a mysteri-ous process of natural justice, but certainly it has nothing to do with visible trading. The article is about a herdsman at the Tuldun State Farm who had been refused a change of house by the farm bosses: "As we see, the question of housing moves into the sphere of politics. True, they do not now put people in prison for politics, as was the case in times of yore, but now the market can inquire about political malpractice. For the market is created by the producers of material wealth, and not by trader-speculators and not by shady dealers. The Tuldun bosses, having cheated the producer, are sabotag-ing the triumph of the politics of the market" (Ubeev 1992). Much is unclear in these remarks (the impression is that the author is toeing some political line he doesn't quite understand); however this may be, "the market" is clearly a good thing, therefore allied with producers and their labor, while traders are a bad thing and their activities do not create "the market."

With these attitudes still prevalent, it is not surprising that to engage in trading professionally is to step over some invisible line of decency. This, in my view, is one reason why cheating, protection rackets, and gang violence have accreted to markets and trade. Traders live metaphorically in a different layer, the layer of grease (the slang for profits is *navar*, the grease on top of soup). Society was unprepared for morality, let alone legality, in this sphere. Public markets have become like huge fairs of disingenuousness, spreading wider and wider as people set up booths here and there or turn their flats into little shops. Petty traders are too insecure to turn their backs on trickery and quick profits: not only do they have to pay bribes and protection money, they are also the "last in the line"—they stand to lose or gain personally from every transaction. Those who make serious profits from all these activities, the New Russians, glide past in their Mercedes, keeping well apart from the peddling on the streets.

Thus the New Russians are dividing into different groups. It might seem that New Russian consumption is continuous with the blatant opulence of the old Soviet high-ranking officials. However, we should be careful about making such an assumption. Top managers and ministry officials, it is true, were the first to be able to take advantage of privatization. But their selling-off of state assets for their private benefit has been surprisingly little resented, especially as they have normally carried on as local bosses and patrons of great power. It is the *New* Russians people dislike, the jumped-up youthful businessmen whose education is being used to no one's advantage except their own, and whose conspicuous consumption is no longer a marker of rank or ability to pull strings in the system.[16] We can now perhaps discern four groups, the old managers, their young entourages of kin and clients, the high Mafiosi, and the aspirant traders and racketeers of the kiosks.

All of them love sheer wealth, but different styles are beginning to emerge. The old managers retain sober suits and put their money in opulent furniture and bushy fur coats for their wives, while their younger kin prefer sleek brand-name Western clothing. The seriously wealthy Mafia buy private aircraft, whole plumbing systems for their houses, or new kitchen systems. The aspirant traders affect black leather, dark glasses, and sports clothes. Behind this lie different rates in the appreciation of the importance of information technology. The old manager would get a gold-plated dinner service and then a fax machine. The new business people first get English lessons or acquire a Mercury telephone line to the West, and only then branch into conspicuous consumption (which, I am assured, includes an obligatory mistress as well as a wife). In any field involving large amounts of money the different interest groups meet and carve out their domains, so the high bureaucrats, old managers, and new Mafia are not strangers, though they may be enemies. But the public at large knows little of this and reserves its dislike for those New Russians who seem to have become rich by invisible and foreign means. Theirs is regarded as unjust consumption, the outcome of some unfair magic, outside the huge struggle to move upward in the power game of Russian society. It is this that makes saving and consuming "ours," be it from choice or necessity, a political statement.

Conclusion

This chapter suggests some connections between the constitution of the consumer under the Soviet regime and present patterns of spending. The Soviet person was ideologically constituted as legitimately producing and consuming only within the state sphere. Thus consumption was in theory not alienated. The terms "ours" (*nash*) and "native" (*otechestvennye*) referred to the products of Soviet state enterprises, not to their ethnic or cultural origin. It followed that nonstate products, or goods whose social life had been transformed through the black market, were in this ideological sense "not ours." This nicely coincided with the fact that the vast majority of black-market consumer goods were of non-Soviet origin. Even stolen state products were tinged with the otherness of "speculation." Consumption thus was not a unified activity but one which took place in two different modes, that of struggling to get one's due (the state allocation mode) and that of battling to obtain something extraordinary (the black-market mode).

In the present period of bewildering change, consumption and the refusal to consume are creating a heterogeneity of culture. "Ours" and "other" are changing places, and the old coincidence between foreign goods and foreign traders has ended. In the early years of reform, it was easy for Central Asians, Caucasians, Chinese, Vietnamese, and others to take on the role of alien "speculator" set out for them. Now, the foreigners have been largely expelled and Russian traders are overseeing a flow of imported goods that is seeping even into the sphere of basic foods. The great redistributive mechanism of the state is faltering in its attempt to contain the social consequences of this rush of new transactions. In this suddenly open field millions of consumption decisions are producing a differentiated culture, crystallizing into new patterns. To understand what drives the actual practices of consumption I have suggested that we can look at certain value-laden perceptions held by Russians, all of them specific to recent historical time: the experience of deception, the instants of exposure to global values, and the projection forward of moral ideas concerning the political economy. The Russian economy is as deeply "embedded" as it ever was, not only in the politics of the struggle for rank and power, but also in the ideas of what lies beyond. The global economy is seen by most as the domain of the great deception, the more so as it seems to be producing new (and dubious) kinds of Russians.

PART II
STRATEGIES BEYOND THE LAW

INTRODUCTION TO PART II

Peering below the easy surfaces of key forms of economic practice in postsocialist Russia—small-scale trading, protection rackets, and bribery—the chapters that follow reveal the intricate structural and cultural mechanisms which reflect and reproduce crucial elements of Soviet (and pre-Soviet) society while dismantling or radically reconfiguring them at the same time. Central to all of Humphrey's analyses of socialist and postsocialist economies has been her unswerving emphasis on a triple mode of inspection, one that simultaneously employs close description of the details of everyday economic practice, a nuanced discernment of the social/historical roots and wider structural contexts of those practices, and careful interpretation of the ways in which such practices are represented by people engaged in them and people observing or experiencing them from various degrees of distance. This method of weaving across explanations of function, system, and meaning provides a vivid sense of the idiosyncrasy of post-Soviet/postsocialist institutions, which seem constantly to be reinventing themselves, as new forms of practice accrue out of familiar cultural and structural modes, and out of novel engagements—however tenuous—across borders of status and state.

Eschewing universalistic categories of market processes and identities, Chapter 4 charts the indigenous classification (and local moral evaluation) of institutions and persons engaged in trade in the Transbaikal region. The analysis here speaks to conditions and practices in most provincial regions in Russia, where the unreliability of the money economy has produced immeasurably complex systems of barter, institutional welfare, and entitlement and a personalization of transactions which owes much to Soviet *blat* circles. Humphrey enumerates the main categories of persons engaged in the market, defines the particular niches which they fill, and assesses the local moral "spin" placed on each category. As became clear in Chapter 1, when the state has severely retracted, local resources are jealously protected at every level and their outflow is resented as the "carrying out of valuables." In the meantime, shuttle traders and others bringing cheap foreign goods into the region to sell are devalued as importing "disorder." The kind of market paralysis that results from this conceptual framework (and frame of practice) serves both to protect communities from the severest ravages of impoverishment and to constrain the possibilities of systemic rationalization.

Protection rackets have been a key feature both in sensational Western depictions of the post-Soviet scene and in local popular culture, lately full of a range of types of Mafia bandits, thieves in law, and uncontrollable young hoodlums. Some scholars have argued that the protection rackets serve critical functions in the absence of effective state power, and while Humphrey acknowledges key structural-functional features of the protection regime, she also seeks to understand the ways that meanings of state authority and legitimacy are contrasted with people's "diverse imaginings" of the mythicized "law" of the racket. A crucial theme in this analysis is the connection between the protection phenomena of postsocialist society and its particular roots in the patronage structures of the Soviet bureaucracy, which were sometimes deeply interconnected with the shadow economy.

As with trading and running a racket, so with bribing: a single concept, seemingly straightforward, opens up on inspection of its various contexts and meanings to appear as an umbrella term covering a host of related but quite different functions, each of which is morally weighed in very particular ways. Crucial in this case, as with the cases of trading and rackets, is to see practices of bribery as situated in networks and collectivities, within which these practices function both pragmatically and communicatively, in the end also serving to distinguish social arenas as public or private, state or commercial, impersonal or familiar. In the process of exploiting, denying, hiding, or masking a bribe, persons navigate newly challenging shoals of identity, belonging, and conscience.

B. G. AND N. R.

CHAPTER 4
TRADERS, "DISORDER," AND CITIZENSHIP REGIMES IN PROVINCIAL RUSSIA

After sixty years as an instrument of the state plan, trade in Russia has irrupted as one of the most volatile elements in the present economy and society.[1] This chapter describes the new forms of trading and investigates what can be learned from them about the current social transformations in provincial Russia.

Burawoy and Krotov (1993) suggest that the post-Soviet Russian economy is dominated by "merchant capital," meaning that enterprises seek profit from commerce rather than through the transformation of production. In the sphere of production, much of the old Soviet structure remains. Furthermore, merchant capital, Burawoy and Krotov argue, does not spontaneously evolve into modern capitalism; rather, like the past alliance of merchant capital with feudal dominant classes, the present cliental links between Russian managers and organs of political power prevent the growth of an autonomous bourgeoisie (1993, 65). I argue here that Burawoy and Krotov are correct about the persistence of the earlier organization of production and are right to query the assumption that when liberalized, trade inevitably takes a Western modern capitalist form. But events since the early 1990s have overtaken their diagnosis: new players on the scene are unaccounted for by Burawoy and Krotov's scenario. In any case, we need to think in different theoretical terms.

The 1990s in provincial Russia brought an enormous burgeoning of petty trade, unforeseen in the merchant capitalism scenario. Significantly, a large proportion of petty trade is international and consists of "shuttlers" (*chelnoki*) traveling abroad to bring in manufactures for sale. Directly related to the explosion of small trade are the breakup and subdivision of former state enterprises, which have shed much of their labor. The dynamics of petty trading are highly volatile: successful individuals move into small whole-saling, and then into large wholesaling, but many small traders fail. Despite this, there is an endless sporadic flow of people into trade, prompted as much by absolute necessity as by the desire to make a profit. Although some wealthy private firms have emerged in the economic interstices where money can be made, in the provinces their number is small.

These days, the idea of merchant capitalism applies perhaps least of all to the former state and collective enterprises. Even relatively successful enter-prises of this type have strong incentives, for reasons explained later, not to show a profit. The majority totter on the edge of ruin or are bankrupt. They experience a great shortage of money, and many operate almost entirely by barter (Woodruff 1999).

In the summer of 1996, industrial workers went for months without being paid, but agricultural workers in many areas had not received money wages for years. Meanwhile, the subsistence sphere greatly expanded. Ordinary peo-ple—whether in industry or agriculture, whether urban or rural—rely on their own vegetable plots, exchanges with relatives, and forest gathering to provide basic food. By contrast, petty trade and the wealthy private firms—the sources of clothing, domestic utensils, cigarettes, and alcohol, on one hand, and oil products, cars, and luxury goods, on the other—operate en-tirely by money. This need for cash in a barter-and-subsistence economy is one of the main sources of "traders," people who need money to purchase things they cannot produce themselves.

Many provinces of Russia cannot balance their budgets. They rely on financial subsidies from Moscow. This means that, very generally, money cir-culates through regional governmental budgets only to certain parts of the population: key industries (power, transport), state employees (administra-tors, doctors, teachers), and state dependents (pensioners, invalids, war vet-erans). Successful traders reap this cash, giving rise to a number of support industries for the rich New Russians, as they are called, such as car-repair firms, security teams, and builders of their new houses. These money flows do not penetrate far, however, and great numbers of people have irregular access to money and, in the countryside, virtually no access.

The intellectual problem in analyzing this situation lies in trying to com-prehend an unprecedented and fluid set of circumstances. Unlike China, where a centuries-old pattern of petty capitalism quickly reestablished itself after the reforms in the early 1980s (Gates 1996), Russia does not appear to be reverting to its prerevolutionary combination of family merchant houses and great periodic fairs. In fact, Russians seem surprised by what is happening with their trade. In comparison with China, Russian trade is atraditional, in the sense that it is inventing its own new culture as it goes. It is doing this, however, not in a blank field but in an economic terrain inhabited by the disintegrating and unwieldy former state enterprises, as well as by local governments desperate to keep at least some of those enterprises alive.

The vocabulary of holistic schemes seems inadequate to explain what is happening. If a term like *the transition* is debatable because it is often taken to imply that postsocialist economies are coming to resemble Western capitalist economies (but which ones?), how much more questionable is a term like *merchant capitalism?* Not only is an analogy between Russia in the late twentieth century and the distant past of Europe debatable, but the theoretical concept of a stage or an epoch characterized by an interrelated structure may limit our understanding of the current circumstances of widespread and erratic change. Woodruff's seminal article, "The Barter of the Bankrupt" (1999) points rightly to the need to understand the uncertain dynamics of local politics and its fitful relationship to—even its frequent contradiction of—Moscow's attempt to regulate the flow of money.

Above all, applying the idiom of Marxist historical schema to contemporary experience almost inevitably denies the ethnography of representations. The notion of a class-based, stable ideology cannot deal with those features to which anthropologists have access and that are peculiarly important in the unstable conditions of Russia today—namely, the nontheorized and most various frameworks and values through which people understand the world. It is essential, in my view, for an ethnography to include these representations, since they both inform economic action and create reactions to that action. I argue that the forms taken by the surge of mass trade are greatly influenced by these views.

The reactions to the facts of trade emerge from the underswell of the habitus of people's life, which was formed in Soviet times but is now undirected and contradictory. The great difficulty in describing this phenomenon lies in its inarticulacy and emotion-driven character. It may seem surprising to use such terms in relation to trade, but it should be remembered that present trading activities developed from an illegal pursuit, without a vocabulary of its own legitimacy, and that Russian precedents for "normal" trade lie in the generations before the longest memories. This means the stereotypes characterizing trade from the outside (from people who are unfamiliar with it) are more powerful than the emerging idioms to conceptualize it from inside. Contrast, for example, the modest domestic expression traders use for their profit, *navarka,* the grease that emerges on the top of soup, with the passionate, generalized denunciation of an elderly peasant family (one of many who made similar statements): "What is the source of Russia's misfortunes? Traders. They should be put away. They make money just for themselves, not for society." Since the early 1990s, governmental responses have again repeatedly controlled, liberated, and abruptly regulated traders in various ways. These public reactions have various immediate purposes, but I argue that their ultimate sources lie in evolving ideas of order, in concepts of identity and territoriality, and in different political cultures. An ethnographically adequate account of trade in present-day Russia therefore has to describe not only the various trading activities but representations of those activities and, most difficult of all, the sources of such representations, and it should be phrased in a way that incorporates the reactive and dynamic nature of the phenomena.

To get at the contradictory dynamics affecting trade, it is necessary to uncover the emotion-charged, unrationalized values that are derived from people's ambivalence to the realization of the Soviet state structure. The state's organization penetrated the consciousness of all people, but here it underwent a culturally varied transformation (sometimes oppositional in character, especially among non-Russians; Humphrey 1989). I argue that the historically formed sense of "us" against the state—that is, an identity defined by the state but required to act in relation to it—has given rise to a plethora of localisms. These localisms exist at district, county, and provincial levels and have deepened and become mutually competitive in recent years with the weakening legitimacy of all-Russian structures. Soviet organization of production and distribution gave each unit the ideal character of a self-reproducing social whole, and this tendency has only been strengthened by the local "self-government" rhetoric of Yeltsin's program.

This chapter shows how uncontrolled movement violates the sense of order pertaining to such bounded wholes. Defensive territoriality now exists in incoherent confrontation with the simultaneous realization of globalized desires and demands. Trade brings in desirable goods, but it also carries out valuables, and it inevitably breaches the frontiers of jealously guarded domains. International trade, including that with the states of the former Soviet Union, arouses both the most desire and the most anxiety. Markets and border crossings are places where "disorder" (*bezporiadok*) is feared. I argue that the acute confrontation of trade with localism is an active component in the emergence of new citizenship regimes in Russia. In addition, I try to explain why Russians link stereotypical traders together with smugglers, profiteers, speculators, racketeers, and "criminogenic elements," and how the vast accumulation of legislation regulating trade is actively affecting what it means to be a citizen in Russia.

The Expansion of Cross-Border Trade

In the historical long duration, Russian state policy toward trade has been characterized by autocratic, centralized control with a few temporary windows of quasi- free trade. Even if short-lived relaxations were sometimes more or less forced on it, the tsarist government succeeded in retaining a remarkably constipated trade policy. At the tiny number of international border trade posts, the fiscal demands of the state always tended to outweigh the need to keep prices down and goods flowing.[2] However, after the Soviet era in which trade was under state control *tout simple,* the liberalization of international trade and visa regulations in the perestroika years led to a probably irreversible change. Beginning in April 1991, all Soviet citizens were allowed to take part in international trade (Butler 1991, xxiii).

There was an immediate rush of small traders to bring back foreign goods for sale. Six years later, large numbers of people still engage in this trade. It was estimated, for example, that in 1992 about half the population of Irkutsk took part,[3] and in 1996, according to information from the Business Round-Table of Russia, around 30 million people (41 percent of Russia's working population) were engaged in the international shuttle trade in petty commodities and services tied to that trade (Nikitina 1996).

On the whole, the export of Russian goods is not carried out by the independent shuttlers. Rather, the collapse of many industries and the complex, often covert, process of privatization has provided an unprecedented opportunity for unscrupulous officials and managers. This process involved the extraordinarily widespread selling off and removal of former state property, seen by many as a gigantic rip-off in which not only the goods themselves but many of the profits have been transferred outside Russian frontiers—that is, to hard-currency accounts.[4] It has been estimated that values equivalent to the total state reserves of dollars and gold are removed from Russia each year, often by illegal means.[5] The breakup of the USSR also encouraged the illicit removal of goods internally among republics because they did not take action against crimes committed on one another's territory (Handelman 1994). Recently, an ever-increasing number of goods has been designated as having strategic value and not to be exported.[6] But previously, entire regional governments (for example, Kalmykia in 1992) were involved in the turning of state (that is, "no one's") property into marketable commodities, and violations of the export regulations continue to be widely reported. At present, much energy at federal and provincial[7] levels is expended to control the outflow of goods.

The mass character of trade gives the subject its importance in post-Soviet society. In the context of post-Soviet values, the voluntaristic, profiteering, and boundary-crossing character of trade still makes it seem nonroutine, almost transgressive, and for that reason trade is becoming the site of citizens' conflicts. Only as of 1995 or so did a few organizations emerge that dared to mention traders' rights. These groups are often in conflict with provincial governments. Two such groups in the city of Ulan-Ude in Buriatia are *Grazhdanskoe Edinstvo* (Civil Unity) and the Association for the Support of Small and Middle Entrepreneurship of Buriatia. In 1996, these groups were struggling against a recent Buriat government resolution that replaced the existing system of licensing alcohol sales with a "humiliating" auction of licenses and other restrictions. Significantly, and presumably because traders include such a large part of the population, Civil Unity argued that the resolution is contrary to federal law and contravenes the civil rights guaranteed in the constitution. The group proposed to organize a mass referendum of the population, the only way to force the provincial government to reconsider the issue.[8]

This paper focuses on the individuals and firms I call "traders," defined as those who aim to make a profit from middlemen activities involving goods and services. This category is heterogeneous, with a number of rapidly changing forms, but it has the advantage of coinciding with the indigenous concept of *torgovtsy* as people not involved in productive labor. In terms of functions, it might be feasible to make the familiar distinctions among wholesalers, retailers, brokers, financiers, and so forth, but in Russia today individuals and firms may take on one, some, or all of these functions. From an anthropological point of view, it is more useful to try to discover the evolving types of traders defined by indigenous categories, as this can tell us about how traders are beginning to fit into and generate an emergent citizenship regime. Later I outline the dynamics of six such types: *biznesmeny* (business people), *brokery* (brokers), *predprinimateli* (entrepreneurs), *chelnoki* (shuttlers), *kommersanty* (trader-retailers), and *perekupshchiki* (resellers) as a first step in this rather uncharted domain. A further highly important indigenous category is that politely known as *torgovye men´shinstva* (trading minorities).

Some Terms for a Contextualization of Trade in Russia

The economic environment in which traders operate is dominated by productive enterprises such as the extractive and processing plants, collective farms, and factories that were state-managed under the Soviet regime. I refer to them as corporations because since the reforms they have charters legitimizing them as separate legal entities with rights distinct from those of their members.[9] Such production units now engage in buying and selling, bartering, and so forth. I argue later along the lines of Clarke (1992), however, that in the post-Soviet economic collapse these enterprises are not dominated primarily by the profit motive but rather are concerned with survival and the social protection of their members. There is a spectrum here. Perhaps the majority of corporations in rural areas could be called "neosocialist corporations," because socialism (as indigenously defined) is not dead in Russia. Other enterprises, which enter the current fray with a mixture of communitarian, strategic, and commercial motives, might be termed "postsocialist corporations." A third, small category of corporations consists of firms created by independent entrepreneurs that are frankly commercial in outlook. The aim of these distinctions is not to make an absolute differentiation between institutions on the ground, which would be difficult, but to problematize the different ways in which Russian citizens are constructing new economic institutions.

Along with production corporations, the other major actors are the state organizations—including government and municipal bureaucracies—and educational, cultural, and health institutions. It is a peculiarity of Russian life that many of these organizations also act like economic corporations. For example, a rural middle school often has its own housing, agricultural land, tractors, and livestock; supplies its own food and heating; and engages in trade within the district. The trend toward institutional self-sufficiency has increased recently with ministerial budget cuts and late payment of running costs and wages. Nevertheless, state employees (the *biudzhetniki,* as they are known) are much envied since, along with pensioners, they are essentially the only people in rural areas with access to money wages.

Trade is giving rise to new social categories. It is in this context that I employ the idea of the *citizenship regime*.[10] The term refers to the political categorization of citizens by government agencies, even if such a classification is not set out in any document. The term thus refers to a practice rather than a charter. At present, a post-Soviet citizenship regime is being formed. A flood of new laws constantly appears; these laws are of several types and originate from various levels of government, thus affecting the legal capacities of people of various statuses. For example, in Moscow in one week in November 1995, the following were issued: one codex, five decrees, fifteen resolutions, one instruction, one law, and thirteen orders; and these applied variously to citizens of the Russian Federation, citizens of Moscow, Russian citizens living permanently abroad, pensioners of Moscow, citizens of Kalinin Oblast, and so forth.[11] With the declaration of sovereignty by various constituent parts of the Russian Federation, local regulations now elaborate—and sometimes conflict with—those from Moscow. Many laws are ignored or not known about, but a basic bureaucratic portfolio is still part of post-Soviet life, notably papers proving one's place of birth, official ethnicity, and membership in a corporation; passports for internal and foreign use and for registration of domicile; work record; housing entitlement; and professional qualifications.

To engage in trade, one must acquire the status either of a "physical person" (*fizicheskoe litso,* the right to trade as an individual) or a "juridical person" (*iuridicheskoe litso,* the right to trade as a company). In Russian parlance one "buys" these rights; that is, one purchases a license for a given period.[12] Even someone who sells pine nuts on a street corner must have a license and is supposed to keep a book showing the source and cost of acquisitions, the price of each sale, and the profit on each transaction. Taxes are charged on all profits.[13] Physical persons are limited to a small turnover. Juridical persons are subject to dramatically increased tax on profits, reaching 90 percent in larger firms, and must also keep a professional accountant and a further set of licenses, such as licenses for import, export, storage, and sale premises of various kinds; employment of laborers; compliance with sanitary regulations; and so forth. The amount of regulation is difficult to comprehend and impossible to describe fully here, but one example is that a truck must have a license to be on the road but also to travel to given regions. A trader I know was greatly hampered by the fact that her truck was not licensed to go into the neighboring province in Russia.

Such regulations are widely flouted, thus putting traders in an uncertain relationship with the law and placing them in the hands of alternative networks. A further concept to introduce at this point involves social relations of trust. In trade, these relations tend overwhelmingly to be personal relations and are conducted in a different modality from the structure of state posts, even by people who are trading on behalf of state or former state institutions.

After a brief window of liberalization in the period 1991–93, in which it was hoped that free trade would encourage Russian manufacturing, state policy concerning the role of trade has wavered. Indeed, the official import-export trade, from which the state derives considerable income, is generally estimated to be far outweighed by the illegal flooding of goods in and out.[14] Now, the Russian government sees nonpayment of taxes and customs duties as one of its major problems. Traders are viewed as uncontrolled elements to be pounced on for fiscal purposes. An example is seen in the resolution of the Russian Federation, brought into force on August 1, 1996, limiting the untaxed import of international goods by physical persons (shuttle traders) to a value of U.S. $1,000 and 50 kilograms. The Government Customs Committee hopes this law will bring increased customs duties of 2 trillion rubles ($400 million) per month into the state treasury. Russians laugh at this. They predict the new law will only put weak traders out of business, whereas the others will double their normal bribes to the customs people, and prices on the street will go up (Nikitina 1996). The almost universal attitude is that trade is not only largely unprotected by the state but is carried on more in the face than under the aegis of state laws and policies.

In any event, traders have long since elaborated their own means of establishing trust in the context of their particular activities. At the very least, you can trust yourself. The phenomenon of the lone shuttler, someone who personally travels to Turkey, China, and other countries to buy and bring back goods, is one result. Shuttlers often use close kin to sell for them while they go on the next journey, but for the wider links required to obtain start-up capital, establish reliable sources of goods, obtain licenses, find "friendly" customs and railway officials, and so forth, a range of new ties are emerging that differs in various communities, as is described more fully later. Among Russians, family feeling is often no longer strong enough to support these functions, and the ritualized trade friendships which flourished between Buriats and Russians, Russians and Chinese, in prerevolutionary times no longer exist. Bruno (1997) has made the interesting point that women often attribute their success as entrepreneurs to their ability to deal with people and their reputation for greater trustworthiness than men. Banks are still widely avoided—it is feared that they may crash or arbitrarily freeze personal accounts. As a result, even in fairly large transactions payments are commonly made in person and in cash.[15] Anyone with a departure ticket at an airport can expect someone in his or her network of contacts to material-ize at their elbow, such as that old school chum with a mysterious wad of cash in a plastic bag to be delivered to the "red-haired women with a Mc-Donalds T-shirt" at the other end.

Both barter deals and the pursuit of cash make peculiar demands on per-sonal trust. Barter requires security for future and repeat transactions and engenders local dependencies (Humphrey 1991; Woodruff 1999), but it is worth mentioning here that money, which is so scarce in present Russian cir-cumstances, also becomes a barterable commodity. To obtain it, personal networks must be scoured. I was present when my Buriat host, the long-standing director of a government horticultural research station, needed money to pay the electric bill. Last quarter she had paid the electric company with several thousand fruit tree saplings, but this time the company insisted on money. Indeed, it had cut off the electricity for a weekend, to my host's in-dignation. After several telephone calls to the director of the electric com-pany, an old friend/enemy, to no avail, my host said, "Well, I'll try Lydia Ivanovna for the money, though she's a devil, because she owes me for those black currants last year." The call went: "Lydiushka, my dear, how is your health? And your wonderful daughter Tania, how did her exams go? . . . The thing is, I need money, just a few million, by next Tuesday. What, you haven't got any? Now I'm sure those workers of yours would appreciate some rasp-berries, they are really exceptional this year." Appealing to every known tie and blandishment is one technique (with strategic use made of the for-mal / informal word for "you"), but equally possible, according to the rela-tionship being played out, are threats and shouting, groveling, haughtiness, or exercising naked power. Such personalization of transactions is common virtually throughout the economic field, which is one reason why it makes no sense to divide the Russian economy into informal and formal sectors.

The pervasive atmosphere is one of fear of infringement, theft, and vio-lent robbery; and indeed, these are common. This fear is seen in countless incidents, from seemingly trivial threats, like the roadside trader who scratches a skull and crossbones on his temporarily vacated space, to confrontations over disputed use of former state property ("Do you want to kill me with that bulldozer of yours?" as one factory manager screamed dramatically, hoping to deter some "wretched Armenians" from digging up pipes on "his" territory). No one seems to consider calling the police; most common is the appeal to higher power—in other words, to protection. Here it is interesting that Russians refer to both patrons in the legitimate power structure and to racketeers by the same term, *krysha,* meaning roof. A small enterprise manager needs a "roof" up in the ministry or among the circle of the province bosses. For street traders the "roof" is much lower and of more dubious help. Without exception, traders pay both legitimate site fees to the town council ("for clearing rubbish and keeping order") and payments to racketeers who divide up the streets ("to keep others off your patch").

The term *mafiia* is also widely bandied about, perhaps because although criminal organizations clearly exist with histories that go back to Soviet times, today the shadowy tentacles of armed protection are evident in the most respectable areas of public life—and the two are not easily distinguishable.[16] All banks have their own, normally immaculate armed security guards,[17] as do hotels for foreigners and shops with expensive imported goods. But the protection racketeers also cultivate an aura of reliability and popularity (in Ulan-Ude they are "former sportsmen," gangs called the Boxers, the Wrestlers, and the like who have divided up the town). Cossacks and quasi-military squads also stalk the markets "to keep order." Although Russians do distinguish legitimate protection from illegitimate at the ends of this spectrum, it makes more sense to recognize that a widespread need for security exists and that provisions for protection can arise from within ordinary social groups, as well as being provided by outside agencies (Varese 1994).[18]

Some traders are linked with criminal activities, notably making fake vodka, counterfeiting money,[19] and selling drugs.[20] Furthermore, the boundary that had separated protection from trade, tenaciously upheld in most criminal circles during the Soviet period, has been greatly eroded, which means racket organizations themselves sometimes engage in trade (see next chapter). But the almost hysterical fear of criminal deception among ordinary people—the feverish inspection of dollar bills, the countless ingenious tests for "real" vodka—seems disproportionate and has deeper cultural sources, as Lemon (1996) argues. Petty traders are vulnerable in their interstitial position. The more they employ protection, the more society in general tends to mistrust them.

To summarize, I have suggested that to understand everyday forms of trade in Russia, we need to have in mind the following conditions: the continued presence of state (or former state) enterprises, the emergence of new citizenship regimes, the legal categories of trading actors, the uncertain attitude of the central government toward free trade, the new networks of trust, the personalization of economic transactions, and the climate of fear and widespread felt need for security.

Disintegrating Corporations

This section describes how the breakdown of enterprises as social groups is generating peculiarly post-Soviet forms of poverty and anxiety, and how the combined effects of these are generating new forms of trade.

In southeast Siberia, despite the reforms, not all enterprises have changed their status to privatized types.[21] Especially in agriculture, many Soviet enterprises simply remain in place, and even those with the new status of joint-stock company or farmers' association are still referred to colloquially as *kolkhozy.* In industry, many of the huge monolithic organizations of Soviet times have been broken up into their constituent parts. The former Trans-Baikal Timber Corporation, Zabaikalles, for example, has become a series of separate production and processing units located all over the republic (Kurochkin 1995). In either case, my material shows that such a provincial enterprise still sees itself as a productive unit concerned with reproducing itself as a *kollektiv.*[22] There thus seems to be a significant lag between popular values and juridical changes, which affects how people act. What the corporations are reproducing is not a monetary fund or an economic capacity to supply a product but a social community that is specific in its localization at a certain place and in its occupational characteristics. Clarke (1992, 7) aptly refers to this as "the primary unit of Soviet society" and argues for the continued vitality of this "state within the state" in the postsocialist period (1992, 27).

One reform that is changing the social nature of the corporation is the relinquishing in 1993–94 of a range of social functions to the local administration, the lowest branch of the state.[23] Pensions, insurance, education, and medicine have gradually been handed over. This removal of social responsibilities has been the first step in the disintegration of the enterprise-based *kollektiv.* The dire economic situation of virtually all agricultural corporations has forced them to make bitter decisions, and in this situation the crumbling of the boundaries of the community creates anger and anxiety.[24] The cumulative destabilizing effects of the economic crisis and the shedding of social responsibilities can be seen clearly in the following example.

The Onokhoi Wood-Products Company, formerly a branch of the giant state firm Zaibaikalles, has a population of five thousand people, and its situation is desperate. When it decided to privatize as an open joint-stock company, 51 percent of the shares were taken over by the *kollektiv,* 20 percent were retained by the state, and 29 percent were sold on the open market. "All would have been well," people now say, if the open shares had not been bought up by outsiders, the "Tiumen representatives," who also succeeded in having their leader chosen as director. As things began to go wrong and salaries were not paid, some members of the *kollektiv* began to sell their shares, which were also quickly bought up by the Tiumen people.

The battle for control between insiders and outside shareholders is a common occurrence in Russia (Clarke 1992, 13–14), and one reason for such tension is the feeling that only insiders will care for the corporation as a whole. In fact, the explanation for the failure of Onokhoi lies less in callous decisions made by the outsiders from Tiumen, as local people feared, than in the disappearance of purchasers in Kazakhstan, the Urals, and other regions with the breakup of the USSR. This situation was compounded by rising interest rates on loans, the high cost of electricity, increased customs charges, and higher federal and local taxes. By late 1994, a product sellable for a ruble cost 1 ruble 35 kopeks to produce. Still, it was decided "at any price to strive to preserve the *kollektiv* and survive until better days." As there was no money, wages were paid in furniture. "Take it, sell it, and survive!" workers were told. Meanwhile, management also tried to supply the members with food, obtained by barter for Onokhoi wood products.

The Onokhoi workers went on strike in August 1994, demanding work and wages, and the Tiumen director was replaced by a local man. But try as they might, management and the trade union were unable to preserve the *kollektiv* as a source of work. Half of the 2,150 jobs were eliminated, and many of those with jobs were put on short time or given obligatory holidays. The director expressed the hope that those out of work could manage on the private plots provided by the firm and on the "gifts of the taiga forest." His next words are telling with regard to attitudes toward enterprise-based trade:

> "In the recent past the company processed 250,000 cubic meters of timber in six months, but in 1994 this was reduced to 17,500 cubic meters. And although our main suppliers remain the same, the Kurbinsk and Khandagatai forestry companies, no one is going to give raw materials for free. So to provide work at least to our sawing workshops we were forced, true in only small amounts, to obtain unconditioned wood from Irkutsk Oblast and even from commercial traders from the Amur. And it was just the same with selling. We had no way out but to sell to private traders, or to barter our goods for food." "The Onokhoitsy are flapping like fish on ice," observed the journalist sadly. (Nikolaev 1994)

Some significant points emerge from this example with regard to the conditions for trade. Even though the firm has undergone a major change in status, having been freed from state control,[25] (1) the aim of both buying and selling is not to establish a slimmed-down, efficient firm but to provide work, food, and other sustenance for an existing community; (2) nevertheless, forced by the economic crisis, the firm sheds jobs and puts people on short time; (3) there is a reluctance to trade with new partners, particularly with private traders; and (4) large numbers of people, still in some sense in Onokhoi, now have to fend for themselves.

Trade by such firms is enmeshed in governmental regulations that make it disadvantageous to show a profit. Visible profit of juridical persons, as mentioned, is very heavily taxed, and a profitable enterprise might be refused government commodity credit). This is the system, especially elaborated in agriculture, whereby the government secures a supply of future products in return for loans in the form of gas, spare parts, and other commodities. Enterprises are forced to participate because they cannot find alternative buyers willing to gamble on future production. One of the aims of the commodity credit system, as a government official told me, is to keep enterprises going while not making money available to them, because in their theoretically independent status they are not trusted to use it "in the right ways." All this reduces the former state enterprises' capacity to trade. But many people justify the system ideologically. For the old guard there is simply a stark opposition: there are "two ways of living one's life," one based on honest production inside the corporation and the other on nonproductive, selfish business which provides no work for anyone else (Shelkunova 1995).

Thus, many people are forced into petty trade. They belong to a corporation, live there, and yet have no employment there. Others work but receive no pay. "How do you manage when the wages are not paid?" I asked one librarian. "What can I do?" she replied. "First I borrow. Then I stand on the street corner and sell things."

The Sense of Place, Frontiers, and the "Great Trash Road"

The Soviet regime introduced a powerful administrative hierarchy of functional departmentalization combined with territorialization. A citizen's status came to be defined most notably by attachment to a work collective, a unit located in an administrative subsection of the state (republic, autonomous republic, oblast, raion, and so forth). At each level, from republics downward through the administrative hierarchy to enterprises, units were recipients in the redistributive economy (Verdery 1991). At the same time, units were territorially defined. Although there were important social exceptions to the principle of territoriality, such as ethnicity, professional qualifications, or membership in the Communist Party, an entire range of control policies in the late Soviet period had the effect of deepening that principle (policies involving registration of domicile, access to work, wage differentials, and housing).

I suggest here that after the collapse of the USSR, the disintegration of the Communist Party and many all-union departmental structures left regionalism to flourish in new ways. Not only has the old residence permit been replaced by an even more stringent registration system, but an emotional identification with place has emerged with articulate force and has become an active generator of the emerging citizenship regimes. The raising of the status of certain provinces, local elections, the unilateral declaration of free trade zones, the publicity given to provincial budgets, wide differences between regions in the buying power of the ruble, and so forth have contributed to this emergence. A symptom is the recent formation of numerous *zemliachestva* (societies of people from the same district). These groups exist at different levels in Russia as a whole but also within provinces. In Buriatia, for example, there are societies for people from Barguzin District, Ol'hon District, and so forth. Whereas their overt aims are usually cultural, the *zemliachestva* also seem to act as lobbies and networks.[26]

Yet the specter of further splitting apart has made frontiers the focus of tension. The "sacred frontier" of Soviet times has not disappeared, although it has been displaced from the USSR to the Russian border, and it is credited with a long pre-Soviet history. For example, in an article entitled "Ashamed on Behalf of State Power . . . " (*Za derzhavu obidno . . .*), Gomelev (1995) describes how the proud customs service battles at its frontier posts to maintain the Russian Customs Charter of 1633—a charter more legendary than practical, one imagines—against the disorderly flows of goods. At the same time, seamlessly attached to the official ideology but different from it is the people's attachment to their places. Place, people, and local enterprises, all tied together (as workmates, schoolmates, *zemliaki*—district co-residents—and so forth), are the social sites for these "natural" attachments, and they can also emerge at different levels, from the brigade seen as a *kollektiv* to the enterprise, the district, the republic, and to Russia itself. A Buriat colleague told me he was traveling in Chita Oblast with a young nephew. When they were returning home, the boy looked eagerly at the map to search for the boundary with Buriatia, and as they passed through an absolutely undifferentiated steppe he saw a signpost and announced happily, "At last we have entered our homeland!" (*rodnaia zemlia*).[27]

The existence of traders, I argue, cuts right across the territorial loyalties sharpened in the new battle for existence. Not only do traders not "earn their rights" by productive labor in one or another corporation, but they cross institutional / territorial boundaries and make money from the very discontinuities other people feel obliged to observe. They jar against people's sense of identity. They are thought to *take out* the property felt to belong legitimately to honored collectivities that are above mere law. By contrast, as will be shown later, what they *bring in* is disvalued.

A 1996 Russian presidential decree illustrates the crystallization of the concern with communities, borders, and illicit trade. According to this decree, 1,500 kilometers of unprotected state frontier in Trans-Baikalia is to be guarded against incoming "contraband, narcotics, weapons, and illegal immigrants" by a new frontier guard consisting of local volunteers, first Cossacks but also hunters, shepherds, and others. These people will be given various concessions, but, more important, they will have the right to verify documents, stop transport, and "control the border regime." The local community will be "full owners" of the border zone.[28]

Border anxiety translates from the international frontier to certain territories and sites inside the country. The frontier of Russia with China and Mongolia physically consists of a high fence and a ploughed-up strip of land on much of the Russian side, with watch posts and lights near crossings. Foreigners are not allowed near border zones. The border is also furnished in places with infrared, radio-wave, electronic surveillance equipment, and "automated control of the activity of security personnel" (Fedin 1995). These same techniques are being borrowed to provide security perimeters for large installations and enterprises inside Russia where theft has become endemic, ranging from gasoline stations to gas suppliers to nuclear power stations (Fedin 1995, 1). No technical measures, however, can counteract the disloyal trade that operates from inside an enterprise or administrative unit. Compounding this sense of uncontrollable flux is the fact that not only people but goods are changing status: products that were formerly "ours" are now foreign (such as Armenian brandy).

A symptom of the contradictory obsession with territoriality is the continued existence of GAI, the State Transport Inspection. GAI posts still exist on every main road out of all cities, ostensibly to check vehicles for roadworthiness and similar factors. In fact, the GAI regularly stops trade vehicles and exacts "tribute" (*dan'*, as people say) simply for passage. Larger sums are taken for the slightest infringement of traffic regulations or the appearance of carrying smuggled goods, provoking the cynical view that the more restrictions exist, the more can be milked from them by the very people who are supposed to uphold them. This is a vicious cycle. Provinces create their own economic conditions, differences between these conditions give rise to trade and smuggling, regulations to counteract smuggling give rise to bribery and tribute taking, and the effect is sharpened differences between the units, since prices are hiked up in the places for which goods are destined. So it is no surprise that at a higher level of operation republics, too, act as arbitrary requisitioners (for example, the Ukraine takes 10 percent of the electricity Russia sends to Chechnya; Polukeev 1995).

If there is one prevailing fear that valuable goods are flowing out, there is another that "rubbish" is coming in, brought by human caravans.[29] This explains the expression "the Great Trash Road"[30] (alluding to the Great Silk Road) that brings a current of flimsy clothes and trinkets into Russia from "Asia"—a vague concept here including China, Turkey, and the Near Abroad (the successor states of Central Asia and Trans-Caucasus). One senses several multilayered evaluations of this situation. On one hand, it is perhaps seen as a fatal weakness for Russians to desire such things, as suggested by the derogatory words used for the goods. But on the other, consumption of these items of international currency gives Russian citizens the feeling that they are at last participating in the global arena of fashion and technology. Perhaps most prominent is a third sense of being cheated, since most people are well aware that the flaunted labels of Adidas, Coty, or Levi-Strauss are counterfeited in the shadowy sweatshops of "Asia." As a result, the impulse is to reject the "trash" and search farther afield to South Korea, Malaysia, Japan, and Western Europe for genuine goods of high quality.

Six Types of Traders and Their Dynamics

To obtain some heuristic purchase on the confusion of current economic life, I have divided traders into six categories, but this is not meant to imply that they are altogether separate from one another on the ground or that the types are fixed and permanent. The first two categories are "business people," the managers who run new private conglomerates, and "brokers," those who trade on behalf of state and former state enterprises.

The Siberian provinces are unlike the metropolitan and industrial regions because of the relative absence of private business conglomerates. I know of only two in Ulan-Ude: Arig Us, which developed from the former state trading organ into a construction firm that also sells gasoline and other commodities, and Motom, which began as a Lada concession and expanded into car repairs, furniture making, banking, and retailing. Both are at least temporarily highly profitable, have wide national and international trade links, and are multifaceted operations. But even at the cutting edge of provincial capitalism, these firms have close relations with the Buriat government.[31] Arig Us, for example, no doubt benefiting from government concessions, joined with the government to set up Prodsoiuz, an organization to help the faltering stalwarts of state industry (engineering, sugar, wool processing, and so on). Prodsoiuz has a special relationship with a clearing bank (the Oktiabr' Bank, no less) to reschedule outstanding debts between the various participating companies and allow them to borrow from the clearing bank at low rates of interest. Local people suspect the association of "monopolizing credit," to the disadvantage of small competitors. The new capitalists are thus tied into local political-economic structures, and their financial clout allows them some leeway in manipulating their immediate trading context.

Operating at the level of the single enterprise, brokers typically take charge of marketing part of the main product or subsidiary products in return for difficult-to-find inputs. They travel around, search out buyers, and let people know of goods available at their own enterprise. For example, in 1993, a broker from a collective farm in Chita Oblast arranged to sell milk from his company to a dairy in China for the next three years in return for supplies of flour, rice, and sugar. The brokers involved in such deals are almost always close associates, relatives, or friends of the managers or local government officials. Their career origins can often be traced back to the crafty "suppliers" (*snabzhentsy*) of Soviet days. Taking a wage and modest personal profit from these operations, the "broker" strives to set up regular agreements, although this is often impossible. Many brokers take pride in supplying their community with much-needed goods ("I feed the whole *kollektiv*"). Brokers, however, have also been agents in illegal strategies to move local goods across the frontier to the golden land of China.[32]

With regard to citizenship regimes, both business people and brokers are understood to be representatives of corporations, and they are well supplied with the legitimating documents of core citizenship. Their being personally known is the guarantee of their trustworthiness inside the corporation, and its weight is behind them in dealings with the outside. Some significant factors, however, differentiate the two groups. The business people tend to be young and well educated, sometimes with training in the United States or other capitalist countries. They often have an unorthodox entrepreneurial spark. For example, Motom started when two young Buriats were sent to buy sheep but used the money instead to buy tires and eventually set up their own company dealing in secondhand cars. Motom's present retail business, two sleek supermarkets, monopolizes the small niche for expensive foreign goods which are otherwise locally unavailable. Furthermore, the personnel of government and big business is interchangeable: the career of a likely young operator moves easily among posts in the postelection administration, major firms of the locality, and government agencies acting in a commercial capacity.

The reverse is true of brokers, whose future seems less secure. Breakdown of trust ("We found he was trading on his own behalf!") has led many state and former state enterprises to get rid of their brokers. The functions of trade often devolve onto the directors, who are normally trained in manufacturing and unused to trade. Many complained to me that they are unable to attend to production, as they spend most of their time traveling around searching for buyers or negotiating for credits. Barter deals can include the very fabric of the enterprise. "I have a lot of buildings," said one director. "People often ask me to pay in buildings, but I don't agree—or at least I haven't agreed yet." Finally, the rapacious environment of the present virtually compels successful business people to employ their own security. The faltering enterprises, however, cannot afford that luxury. They are regularly subject to theft, often by their own employees. The director-broker thus has to negotiate both internally and externally to keep the workers on his or her side. "One of my biggest headaches is to find flowers for Women's Day," the same director told me. "Where the heck can I get them when I only have flour to pay with?"

Turning now to discuss traders outside the corporations, it is necessary to give a brief résumé of post-Soviet mass trade. The era began with the relaxation of border restrictions around 1988–89.[33] By train, plane, and coach, tourist groups would set off for Mongolia; in fact, they were trading caravans, often sent by farms, factories, or institutes.[34] Curiously, they returned stuffed to the roof with Soviet-produced but unobtainable (*defitsitnye*) goods. The reason for this is that Mongolia had been sent large quantities of such high-quality products by the USSR for the privileged specialists and army officers based there, but these people were now leaving the country. The Soviet goods soon ran out, and the buses carried back Mongolian leather jackets, hats, and winter coats. Before long, every family in Trans-Baikalia was replete with Mongolian goods. By 1991, the shelves in Trans-

Baikalia were empty of goods to sell in Mongolia, and a coupon system was introduced. Local residents were limited, for example, to buying one school exercise book, and even for such a trivial purchase one had to stand in line and show a passport and residence permit.[35] Subsequently, the policy was reversed and prices rose.

In 1991, the China trade opened up, although China never became a mass destination because of language problems and the unfamiliar culture. The trade with China suddenly expanded enormously, but it was carried out by increasingly professional operators. At this point, we see the crystallization of the more or less distinct categories of independent traders whom I call resellers, shuttlers, entrepreneurs and trader-retailers.

I begin with *shuttlers,* whose activities are a direct outcome of the history just outlined. Shuttlers are so called because they personally travel with the goods they buy and sell. Their Mongolian equivalents are called *gahaichin,* which means "pig keeper" (a pejorative term for the manly pastoralists of the steppes), but the pigs in question are huge bales of goods, almost too heavy for two people to carry. In China the Russian shuttlers are called vacuum cleaners because of their habit of buying everything on sight. They take back mostly clothes, trainers, and cheap brand-name products to sell. Shuttlers travel in groups for reasons of security, and as regulations on the border are tightened they have to make illicit arrangements with customs officials and train guards to accommodate their goods. What is in demand in China is not Russian consumer goods but Western money, and this is what shuttlers export. In Russia they sell Chinese goods at kiosks or at the market for rubles, change the money into dollars, fly to China with the dollars, buy a new bundle of goods, and head back to Russia or Mongolia by train.

It is more difficult for the Mongolian *gahaichin.* In the period 1990–92 there were trading rows of Mongols in the Ulan-Ude market. But they were forced to pay extra-high protection money to Buriat gangs and were shortly forced out by local shuttlers, so they spread their activities deep into Russia along the railway lines and up to Moscow. Their numbers were later curtailed by laws reimposing visa restrictions for Mongolian citizens in Russia. Completely unprotected, they are often attacked and robbed. When addressed they say they are Buriats, as Russian citizens are subject to fewer fines and less violence from foreigners.

Meanwhile, local shuttlers have flourished, but there is high turnover in this category. The shuttlers are restricted by the personal nature of their business: an eager crowd of relatives and friends awaits each transport in the expectation they will be given a share. At the petty sales end, marketplaces tend to be glutted, and shuttlers are unable to spread out into the countryside to make sales; at the upper end wholesalers are increasingly taking over trade routes. The poor quality of most Chinese goods has caused a fall in demand. As a result, shuttlers are flying to South Korea, Singapore, Turkey, or even Japan. To break into wholesale trade requires storage space, licenses, vehicles, and so forth—in other words official contacts, which most shuttlers, archetypal marginals who sail close to the wind, do not have.

Resellers are mostly people who can no longer depend on corporations. They include pensioners or children with highly limited routes (buying in one part of the city and reselling at a higher price somewhere else), people who sell domestic products such as honey or knitted shawls on behalf of relatives, and people who trade vodka on credit to circles of neighbors. Most resellers act as individuals or tiny close-knit groups and often have no license, but they are not totally estranged from the society of trade. They have client-like relationships with their suppliers.

Trader-retailers have the capital to purchase a kiosk in town or a vehicle to travel to the villages, buying local products such as meat, as well as selling vodka and other goods. The future once seemed bright for them, but that is no longer the case. The days of the sell-off of collective-farm livestock have ended,[36] and people now never sell their own meat through a trader if they can sell it themselves. Furthermore, the lack of money in villages means that buying consumer goods there has virtually ceased. A typical village has one or two bright little private shops belonging to trader-retailers that are now barely trading or are even boarded up, together with a store belonging to that old Soviet stalwart, the consumer cooperative.[37] Both types of store probably make most of their money from vodka; but villagers say they prefer the co-op, although it has higher prices, because it retains the old "reliable, honest" bureaucracy and sells unprofitable but useful things like matches, unlike the shady trader-retailers.[38]

The most dynamic actors are those freelance traders I call *entrepreneurs.* Some are rich and powerful; others lead a precarious existence. In general they operate on a larger and more irregular scale than the shuttlers, which allows them to make windfall profits from international import-export.[39] Many entrepreneurial firms are joint ventures with roving Korean, Vietnamese, or other foreign businesspeople who supply the initial capital and international links. When demand plays on globalized desires and fashions, the entrepreneur needs access to fast travel and communications. Adept manipulation of the legal system, an aptitude for risk, and a thirst for the freedom money offers are characteristic of entrepreneurs. It is my impression that opportunities for risky major deals are becoming scarcer; there is too little money in the provinces. Entrepreneurs fall back on safer options, wholesaling if they are successful or purchasing a kiosk or a concession[40] if less so.

It is significant also that many people are latent traders—that is, they have purchased licenses to trade as physical persons without actually doing so. This seems to indicate a change in attitude toward trading. Not only does trade, unusually, now appear as a safety net for those in danger of losing their jobs, but the idea that having a license provides possibilities for economic good fortune is highly important to many people.

This mirage-like image goes along, in my view, with striving for the sense of freedom gained from having money. As Simmel wrote (1978, 306–312), having money is different from having specific objects, in that whereas the latter constrain the owner, the abstract nature of money allows maximal enjoyment of almost any object and the pleasure of further use and fructifying of money itself. Woodruff (1999) points out that this implies the presence of a fully monetized economy. In the context of Russia, which is very unevenly monetized, the dollar is much more "moneylike" than the ruble; it gives a greater sense of mastery—the ability to be an actor in the world market. This explains to some extent the eagerness of entrepreneurs to set up foreign dollar bank accounts and their reluctance to trap good money in productive investments at home. Yet, as Lemon (1996, 60) demonstrates, the dollar also has a powerful antivalue: "Trade for dollars," she writes, "drains the nation of its characteristic treasures. . . . For Russians, it is the self as a 'national being' that is alienated or thought endangered by wrong exchanges and foreign currency." The Russian government is currently developing laws to block currency transfers abroad, and it is widely believed that these laws will harm small traders.[41]

Trading Minorities

The ambivalence aroused by trade in general is crystallized into antagonism in the case of diaspora traders, who are accused more than any others of creating "disorder." Localism reinforces itself with racist stereotypes. In southeast Siberia, the two main diaspora groups are the "Kavkaztsy"[42] and Chinese. Each has an established economic niche, which differentiates them from the wide-ranging ad hoc operations of the entrepreneurs. Socially, the two diasporas are very different from each other. The Kavkaztsy established a market role in Soviet times as purveyors of fruit, vegetables, and flowers, and they expanded through the now half-forgotten perestroika cooperatives to dominate marketplaces in a series of towns. The Kavkaztsy of Irkutsk fought off an attempt at penetration by Central Asians in the early 1990s (Diatlov 1995, 5–6). When military events erupted in the Caucasus, supply lines were cut, leading the Kavkaztsy to operate as middlemen buying supplies from Central Asian wholesalers at low prices. But they managed to send money back to their republics. They have begun to divide functionally and fight among themselves: the Azerbaijanis control the marketplaces and keep the Chechens out, whereas from 1992 onward the Chechens have taken over finance (including forging promissory notes and counterfeiting currency). In the spring of 1993 police discovered 500 million rubles in the possession of a Chechen group in Irkutsk, along with twenty-five false promissory notes worth 6.5 million rubles (Diatlov 1995, 9–10). Russians feed on such news, which adds to their stereotypes of the Kavkaztsy as flamboyant, sexually disgraceful, and violent. Around this time, the mayor of the city said, "A Chechen mafia controls the whole of Irkutsk."

It is far from clear, however, whether this is really the case. As Diatlov establishes (1995, 6–10), the vast majority both of criminal groups and of crimes in the city[43] are attributable to indigenous inhabitants. Nevertheless, the general assumption is that the Kavkaztsy "generate crime."[44] As a result, the Kavkaztsy have had to find Russians as fronts under which to register their companies and to hire indigenous people to man their kiosks. "They are there, although you can't see them," is still the assumption. In this connection, special measures were enacted by the Irkutsk City Soviet in 1993 to control and establish residence quotas on citizens from the Near Abroad and the Caucasus. Thus by 1994, when fears of Chechen terrorism had been added to the mix, the MVD (Ministry of Internal Affairs) felt it necessary to state that all 250 Chechens in the city were known and controlled, all had residence permits and established businesses; therefore, they would be unlikely to engage in terrorist acts (Diatlov 1995, 10).

By 1996, it was no longer the Chechens but a Georgian gang that was the focus of fear. In June, seven members of the gang were shot in a cafe by Russians. A police report makes it clear, however, that the issue was one of territorial dispute rather than ethnic conflict. Both groups are multiethnic; the "Georgian" group in Irkutsk includes Russians, Buriats, and Jews as well as Georgians. Interestingly, the war is largely ideological, concerned with the old criminal traditions that separate theft and antistate crime, on one hand, from business-related crime, on the other (see next chapter). The Russian gang is headed by a "thief in law" nicknamed Tiurik, who owns shares in the Bratsk aluminum factory and now lives in Spain. The Georgians, by contrast, advocate the older, "pure" criminal tradition that eschews contacts with business.[45] Despite such newspaper reports, people in general firmly link trade, crime, and disorder with "blacks" in a mutually self-reinforcing circle.

The Chinese traders create no such fears of violence, but they have also evoked the erection of severe new barriers in the citizenship regime. The fear here is akin to the old yellow peril myth, that Chinese economic penetration will be followed by a demographic expansion with millions of immigrants swamping Siberia. Chinese are said to be already present in great numbers as market sellers, guest workers, entrepreneurs, retailers, cleaners, and students.[46] Many are hidden from officialdom, as they live on expired visas and pay no taxes. As with the Kavkaztsy, it is rumored that, as they are not apparent in cities, a large number of Chinese live in outlying towns and villages. Chinese traders are said to have moved on from shuttling to create a solid infrastructure of their own markets, joint ventures, hotels, restaurants, shops, dormitories, and undercover financial institutions in most Siberian cities; and anxiety is expressed that they are widely buying immovable property behind Russian names.

In fact, it seems that Chinese contract workers and students, both invited by Siberian institutions during the early 1990s, greatly outnumber traders. In those years Chinese traders bought timber semimanufactures, gasoline, and technical components and sold the usual clothes, shoes, and consumer goods. More recently, they ceased buying Russian goods and exported the money from retail sales back to China, a procedure said to involve an underground banking system (Diatlov 1995, 16–24).[47] Since early 1994, Chinese economic activity in Siberia has been cut drastically by local authorities eager to "protect national interests." Contract workers have been sent back to China, Chinese business investment has virtually ceased, and Russian sales in China have been correspondingly cut—all of which has created an economic disaster for the region (Minakir 1996). A policy of harassment (*bytovaia nepriiazn*) was instituted throughout the Far East toward those who had obtained legal residence status (Minakir 1996, 22). Petty traders have been reduced to a trickle. In Ulan-Ude in 1996 I estimated that only thirty to forty Chinese traders and one large Chinese shop remained.

Unlike the Kavkaztsy, the Chinese traders in Siberia do not have their own mafialike protection gangs, perhaps because of a different solution to the problem of trust. With their family ties and internal discipline (perhaps related to the still fearsome political regime in China), the Chinese are mutually collaborative. The Kavkaztsy, in contrast, belong to antagonistic ethnic groups and to different clans with traditions of armed revenge. With mistrust pervasive among their traders, the Kavkaztsy have tended to secure their transactions through more violent means.

The Chinese are not accorded the frightened respect given the Kavkaztsy. Rather, despised for their strange mildness, they are often attacked by local nationalists. In Irkutsk the annual holidays of the Special Air Forces, the army, and the Cossacks are occasions for regular attacks on the Chinese markets (Diatlov 1995, 24–25). During 1993, some patriotic organizations associated with the nationalist Vladimir Zhirinovsky's party were set up to "strengthen Russians" and to combat the presence of foreigners, "who have many rights and no responsibilities." A militarized terrorist group, calling itself Partner Ltd., founded a special Freedom Movement sector to "liberate" the region from foreign mafias. More broadly, continual complaints were made to the authorities about speculation, nonpayment of taxes, fictive marriages to obtain residence permits, and so forth on the part of the Chinese traders. In December 1994, the Irkutsk administration reacted with yet another crackdown, despite the fact that new regulations had been put in force in 1993. State security organized two massive operations, named Foreigner and Signal, that checked all firms, markets, and dormitories. The relatively small results, only 302 Chinese deported and 1,380 arrested, were said to reflect the cunning of the incomers and the corruption of local officials in hiding presumed illegalities.

This is not an isolated instance. In Ulan-Ude in the summer of 1995 there was also a crackdown on all foreign retailers of consumer goods in the central market; all were deprived of their licenses. This action aroused some protest and engendered a call for setting up a new committee to protect the rights of entrepreneurs against administrative organs.[48] By summer 1996 Kavkaz retailers were rarely seen in the city, and Chinese traders had been confined to a market in the Elevator District of the city, where they were sequestered humiliatingly in their own compound behind a wire fence. Nevertheless, this was by far the busiest part of the market.

The Aesthetics of "Disorder"

The familiar Soviet landscape of the city, replicated in town after town, seems to arouse an unexpected protectiveness. The city should develop and reproduce itself as an expression of the people's progress, it is felt. Thus, neither unfinished municipal buildings, with heaps of bricks and tangled, unused pipes, nor the disintegrating fragments of the past are regarded as constituting "disorder." Old boards of honor with half of the letters gone, rotted plaques of Lenin, and the broken swings and playthings of a closed kindergarten are left just as they were, and people pass them without a comment.

But the physical evidence of new individual economic activities is not seen as the people's doing. Trading is kept away spatially from government buildings and otherwise seems "disorderly" wherever it happens. Pavement sellers by a shop door "get in the way"; when confined in a market, they "create dirt." A foreign or colorful appearance is noted immediately, registered, and resented. In Ulan-Ude the result has been that original-looking trading stalls have virtually disappeared. Kiosks and stalls, by local regulation, must be of a given size (recently increased, to the traders' irritation). Many places have lines of identical stalls, nameless, and all painted the same color. Seeing this, people say with satisfaction, "At last there is some order in our markets."

I am much taken with Lemon's interpretation (1996, 45) of the post-Soviet market as a quasi-theatrical stage on which roles are played. This description

6. *"Disorderly" pavement traders in front of a state store, Moscow, 1997.*

7. The creation of order: market traders in rows of identical kiosks, Ulan-Ude, Buriatia, 1996.

seems to be borne out by the numerous street traders who are beginners; unlike the blasé professionals, they often look apologetic, uncomfortable at being there at all.

In general, in Russia laws and bureaucracy are popularly seen as the outcome of the desire for order. People are willing to tolerate what might seem to be excessive proliferations of rules because those rules represent civilization, which tames the seething, disorderly nature of the Russian people. This disorganized, passionate nature is something people are also secretly proud of. But in the cultural structure of self-analysis, there are always scapegoats for the negative aspect of disorder. For many people, even those engaged in it, trade plays this role.

Conclusion

Trade in Russia has evolved in a particular direction. The functions of state-planned internal exchange have not been efficiently replaced by trade but limp along in a crippled version of the Soviet system. Meanwhile, mass trade—with its search for any kind of profit—has been produced, but is also limited, by the drastic reduction of incomes. What success has occurred in trade is closely connected to consumers' expanded horizons to embrace the entire world. As a result, although a few large firms linked to government have been able to dominate profitable aspects of home production (oil products, cars, and similar products), the activity of small traders is overwhelmingly concerned with selling imports and images of foreign glamour. Since the early 1990s, demand and desire have moved to sources further and further outward. One after another, the earlier suppliers failed to satisfy—Central Asian underground workshops, Eastern Europe, Mongolia, and China, in turn, came to glut the markets and be pushed aside. The expansion of the network of suppliers to distant and expensive places will probably result in a gradual professionalization of the import trade and the relegation of the new traders-in-desperation to the lowliest reselling roles.

Simultaneous with this process is another, conceptual one that is also progressive. Here native Russian products are valued—almost supervalued, as though nothing the rest of the world can produce can compensate for their loss (Humphrey 1995, chap. 3). As the products of native labor, these goods have an almost noneconomic value. It is acceptable for other people to want these excellent products, but it somehow seems immoral when they are traded away. Simultaneously, incoming goods are devalued. Is this what years of learning the labor theory of value have come to? In fact, such an inchoate sense of value parallels the real selling off of (mostly state) property hastily and disadvantageously. Indignation at this process taps the contradictory facts that, on one hand, Russians do cherish concepts of production collectives to which they are attached, and they feel loss if the *kollektiv* itself disintegrates, but on the other hand, it is they themselves who stand at the warehouse doors ready to make a deal. When identifiable "traders"—people defined as not engaged in production—are perceived as the perpetrators, however, the sense arises that now there are "outsiders" on the raid. Thus, added to the thicket of legislation by which the nested sovereign units of the country seek to define themselves is growing regulation concerned specifically with defense against the types of trade that have become so prominent in Russia. Taken together, this legislation is producing new citizenship regimes. These serve not only to exclude trading diasporas but also to limit the activities of home-based traders.

I argue that this process marks a fundamental shift in the way society is perceived to be organized. If the perception of tsarist times was of a vertical hierarchy, which was replaced by the Soviet pyramidal territorial structure, the recent shift is to a more horizontal, relatively egalitarian territoriality.[49]

The jostling for equal status relates to obtaining subsidies from Moscow, as well as to regional freedom of action, but the upper linkages with the center have become shifting and uncertain. The collectivities invoked in contemporary loyalties and exclusions are essentially those created by the Soviet administrative structure. It is significant that with all the historical revelations of the arbitrariness of these created administrative units and the alterations and amalgamations the Soviets themselves introduced, few boundaries have been changed since the collapse of the USSR. What did collapse in the early 1990s was the former solid pyramid defining the relation between units. Revealed now by the retraction of Soviet homogenizing governmentality is the variety of idiosyncratic resources (ethnicity, culture, environment, religion, and the like) that can be used in defining regional identity.

Trade in general operates by making a profit from the difference between the state of affairs in one place and that in another, and this means that traders, almost by definition, will infringe the boundaries between regionally defined units. The peculiar position this situation creates for traders in Russia defines their essentially post-Soviet character. I have tried to show in this paper how, from the smallest units such as the Onokhoi Wood-Products Company to a large city like Irkutsk, trade is generating anxieties of several kinds. The resulting citizenship regime, first, creates privileges and subsidies for core members (these have varied during the period under study but include distribution of goods, allocation of vegetable plots, entitlement to coupons, differential wage structures, and access to government loans) and, second, discriminates against various categories of outsiders (for example, through quotas on residence, refusals of licenses and charters, strategic tariffs on imports, and arbitrary removal of trading rights). The legal citizenship regime is nevertheless benign compared with the torrent of aggression traders suffer in everyday life.

Regionalization is further promoted by the mass exodus of industry and agriculture from the price mechanism and the substitution of barter for money transactions (Woodruff 1999). The information required (who wants twenty thousand saplings or fifty easy chairs?) and the networks of trust necessary for ongoing barter tend to be local. Furthermore, barter, although a type of trade, undercuts the existence of traders; it always seems cheaper in the short run to exchange goods than to pay traders' profits. Yet, in the Russian provincial economy today, only state agencies and private traders have money. Provincial governments have seized what they see as a double opportunity: if electoral popularity is enhanced by accommodating local sentiments regarding "order," the fiscal coffers can be filled by hitting traders hard. As a result, small traders are hedged around by taxes and restrictions on every side, and the few profitable firms are supported in quasi-monopolistic positions. Perhaps the fact that they have money—money that can be spent in China or Turkey, money that can be "used voluntaristically"—is what makes traders seem so enviably dangerous. They are a challenge to governments that seek to maintain power by controlling the distribution of money. But, paradoxically, if trade were to be freed up and supported by positive public images, the separatisms that are a much more real danger for Russia today would have less foundation in economic practice.

CHAPTER 5
RUSSIAN PROTECTION RACKETS AND THE APPROPRIATION OF LAW AND ORDER

In Russia, perhaps more than in other countries, it is clear that the category of people who engage in activities defined by the state as illegal do not necessarily define themselves as criminals.[1] Stalin's harsh legal policies, which defined actions such as tardiness at work, aiding abortions, or accidental loss of secret documents as crimes (Solomon 1996), reinforced the long-standing Russian attitude that divorced community from state notions of law (*zakon*). Some people, however, joined self-defined bandit gangs. These groups existed, and still exist, both in prisons and camps and in ordinary "free" life, not accused of any crime. In this chapter I attempt an anthropological study of the politico-economic logic obtaining in these groups, in particular their discourse and practice of their own "law" (*zakon*) and the emergence of the protection racket (*reket*) as their central activity.[2]

Practices of "law" within the bandit bands differed significantly from those employed by the Soviet state in the Stalinist period, thus producing a social understanding that there were two worlds. Increasingly, from the "period of stagnation" of the 1970s to the mid-1980s onward, the mainstay of the politico-economic practice of the gangs came to be racketeering. What is the protection racket? In simple terms, it is the extortion of regularly paid dues from enterprises in return for "protection" controlled by a person or group known in Russian slang as the "roof" (*krysha*). The racket, it will be suggested, was a practice that bridged the two worlds of the criminal gangs and public life. In the current post-Soviet period, racketeering has burst the boundaries of the criminal groups, with a variety of "roofs" found among the police, politicians, and private security firms, as well as among the traditional criminal bosses. This is not a situation arising merely by function but is driven by post-Soviet anomie and cultural attitudes to the state. The practices of the racket are dynamic and unstable. They are at once expansive and implosive. At the same time, violence from young street bandits, called (literally) "thawed-outs" (*otmorozhennye* or *otmorozki*) in Russian slang, attacks the racket structures but also serves to reproduce them. As with the rackets themselves, the actions here can be seen as the product of particular kinds of persons constructed by the post-Soviet socio-cultural environment.

From a theoretical point of view, the Russian case is interesting in regard to several questions raised by Smart (1988, 91). In particular, Smart asks how illegal economic activities persist in a situation of regulatory vacuum, that is, without state support for property ownership and the sanctity of contracts. What substitutes for the state? Varese (1994) addresses these questions as regards contemporary Russia. He argues that the post-Soviet spread of property has not been matched by clear property rights legislation, and that the state authorities are ill-equipped to enforce what rules do exist. This situation reduces trust in the state and fosters a demand for protection. Although in principle such a demand might not find a supply, in the Russian case there is a ready flow of individuals trained in the use of arms and without other employment, such as disbanded army soldiers and former police and KGB officers. This is an argument based on the "rational choice" of the users of protection, and it suggests that protection rackets only emerged after perestroika when such a need was established.

There is another version of rational choice theory, which moves from an economic argument to a more political one. Volkov (1998) argues that if the key to state formation is the monopolistic control over organized violence and taxation, then the degree of disintegration of the state correlates with the extent to which it relinquishes control over these two monopolies. In Russia, nonstate enforcers of rules (such as rackets and mafias) have to a considerable extent displaced the state in the process of postcommunist transformation because they have been doing a better job than the state in reducing the transaction costs of exchange and production. Pejovich (1997) suggests that the arbitrary nature of the Russian state is an important reason for its inefficiency: it promotes policies for its own purposes that do not accord with the informal, endogenous heritage of popular rules; such policies are difficult to enforce, and this raises their transaction costs. Nongovernmental rule enforcers, in contrast, are more efficient than the state because they are less arbitrary, closer to ordinary peoples' lives, and, significantly, have incentives (their own profit) to relate the costs of their own activities to the benefits of those to whom the rules are related. Agreeing with this view, Volkov writes that the result is what he calls the "diffusion" of Russian state functions, including taxation (which people now often choose to pay to the mafias) and rule enforcement. By the late 1990s, the struggle for control of violence has largely settled into dispersed spheres of power. Although in principle the state might regain full control, the radical outcome may well be that, while the state continues to display its integrity on the international scene and still manages to maintain its symbolic façade, it ceases to dominate in terms of its key domestic functions: protection, taxation, and rule enforcement. Instead, a number of actors perform these functions, the state being only one of them.

These are valuable contributions with which this chapter concurs, but here I would like to take a slightly different tack. The protection racket is found throughout the world and may well be best seen as an activity with its own independent and systemic characteristics, not a cultural category emerging in each case from a combination of local features. However, to see the problem as only a functional one (the securing of contract and property rights, rule enforcement, and so forth) is to neglect the specifically Russian history of criminal culture/society. It is possible analytically to distinguish the structure of the racket from the values, symbolism, and legitimacy attributed to it and from the social production of the kinds of persons who engage in it. Thus, rather than seeing racketeers only as agents who happen to have appeared on the scene, this chapter examines the historical dynamic of a criminal culture that has its own momentum and attracts certain people to take part in it. The protection business today includes people from many backgrounds, including the army and the police, but there is evidence that they too are drawn into the ways of thinking, the language, and the practices of the gangs that form its backbone.[3]

This culture is the subject of the most diverse imaginings among ordinary people and has given rise to popular genres of thriller (see for example, Berkutov 1996; Koretskii 1996) and cinema, as well as massive newspaper coverage. Clearly we should not confuse what Verdery (1996, 219) calls "the conceptual mafia" with the "real thing." Analysis of the agendas lying behind the representations of the Russian mafia would have to be the subject of a different work (cf. Pilkington 1994; Ries 1998); and here, acknowledging the diversity of opinions, I have attempted to use a variety of sources to support an argument. This is that the rackets are not only private suppliers of protection, nor simply ad hoc usurpers of state functions, but culturally distinctive groupings that use what we might call techniques of predation and patronage evolved from historically earlier Soviet contexts.

When he was asked recently how Russian organized crime differs from other foreign mafias, Andrei Konstantinov, Russia's most experienced crime journalist, replied, "It differs by its strong historical traditions, whose roots go back to the seventeenth century, by its ideologized character, and further by its intellect and quick-wittedness."[4] Konstantinov's view of Russian mafias as historically specific, fluid, and changing groups that have recently integrated remarkably fast and thoroughly with state structures is similar to Rawlinson's (1997). Both authors point out how racketeering predates perestroika and commercialization, while Shelley (1997) draws a parallel between the structures of control of contemporary organized crime and those of the Soviet state. Here I attempt to draw these threads together, focusing in particular on the equivocal legitimacy and dynamics of bandit traditions in the wider context of law in Russia.

That I am not simply making up this idea that we are faced here with different criminal traditions and not just functional solutions to transactional problems can be seen from the following newspaper report. On July 11, 1996, seven people sitting in a cafe in Irkutsk were shot and four of them killed. This was a gangland "sorting-out" (*razborka*). I quote the paper at some length, since it introduces a series of categories to be discussed further.

> The war between these groups started in Spring 1995, when two "thieves in law" from Irkutsk were "crowned" [for explanations of these terms, see below] in Moscow. According to police information, one of the main reasons for the coronation of the criminal leaders from Irkutsk was to strengthen the position of the Japonchik grouping, which was trying to counteract the growing influence of the Georgian criminal clan. The losses in this war were born by only one side: Soloma ("Straw"), Paata, and Bakurin, all Georgian "thieves in law," were shot.

> In the opinion of officials of the Ulan-Ude UOP,[5] the war between the two criminal groupings should not be seen as a conflict along ethnic grounds, since criminal society in general has an international character. The Georgian group includes people of various nationalities—Georgians, Russians, Buriats, and Jews. It is two different criminal concepts that are in conflict here, varying perspectives on criminal traditions, and different attitudes to business.

> Thus, for example, the Irkutsk "thief in law" called "Tiurik" is the owner of a large packet of shares in the Bratsk aluminum factory, and he

lives in Spain. The Georgian criminal leaders, however, try not to have close contacts with business, and they propound a "purer" thieves' ideal. (Razborki 1996)

The Thieves' "Law"

The internal "law" of Soviet criminals seems to have been based on much earlier peasant and bandit conventions (Chalidze 1977, 8–9; Rawlinson 1997, 33), a subject that unfortunately cannot be pursued further here. However, the specific institution of *vory v zakone* (literally "thieves-within-the-law") is known from the 1920s (Handelman 1994, 26) or early 1930s (Rawlinson 1997, 37; Konstantinov 1996, 85). The situation calls into question several of the dominant stereotypes about the relation between the state and illegal networks. Commonly it is assumed that the state is identified with the law, and illegal networks consist of those people who are beyond either the state or the law. However, such a picture rests on assumptions about the nature of "the state," as if such a body is to be defined solely within the Western tradition.

In the revolutionary Russia of the 1920s, there were two ideological tendencies with regard to the state which reveal its radical difference from Western models. To simplify drastically, these can be described as follows. First, there was an influential concept of the state, whereby it was not conceived as a bounded entity within society but as ideally coextensive with the whole of the people (*narod*). Although the state in the narrow sense of the organs of government was to be ruled by the dictatorship of the proletariat, nevertheless the concept of the revolutionary state was that it should be inclusive, excluding only the "enemies of the people," a political rather than a criminal category. In other words, what we are here calling "illegal networks" were conceived initially not as outside, but as inside the purview of the state. Early revolutionaries borrowed ideas and practices from bandits (such as folk Russian views of brigands as liberators, traditions of secrecy, and nicknames) and the revolutionary practice of expropriation was recognized at the time to be a version of banditry seen in the rosy light of taking from the rich to give to the poor (Chalidze 1977, 20–23; Rawlinson 1997, 37).[6]

Second, and more remarkable, is the tendency of the Bolsheviks to reject the whole idea of law. Law, in the sense of universally applicable rules and regulations, was seen as a bourgeois invention, devised to protect the alien institution of property rights, and it had no place in socialist society. Instead, misdemeanors were to be judged by tribunals and people's courts in which there would be no professional legal officials but rather judgments according to revolutionary consciousness (Solomon 1996, 21–24).

In fact, private property was never entirely abolished, and Lenin almost immediately realized that law was needed in order to accomplish the functions of the new Soviet state. Nevertheless, at the beginning of the 1920s there was fierce debate about the need for a code defining specific crimes and punishments—law, like the state, was destined to atrophy, so why not start getting rid of it now?—and antilaw voices were heard even well into the 1930s (Solomon 1996, 186). We now know that neither the state itself nor the state's law would wither away in the Soviet Union; indeed, to the contrary. But it must be significant that at more or less the same time that the new Soviet rulers were questioning the value of law and setting up their brutal revolutionary variant, at the start of the 1920s, the criminals were systematizing their own conventions and rules and that they did this in the idiom of "law." The links between the Party and the bandits barely survived the revolution. The bandits' "law" came to be utterly and strictly hostile to the state,[7] but it had a solid internal legitimacy. It was an unwritten law that emerged from inside the society of its own subjects.

The bandits' "law" applied within the so-called Thieves' World,[8] and it is apparent that the term we have been using, "illegal networks," is not a good description of the organization of this society. Conceived as a separate "world," its parts also were distinct groups rather than networks. Chalidze's term, *artel*, highlights the importance given to the idea of the collective (1977, 46–47). The bandits themselves came to use the term *bratva* (fraternity). The relations between such baseline groups might be conflictual or alternatively might constitute a patrimonial hierarchy, but in neither case does the idea of a network seem apt.

The criminal artel or fraternity had an egalitarian ethos, and it was headed by a chief who was chosen by peers for his leadership qualities. The senior among these achieved the status of thief in law, and they were "crowned" at a ritual attended by a large gathering. At least two recommendations were required from other thieves in law (Handelman 1994, 29). The basic group consisted essentially of the chief's followers who had sworn to obey "the law." Each member had a nickname which superseded his civil name. In other words, a man acquired a new identity on entering and a new way of life. Even today, gangsters meeting one another for the first time ask, "Are you a *zakonnik?*" (Are you someone who is subject to the law?). These days a common term for the thieves' law is *poniatiia* (understandings). The idea is that these will govern a person's life, so bandits talk about "living according to the understandings" (*zhit' po poniatiiam*); they contrast this with the lives of other criminals who do not live according to the understandings.

One of the most important of the laws was the injunction not to compromise with the state or the Party. It was forbidden to work for any state organization, to serve in an army, or to have a residence permit; even having worn a Pioneer scarf or a badge of Lenin as a child was enough to disqualify a man from reaching the highest rank and becoming a thief in law. Attachments to the ordinary world in general were not allowed. A thief therefore should not marry. In this highly gendered world, liaisons with women from inside the Thieves' World were common, and women could be members of the bands, but they were held in low esteem and usually badly treated. Forcing a man to take the "female" role in homosexual acts was an established punishment, or downgrading of status, in the camps. Someone who it was discovered had compromised with the state authorities was punished violently and called a bitch (*suka*).

In general, this was a world which combined in a peculiarly Russian way the notion of community (*obshchina*) with a highly authoritarian practice in which the younger thieves had to be subordinate to the older men for years, until they gained their own power. It was expected and virtually required that a thief should be sentenced several times. The "zone" was a hardening experience, and a well-shouldered sentence was one way to acquire authority. During their time in jail and camps, men accumulated elaborate tattoos which were allegorical signs of their hopes, memories, and wishes (Baldaev 1989). The tattoos were also proofs of the necessary toughening experience. Thus, when a thief in law was interviewing his potential successor, he might ask him to undress to reveal visual evidence of his suitability for the post (Koretskii 1996, 179).

From the economic point of view, the central institution of the fraternity was the common treasury (*obshchak*). Note the linguistic link with *obshchina*, community. By "law," the gains from theft were to be put into the *obshchak*, which was managed by the leader of the gang. The common treasury was used to give pensions to widows and families of members, support those in the camps, and set up funds to be used on their release. The members of the fraternity, including the leader, were paid enough to live on from the common treasury, and the thieves in law, in particular, were expected to lead sober lives, almost like those of bureaucrats, maintaining order, judging violators of the code and administering the treasury (Handelman 1994, 26).

They might order a robbery, but privately they had to be examples to the rest, incorruptible, disinterested, and without desire for personal wealth (Varese 1998, 4). Likewise, the rank-and-file thieves could cheat any lay person, but they had to be honest with one another. There were many other quirky rules in the "law," and these probably varied from place to place, but the main idea was clear. As a contemporary Russian writer put it, using thieves' jargon which I hope readers are already beginning to understand: "According to the understandings, if you pay money into the *obshchak* and you are not stuck with any bad deeds that sully your honest name, then you are a 'person.' " (Berkutov 1996, 141)[9]

The War of the Bitches

I have relatively little information about criminal fraternities in the 1920s and 1930s, and so must fast forward to the period just after the Second World War when the Bitches' War took place inside the camps. This episode is quite well known from the literature (Handelman 1994, 30–31; Rawlinson 1997, 41; Varese 1998), and so I will mention it only briefly here. The War of the Bitches was a turning point in the relation between the Thieves' World and the state. After the German invasion of Russia, thousands of prisoners answered the call to join the army or munitions factories. Patriotism outweighed the law against association with the state. The thieves in law were aghast and angered, and when these soldiers returned from the war, they were not forgiven. As soon as they found themselves again behind bars, they were set upon as "bitches" (scabs). Handelman (1994, 30–31) reports that during the 1950s hundreds, perhaps thousands, of convicts were beaten or killed in a battle that engulfed the entire Gulag. The "bitches" who lived long enough to leave the camps cut off their links with the old crime chiefs. Having violated one part of the "law," they had little compunction about abandoning the rest of it, especially the prohibitions against going into business and the personal accumulation of wealth. The scene was now set for a close association between the *suchennye* ("bitchified") groups and state officials and production managers.

This episode shows that for many criminals the thieves' "law" was not a supreme value, and there were differences of opinion within the thieves' world. Kabo (1993, 60) for example, describes how when he was in the camps in the 1950s a period of chaotic violence when the "bitches" were in power was succeeded by a time of order with the advent of a group of thieves in law. The leaders of the "bitches" were knifed to death and the next day, Kabo writes, "the reign of law had dawned. The thieves established a strict and—according to their conceptual system—just order in the zone." Samoilov (1993, 36), however, writing of his time in the camps in the 1980s, saw the thieves' law as imposed: "The *vory* are the enforcers of the 'thieves' law'—that is, the criminal morality that they inculcate and impose on everybody. In that morality, it is not labor but rather thievery, robbery, and pillage that are matters of honor and valor; every murder is a heroic act, drunkenness and debauchery are the supreme pleasures, and a real *kaif* (high) is the subject of fond reminiscences, boasting, and envy." Although it is evident that for Samoilov and many other prisoners, the thieves' law was despicable and contrary to general social values, nevertheless he describes it as a morality and indicates that it included a primitive notion of universal justice. For instance, *thieves* had the privilege of taking away any packages belonging to lower-status prisoners, except for the bread ration, which was the blood-sustaining *polozhniak* (vital substance) and could not be taken. Any violation of this rule was instantly punished (Samoilov 1993, 36). In this particular aspect, the faint gleam of the notion of justice for all, the thieves' law differed from the principle of the Soviet state law.

The Law of the Soviet State

While it is, of course, impossible to treat this subject in any depth in a short chapter, one aspect of Soviet law is particularly relevant to our topic: its instrumentality. Soviet law arose after the revolution as a means of government, in particular for the regulation of the economy. The law explicitly applied differently to different classes of people (Solomon 1996, 33). Although the idea of a separate criminal law was established in the 1920s, largely to regulate the New Economic Policy, the law as it developed under Stalin was "distorted" in several ways according to Solomon (1996, 404)—presumably he is referring to distortions of the law as procedures implementing justice. Solomon is not here referring to the Terror, and he argues convincingly that Stalin used two distinct forms, terror and the law, as means of rule. However, even within the sphere of criminal law, instrumentality was primary, tempered only faintly by the scruples of officials administering it.

Soviet law was developed by Stalin to strengthen the state's ability to govern, and this characteristic persisted well into the 1980s and still has its reverberations today (see Shelley 1996, 1997). Used as a political resource, new laws required neither the consent of the public nor that of implementing officials. Regulations and edicts issued by specific leaders or branches of government were frequently used to supplement and supersede existing laws, a practice that continued tsarist traditions of ruling by decree. There was a constant refashioning of law to suit the leaders' immediate needs, with the result that even legal officials often did not know what the law was (Solomon 1996, 415). Furthermore, many decrees were kept secret. The aim here seems to have been to hide regulations whose very existence would have revealed the dictatorial and cruel nature of Soviet rule to the world (edicts concerning women and children in prison camps or definitions of "shirking" as a crime, Solomon 1996, 419). The repeal of laws on shirking, because case loads were too heavy to be managed by the courts, was also kept secret. This time, Solomon argues, Stalin may have been motivated to hide from workers the fact that shirking was no longer a crime (1966, 424–425). In any event, the secrecy of large parts of the law, and its constantly changing content by fiat from above, is evidence that it was the embodiment of a general social morality only in a secondary, refracted sense, that is, a morality which gave precedence to the state as the arbiter of what was lawful.

The Soviet law was the context within which the bandits' "law" evolved. Though some Russian writers have declared that the Soviet Union was a "bandit state," or that the zone was a mirror image of the USSR (Kabo 1993, 63), a closer consideration of the thieves' law indicates that, although there were parallels,[10] it held itself apart from the state's law and preserved some different principles. For a start, one could point to a direct symbolic confrontation of discursive values: gangsters of all types self-identified themselves as thieves at a time when production was the overwhelming Soviet value and theft of state property was an obsession, resulting in constantly changing laws on theft of elaborate cruelty (Solomon 1996, 222–223). Again, the bandits' "laws" were never edicts or regulations emanating from particular bodies or individuals, however powerful. On the contrary, the bosses, the thieves in law, were expected to follow rather than initiate "law." They had to behave in such a way as to deny the merest suspicion that they were bending the "law" to their own advantage. Of course, it is true that the thieves' "law" was already set up greatly to benefit the chiefs; but the point is that individuals could not suddenly change it. Furthermore, the thieves' "law" was not secret, at least within the Thieves' World. On the contrary, it was open. The "laws" consisted quite largely of pointless rules and taboos which showed, by their observance, the general subordination to the law. It was part of the "law" that changes to the "law" could only take place at general assemblies with the approval of the *obshchina* (community). Finally, the concept of "the understandings" suggests that the underlying idea of the "law" was one of legitimacy assured by generalized psychological internalization of the given values. Soviet law, by contrast, being conceived instrumentally rather than normatively, was also responded to by the population instrumentally (this is a simplification which begs many questions, but on the whole it is a valid point in this context).

Nevertheless, the ideological status of the thieves' law, which was that it was handed down untouched from previous generations, meant that it came fairly frequently into conflict with practical solutions to problems.[11] Its quirky rules of etiquette and obedience were more easily maintained in the restricted life of the "zone" than outside. Indeed, one senses in all this that the thieves' "law" was as much a powerful ideological myth as anything else. So far, I have tried to explain that this myth was active in a cultural world that set itself apart from the surrounding context of state-dominated Soviet life. Nevertheless, there were some fundamental similarities in the construction of the politico-economic person in these two spheres. In both cases persons were assigned to ranked categories of power/status. The vast majority of material objects, especially land and buildings, were not owned (products had only a very limited "social life" as private property; Appadurai 1986) but managed and controlled by corporations at various ranks. The economic person was predominantly one whose initial relation with goods (by theft in the case of the bandits, by production in the case of ordinary people) was that of a temporary holder, for the goods themselves were properly at the disposal of a higher social unity, the *obshchina* (community) and the state, respectively. I would now like to look more closely the protection racket, which emerged as a criminal practice from a bridging between these two worlds.

The Principle of the Racket

Chalidze (1977, 33) is of the opinion that there were no organized protection rackets in Soviet Russia, but Varese (1994, 257) points out that the payment of protection money was widespread in the last years of the Soviet regime, when cooperatives were legalized. Estimates suggest that 75 percent of Moscow's cooperatives and 90 percent of Leningrad's cooperatives made such payments. Arkadii Vaksberg (1991), however, sees the origin of the protection racket in much earlier Soviet illegal practices, and it seems to me that with regard to techniques of predation he is right.

The essence of the racket was the payment of a roof for political protection of one's source of livelihood. The illegality lay in the acquisition of the payment as private property, removing it from the sphere of state distribution. One of the main functions of the roof was to appear legitimate, to be the public skin over the operation. In this sense, the well-known scandal of Medunov, the Brezhnev-era Party boss of Krasnodar, who stashed away vast amounts of illicit wealth in return for his political patronage, was an example of the protection racket. Medunov's enemies had obstacles placed in the way of their careers, while his supporters were promoted. Possible revealers of the scam, like the journalist Vaksberg himself, were threatened with violence. As Vaksberg puts it:

> Economic freedom is the first step towards freedom in general. And that is something a totalitarian government cannot allow. The embezzlement of state property was fine in itself, as was stealing from your neighbor. Neither caused the authorities so much as a blink. There was one indispensable condition, however: that the embezzler should co-opt into his band of accomplices and protectors one or preferably more—and ideally more senior—persons amongst those in power. "Cut them in," in the language of the underworld. (1991, 24)

For this to be understood as a protection racket, one only has to make the conceptual shift of seeing career competitors as the potential threat against whom protection is required. Once the racket was in place, the threat also included the ordinary police. But the technique of predation rested on a prior and more immediate threat from the roof himself, "Cut me in, or it will be the worse for you." Such a racket could of course occur without any self-avowed criminals taking part; but if they did, they would take the roles of the embezzler or the protector. In bandit language we have the following scenario:

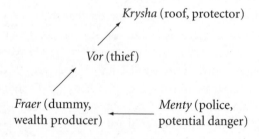

What has made this model so fundamental to current bandit practice is that it has come to apply first and foremost inside the Thieves' World among the gangsters themselves. A bandit group needs a roof with authority among other criminals to be able to operate regularly, without its source of supplies being attacked by other gangs. Berkutov's novel (1996)[12] of bandit life in St. Petersburg in the 1990s is devoted to this theme: it starts with two recently formed bands waiting outside the gates of a distant camp for the emergence of a famous thief in law, each of them eager to engage his protection services as their roof. One of the gangs had for months been feeding him parcels of luxuries paid for from their *obshchak*. By rights they should be the ones he signs up for, but to whom will he in fact offer his patronage?

By the Brezhnev era, gangsters realized that the minor rackets they had been engaged in (prostitution, gambling) could be massively enhanced by moving into the patronage structures of the main shadow economy. A crucial change now took place. Some bosses abandoned the thieves' law to the extent of accepting payments as personal wealth. A leader could still respect the inviolability of the *obshchak*, but accumulate other income on the side.[13] Perhaps, despite the bandit ideology, it was always thus to some extent. Whether this was the case or not in Stalinist times is difficult to tell, but in the period of stagnation, when bureaucrats and managers in the external society became increasingly interested in personal gain, the shift away from the "modest" *pakhan* was also certainly taking place (Vaksberg 1991, 27). Thus, racket systems inside the Thieves' World came to parallel those existing outside, and simultaneously certain criminals moved to bridge the gap between the two.

Handelman (1994, 31–32) argues that the important players in this change were the "authorities" (*avtoritety*) of the groups which had repudiated the hierarchy of the thieves in law, the gangsters known as "bitches" who had flouted the prohibition on contacts with the state. Once linked into rackets, bureaucrats, factory managers, and the like could themselves become "authorities." By the perestroika era in the 1980s the racketeering in the officially protected shadow economy was so lucrative that many younger bandits were attracted to these groups and the authority of the thieves in law diminished. "In St. Petersburg, when the gangster Authorities sit down to talk with the Thieves-in-Law," a police colonel told Handelman, "they are on equal terms. It's like two generals. And the one who wins is the one who is more intelligent, shrewder. And richer" (Handelman 1994, 31–32).

Today, at the street level the racket works in classic form as follows. A given marketplace, let us say, is "held" by gang X. This means that a rank-and-file member of the gang (a bull, *byk*) is assigned the task of guarding the market stalls at nights from drunks, petty thieves, and so on and charged with extracting a fixed sum from the traders each month. The "bull's" benefit, apart from the salary he receives, is the opportunity to graze at will on the beers, cigarettes, and prostitutes of the market he guards. The gathered money is handed over the chief of the gang, who passes it upward to the leader who manages the *obshchak*. The "roof" is paid a generous share.

Although most gangs today also obtain money from other sources (from straight extortion, theft, and so forth at the bottom, through smuggling, the drug trade, and financial swindles to investment in casinos, banks, and the like at the highest level) the street protection racket is still the most stable source of income. The ability of subordinate brigades to "draw up" (*podnimat'*) racket dues is still the source of the bandit leader's authority (Pogonchenkov 1996). In 1993 in St. Petersburg a stable of sixty subject firms was sufficient to support a gang of around one hundred members with a little extra income from prostitution.[14] Racketeering determines to a great extent the social organization of the criminal operation. Thus it is the basis for the *geographical organization* of gangs, since it defines the area or the "points" from which dues are taken (in cities like Moscow these form relatively coherent territories). The protection principle of the racket also implies a *vertical structure*. The requirement for internal trust generates strictly defined *boundaries* and *entrance requirements*.

It is certainly true that most contemporary gangs have appeared relatively recently, and probably none have a direct history as organizations going back to postwar times. However, their culture and techniques were transmitted, mostly in the camps, through "generations" of gangsters. Now, there are also new practices and accompanying jargon. The totality becomes almost like a theatrical repertoire of "acts," which the bandits use both to differentiate among themselves and to relate to people in ordinary life. I suggest below that what these acts reveal is that gangs are fundamentally appropriative institutions, rather than firms selling a service of protection. It is in the bandits' interests, however, to purvey the latter impression.

Predation and Selling "Law"

Quoting the owner of a café who said, "A roof is when I have bandits to whom I make payments so that other bandits don't disturb me," Konstantinov (1996, 174) points out that the café owner thereby expressed three misapprehensions: first, a businessman does not have bandits, bandits have businessmen; second, he does not pay them, they take money off him;

and third, what the bandits offer is not "real protection" but the most primitive form of unofficial policing. If Konstantinov is right, the techniques of threat/protection derived from Soviet contexts have evolved toward violence. Protection is no longer a matter of safeguarding careers but a physical intervention in conflicts over property.

In setting up the arrangement with a businessman, racketeers differentiate between a *probivka* (lit., piercing), which is a polite inquiry ("Are you paying anyone else? If not, you must pay us") and a *naezd* (raid), which threatens the businessman physically or psychologically. In either case, they "load" (*zagruzit'*) him with a certain percentage of his monthly profit. The language reveals the predatory orientation. The protection offered is usually no more than a mobile phone number, but it may extend to stationing a couple of heavies (who have to be paid separately from the monthly dues of 20 percent of the profits) (Konstantinov 1996, 174).[15] That contemporary rackets may virtually dispense with protection can be seen from Hohnen's study of the huge Gariunai market in Estonia in 1994. Hohnen (1997, 114–116) found that stall holders paid the racket large sums two months in advance for tickets for trading sites, while protection was given only to some traders separately at a much lesser rate.

A "real roof" is different. In this case, the racketeers become involved in the business, controlling inputs and agreements, recalling debts, obtaining credits, finding orders, sometimes even investing in the business themselves (Konstantinov 1996, 175–176). Such protection costs from 50 to 70 percent of the profits each month. This "full roof" often does not lessen but increases the risks for the businessman. It may draw the firm into illegal activities or "wars between roofs" that have nothing to do with the business itself and everything to do with bandit rivalries. Firms are sometimes elaborately deceived—for example, by being attacked by fearsome thugs hired by the "protecting" bandits themselves to convince them to pay up. There is also the practice of "fattening the piglet": the firm is cosseted and given full protection for years, while a bank account is opened in its name abroad. When it is judged that no more can be squeezed out, and full protection allows access to the account, the businessman is murdered (Konstantinov 1996, 233).

Konstantinov perhaps gives a too purely predatory description. Rackets must take care to keep the income flowing, though they differ in their tactics in this respect. It is certainly the case that firms and individuals look for roofs as much as having them imposed (Ries 1998). When two firms each have roofs and there is some disagreement, it is the roofs that do the negotiation. What the rackets sell is law, or more correctly, the idea that they are the kind of people who *have law*. I have already described the historical environment of popular Russian ideas of law, and it is worth repeating that in all its variants law is closely identified with control. Hence the mafias' rhetorical cultivation of harsh discipline, which is largely directed at the outside world: "This is what you'll get as our clients," is the message, "and this is what we'll mete out to the enemies too." Thus, curiously, selling legal services is not at odds with predation, since the harsh terms are part of the package of the racketeers' roof. The powerful are expected to dictate their terms and to be jealous and punitive too. Nevertheless, it remains the case that if the firms unwillingly buy into such qualities, the environment allows certain gangs to indulge in predation to an *irrational* extent. This can be seen in what we might call "overpredation" on the sources of income,[16] not to speak of the internecine beatings and killings.

The "Thawed-Out" Gangsters and Dynamical Systems

Among the many sad facts that have had an impact on racketeering is the demoralization of the police and the failure of an independent and incorruptible judiciary to emerge. Varese (1994) shows how, taken together, these have created a vast demand for protection from firms, which as an alternative to mafias may create their own strong-arm branches or employ one of the numerous private security firms that have appeared in recent years.[17] However, another dynamic element in these developments is the appearance on the streets of something new, thugs called the "thawed-outs").[18]

The idea here is that the Soviet regime froze its people, but now young men have unfrozen, becoming somehow inhuman in the process. *"Thawed out"* is slang for people who are cruel, immoral, and volatile, unwise and avaricious. The term conveys the sense that certain people have appeared who are not simply out of work and looking for a way of earning a living but are caught up in the culture of predation, attracted to it, and prepared to take it beyond its limits. Even other bandits see them as *bespredelnye,* literally "limitless," "out of order." Crucially, thawed-outs do not live "according to the understandings," though they may be employed as hit men and so forth by the criminal fraternities. Inside the bandit economy they are contrasted not just with the protection racketeers of longer standing but also with the armed security guards, both of whom are called *profi* (professionals). The distinction is expressed as follows, according to one gangster:

> The amateurs steal from the state. They are not interested in one another's existence and do not think about tomorrow. This is the very lowest racket, when a man is seized by the throat and money is demanded

"from your black eye." They operate carelessly, beat their victims, attack with knives and pistols, and threaten with words like, "Shit, give the money or I'll kill you!" In such a situation, the victim should reply, "Good, I'll get the money tomorrow" and then turn to the police. The *profi*, however, are far-sighted both in their expressions and their actions. They'll show you your bank account and praise the abilities of your young son. They will on no account ask you for more money than you can afford, in case, as they themselves say, "the nonsensical idea entered your head of addressing the police." (Marzeeva 1996)[19]

In other words, "thawed-outs" underlie the protection racket structure with a different type of activity, a dualistic confrontation of direct, violent extraction. I shall return to the relations of the bandit groups, the security firms, and the police; but first I address the question of the nature of gangster power relations and the place of the "thawed-outs" in them. I suggest that the emergence of "thawed-outs" is a vital element in the persistence of racketeering and its dynamics.

Some authors have described a hierarchy, variable in its components, for particular cities. For example, Konstantinov (1996, 206) writes that in St. Petersburg in 1993–94 there were several powerful, well-organized groups with the following vertical structure: brigades (5–10 people), teams (2–5 brigades), groups (2–5 teams), groupings (2–4 groups), and associations (around 5 groupings). The protection racket base seems to construct a stepped series of groups through which resources can move upward.[20] The most evolved groupings have special sections for banking, counterintelligence, economic planning, arbitrage, and law, and they often also include specialized services, such as counterfeiting workshops. At the beginning of 1994 the main groupings of this type in St. Petersburg were the Tambov-Vorkutin, the Azerbaijan, the Chechen, and the Malyshev. At the top of this structure, the criminals may invite the directors of the largest state firms to join in, or they may back pliant politicians for election to office. At the bottom, the lawless "thawed-outs" are not even counted as full members. At all levels, some of the recognized players are in prison or in the camps.[21] Dunn (1997, 64) and Pogonchenkov (1996) do not use a hierarchical model and depict a shifting mass of gangs, of varying sizes and power, operative at the time of their studies (mid-1990s).[22] Dunn (1997, 64) points out that it is essentially meaningless to count the number of gangs, since splits and amalgamations occur.[23] Though there are regional meetings of top leaders, there is no likelihood that one unified structure will appear in Russia.[24]

This is partly because of the persistence of the traditions mentioned at the beginning of this chapter. The *vor* ("thief") tradition is strong in Moscow, while that of sundry *bandity* ("bandits") dominates in St. Petersburg. The main distinctions seem to rest on the willingness to enter legitimate business and on treatment of the *obshchak*. In the "thief" custom, all revenues are paid into the *obshchak* and the gangsters receive shares, while in the "bandit" tradition only a percentage of the profits are paid into it (Konstantinov 1996, 148). The "bandits," often known as *sportsmeny,* have a cult of athleticism and physical strength, involving demonstrative abstinence from drink and drugs. The "thieves" keep stronger ties with bosses in the prisons and camps (where this tradition's authority is still paramount) together with the culture of tattooing, written edicts, observance of "the law," and so forth. So, although he points out that "all rules exist to be broken," Konstantinov (1996, 294) is able to chart significant markers whereby gangs distinguish themselves. For example, he writes that Kazantsy, even though they operate in bandit-dominated St. Petersburg, are oriented to the *vor* tradition, and this can be seen from their use of drink and drugs, their cruelty, and their communitarian treatment of their *obshchak*.

As regards the dynamics of mafiadom, even a well-known grouping such as the Solntsevo gang in Moscow, which has lasted over several "generations" of leaders (about fifteen years) has had changing sources of income over time.[25] The top gangsters are increasingly moving into large-scale financial crime and into major industries (Pogonchenkov 1996; Investitsionnye 1996, 34; Dunn 1997, 64). The eventual effect on the structure of major gangs of such activities and investments, especially the removal of capital abroad and the acquiring of foreign citizenship by the "authorities," is not easy to predict. If we limit ourselves here to the Russian-based gangs operating with a protection racket foundation, it can be seen that the leaders prefer to resolve disputes by peaceful negotiations and to have their subordinate brigades observe territorial boundaries. Nevertheless, the constant advent onto the streets of the lawless "thawed-outs" injects violence from the bottom that can move up through the layers. A brigade is pushed out of one income source and moves into the territory of another brigade, which is defended by a higher group, and so on. The more important point is that this direct street violence establishes the need for protection of the businesses on the street and thereby sets up the conditions of reproduction of the racket.

The predatory logic of the racket entails both intensive and extensive methods: more income from each "income spot" and extension to new "spots"

(Konstantinov 1996, 170). This implies that the metropolitan honey pots will be constantly at risk of outside attack. Thus gangs from the Caucasus (Azerbaijanis, Georgians, Chechens, Ingush, and Dagestanis), known collectively as the "wild animals" by the resident Slav gangs, have moved to Moscow, as well as bandits from provincial cities. The outside gangs get a foothold when an established gang is weakened by the death of a leader. If such a gang then splits into its lower-level groupings, it may be unable to protect its "spots," and gangland wars result. In 1996, the external gangs had not succeeded in carving out their own territories in Moscow, but instead preyed in double or even triple rackets on the unfortunate business spots. The Kiev market in Moscow, for example, was controlled by the local Russian Tagan group but also by the Chechen and Azerbaijani gangs (Pogonchenkov 1996).

Two dynamical processes thus occur. When there is saturation of an area with protection gangs, the result is what I call *implosion,* the competitive homing in on a single wealth-producing spot by several bands. Berkutov's novel *Krysha* (1996) dramatizes this situation. A successful car-parts dealer is the target of three or four gangs. Each hopes to acquire the horrific videotape (of the businessman's daughter being raped) that would give them the hold over him to force him to pay up and enter under their "roof." The novel ends with all the bandits bar one dead or maimed. Similar real-life cases are documented from Moscow in the 1990s.[26] This centripetal process coexists with the process of *expansion,* which is the result of a gang perceiving a wealth opportunity that seems insufficiently protected. This depends on intelligence, and some gangs are better prepared for lateral extensions of operations than others; but in principle a protection racket structure will expand when there are differences in violence-backed power between groups. However, there seems to be a closure to this process; this occurs when the racket reaches unpropitious ground, either where there is insufficient wealth to be vacuumed up[27] or when the ground is effectively dominated by other controllers, such as private protection agencies or the police.

Recent additions to the "understandings" thus concern intergang conflicts, such as priority given to the band that found the "spot" first, holding off while rivals are in prison, prohibition of turning rivals over to the police, compensation for thefts between gangs, and conventions for announcing war. In "law," unresolved matters should be raised openly at intergroup gatherings, where they are called *pred"iavy* (claims), before battle is engaged (Konstantinov 1996, 168). Of course, unannounced violence in fact occurs at the top as well as at the street level,[28] and gang leaders often ignore the understandings. It is interesting that what certain bosses say about the rules ("We have them just to keep the young ones in order") (Konstantinov 1996, 169) accords with the idea that the unwritten ethical code may act as a means of governance.[29] Be this as it may, and even if the rules are often ignored, it is certainly wise to know what they are.

A notable feature of the wider Russian pattern is the provincial town or national republic base of many gangs that operate in the metropolitan cities. This centripetal pattern can perhaps be explained by the close relations of trust inside gangs, which contrast with the more predatory relations between them and their clients. The Tambov group, for example, which operated in St. Petersburg from the late 1980s to the early 1990s, was started by Vladimir Kumarin, who grew up in the city of Tambov, whence he recruited childhood friends, kin, and other fellow countrymen. Like several other bandit bosses, Kumarin ostensibly worked as a barman, using the hotel bar as the gang's intimate place. The grouping grew to include hundreds of associates, not all from Tambov; but it is interesting that the home town is not where the band operated. The parents of one of the Tambov bosses worked as respectable officials in that city (Konstantinov 1996, 147–155). All this suggests that many gangs see themselves as raiders on an outside world, avoiding the complications of predation on home ground. The rather closed social worlds of the bosses tend to be short-lived.[30] Nevertheless, they have a certain glamour for those excluded from them.

The Gang Seen in a Shifting Light

The serious criminal groups are hidden from the street. However, the language, dress, and mannerisms of an imagined mafiadom are fascinating for the kids on the block—and this can mean children as young as ten or eleven. In some cities, certain schools are saturated with rackets (Omel'chenko 1996). If sheer income, as well as outlaw styles, are attractive to youth, nevertheless it is also the case that professional criminalization forces itself downward and engulfs children who would otherwise have had nothing to do with gangs (Pilkington 1994, 149–154). Street gangs of youths produce "thawedouts," who emerge by virtue of their harsh personalities and fighting qualities.[31] Such bands are not normally "under" regular gangs but maraud independently. However, individuals may transfer from one status to another. Films and thrillers celebrate this moment: the big move in a young bandit's life is shown when he is accepted into a regular gang "following the understandings." Proving oneself in the gang can involve "hazing" (such as being beaten up for men, and having sex with all the gang members for women), or rites such as the kissing of a dagger.[32] It is difficult to know whether such initiations really happen; but what I would like to touch on here is the intense swirl of popular suppositions around "the Mafia," which objectify it in various different guises. One picture is that the bandit has a regular, well-paid occupation.

In a characteristically post-Soviet double vision, the new bandit's occupation may be viewed in the old socialist categories. In Koretskii's *Anti-Killer* (1996), the young bandit's mother is delighted when she hears her son has been taken into a *brigada*, because despite her twenty years of thankless labor:

> contrary to her own experience she thought that the brigade was a second family, her native home. That was how working collectives were depicted in numerous films, books, and songs. And the fact that she herself had been unlucky—they were drinking all around, swearing, and pressing her to have sex after the shift—did not alter the general impression. . . . Everything depends on the leader.
>
> "Is your brigadier a good man?" she asked her son.
>
> "O.K.," he stuttered. "We'll see. The work will show." (Koretskii 1996, 6)

In this mode, the boy himself (not just his mother) is depicted as understanding his activities as "work" which takes place in "shifts," and it may even be seen, in bizarrely Soviet terms, as creative (*tvorcheskii*). Here protection is a good, produced like other goods.

However, the post-Soviet perspective in which the *"bulls"* can be seen as regular workers in brigades can change in an instant to the militialike frame of the *"profi,"* where trained and efficient violence is the predominant ideological value. In this case, the *obshchak* no longer has the aura of a beneficial communitarian fund. Instead, paying into it becomes a mark of discipline. As for those who should benefit, equality has long gone: low-ranking thugs are often forgotten when they disappear into the camps. The *obshchak* is for the deserving elite. The brigadier's orders are called *razvod*, an army term for the allocation of duties. The social person of the racketeer depicted in this perspective is a hardened, obedient fighter, vigilantly guarding the "income spots" from raids.

This may seem close to seeing the *obshchak* as an army chest and the gang as a patriotic military unit. However, the Chechens are the only ones who may have openly confronted the state in this manner. All three Moscow Chechen gangs pool a common *obshchak*, thought to contain billions of rubles at any one time (Dunn 1997, 66). While Dunn cites traditional uses for the Chechen *obshchak*,[33] Pogonchenko (1996) states that it was used to finance the war against Russia and fill the coffers of the Republic of Ichkeria. If this indeed happened it was unusual: the mafias in general depict themselves as loyal to Russia (if not to the particular government of the day). Some even see a strong state as necessary to their own strength, like two sides honed in war against one another.[34]

Racketeers are often described as providing more than protection, notably practical governance of street business neglected by government officials. For instance, in Koretskii (1996, 250) the brigadier controlling a market turns up and says to his guards:

> "Four lorries are at the eastern gate with potatoes, and they are not being let in."
>
> "They have pesticide contamination above the norm," explained the head guard and drank a gulp of vodka.
>
> "What? Have you become a sanitary official?"
>
> "No. But there must be order. They want to sell poisoned goods for the same [racket] dues as all the others. I say: let them give 10 percent for the condition of the potatoes and 30 percent for their own dues. And even better if they take their shit to the rubbish dump and don't dirty our market."

The prevailing relation between racketeer and trader is not threat/ resentment, but rather shown as lordly condescension and deferential gratitude. The reason for this is that the trader is usually depicted as engaged in some illicit dealing, which places him in a vulnerable position. When the brigadier mentioned above went to collect dues from an Azerbaijani flower seller, actually a drug dealer, and found himself initially stopped by the dealers' bouncers, the Azerbaijani soon rushed out, saying:

> "I am so sorry, my dear friend, they are new people and don't know you yet," and Hussein met the brigadier with a smile which could have been designed for a beloved brother who had been absent for many years, or for the senior in the clan. "Now they recognize you, they'll love you like a true friend." And turning aside to a hovering servant, "Tea, coffee, fruits, and cognac for my friend!—and make up a bed next door. If the guest wants it, you'll lie with him." (Koretskii 1996, 251)

A slight edginess between the two men never disappears, but the "guest" avails himself of the cognac and the girl, and then wonders aloud why he has not been offered the deluxe room upstairs. Hussein has a secret in this room, as both men know, and preserving it intact is to maintain a boundary, always fragile, between the boss and the client. In such scenarios, "protection" becomes a most equivocal thing, almost an invention, an agreement by both sides to preserve the decencies—for of course the main threat to the Azerbaijani flower/drug seller is that the brigadier himself will ring up the police and betray him. The underlying message in such novels, it seems to me, is about power, which includes the ability of the gangster to withhold violence—to behave decently, in a civilized manner.

The preoccupation with civilization runs through many accounts. A bandit, for example said to Konstantinov: "Yes and generally—we are no longer bandits. Perhaps we could be called gangsters. We are civilized people. We see nothing wrong with the police grabbing various thugs ('untieds,' *otviazannye*) and 'thawed-outs,' who go round with automatic guns and frighten everyone with their terrible haircuts" (1996, 216). In such statements, violence is relegated to a stage in history now left behind, and to the kids on the street who do not know better.

"Roofs" in the Landscape

I move now from discussing the mores of gangland to its situation in the wider political economy. Businesses now often employ their own private security firms as an alternative to, or as well as, paying into the protection rackets (Varese 1994). However, in Russia these firms cannot be completely separate from the criminal structures. As one director put it, we have to work in "bandit" territories, and the system of the "roof" is our economic reality, so, like it or not, we have to deal with the criminal fraternities. Officially we should have no contacts with the criminal world. But it is not our fault that the criminal organizations have become so powerful (Ivanov 1996). The mayor of St. Petersburg, Anatolii Sobchak, at one point tried to close most of the firms, but he did not succeed (Krom 1996). The situation seems to be that the security firms are like a buffer between the police and the criminal gangs. But they are closer to the latter, both in their rationale, which is frankly commercial in both cases, and in their techniques—indeed they sneer at their former police recruits, who "hardly know how to hold a gun" (Krom 1996). Nothing is easier than to slip over from the bodyguard to the bandit role in relation to a business you work for every day. "Frighten them, Vasia, you'll get some money," as Ivanov (1996) put it.

Meanwhile, according to a recent survey of the Moscow criminal scene:

> The police at some point understood that along with guarding of an abstract public kind, for a very nice money reward there could also be the guarding of concrete personalities or commercial structures. Thus the term "police roof" came into play. In view of the corruption of state powers it is now difficult to say where a given man with epaulettes is "kept" by the *bratva* or the converse—the "bandit" is working for the "patron." The methods of the guardians of law and order are just the same as those of the bandits. (Anatomiia 1996)

Hohnen's study of the Gariunai market (1997, 112–117) describes a landscape dominated by a combination of rackets, market managers, and police. As mentioned above, their main income is derived from charging large sums for tickets for trading sites, a task meant to be carried out by the market managers alone. What actually happened was that the managers were left with only a few tickets on the outskirts, which few people wanted to buy, while the rackets commandeered the valuable central places. Soon it appeared that some of these places were also controlled by the police. While some traders said that the police extracted these places as their price for turning a blind eye to the rackets, others maintained that the police had entered the racket themselves and that a "privatization" had taken place in one of their sections. In fact, all of this divvying up was shrouded in mystery. Though the transaction was in a sense "legal," since traders were ostensibly paying for places rather than for protection, the owners of the tickets moved into the shadows. Other traders collected the money, and most traders no longer knew to whom they were paying. It was part of the traders' ethics not to inquire, to look away when neighboring stall was paid a visit, to communicate in "half-words" and shared silences (Hohnen 1997, 124).

Such a situation is part of a destructive cycle that has reinforced distrust of the state and for vast numbers of people induced complete alienation from it. One businessman explained how the moment of truth hit him: he started a firm importing computers, and at the end of the first year he paid his tax. A day later, a *brigada* paid a visit. They made it clear that they knew exactly how much tax he had paid, and insisted that an extra 5 percent of his income was due to them. The businessman was very shaken. He knew that whatever other protection he engaged he would not be able to rid himself of the gang. What was he to do? The only solution, he said, was to count the protection dues against taxes. In fact, why pay taxes at all?

Such calculations—weighing state tax against protection dues as if they were equivalent—is reinforced by prevailing public attitudes, however unjust they may be to those state offices and police departments that work honestly. A journalist writes in the influential paper *Izvestiia,* "We have no state, only a conglomerate of mafias. If the police saves me from the bandits, then who will save me from the state?" She continues in a post-Soviet vein dominated by the underlying expectation that the state should be a provider (but no longer is):

> The state quietly takes the lion's share of our salaries, deducting taxes and percentages from our wages, and we also have to pay for light, gas, our apartments, and telephones. And we have to pay for so-called communal services. And we have to get that bottle for the plumber, and a box of chocolates for the gynecologist. And we have to pay 400,000 [rubles] a month to the English teacher for our child, even though education should be free. No one puts a knife to our throat taking this money. So this is not called the racket. (Marzeeva 1996)

The journalist, who may echo the sentiments of many Russians, continues that she personally would never call providing protection a criminal activity. It is dangerous work, paid at the rate objectively necessary, and "in any case we have never had much understanding of the people they protect" (that is, businessmen).

This last point is important, for it hints at the real gap that the gangs first rushed to fill. It does seem to be the case that in the 1980s no one took very seriously the security of the early traders and cooperatives, who were still generally thought of as speculators. The police saw it as fairly unimportant that racketeers were taking money from such people, and this turning a blind eye, of course, allowed the rackets to grow rich. We may therefore question the idea that it is necessarily a weak state that allows mafias to proliferate (cf. the arguments in Volkov 1998). Rather, it seems that certain actions undertaken by the state, such as prohibition in America in the 1930s or the legalization of cooperatives in Russia, create niches that rackets can exploit. In Russia the government has subsequently hastened to declare war on the mafias, while leaving such niches untouched (for example, the inviolability of deputies has resulted in a new "deputies' roof" for crime).

The police, for the most part, do battle against crime. But they are involved in many situations, like the market traders' tickets, in which it is difficult to tell what is allowable and what counts as corruption. So they fight identifiable enemies, the bandits who appear on the streets. In the absence of popularly legitimized state law, they may see this battle as a question of each individual officer's calling, or in more abstract terms as a fight of Good against Evil.[35] They are disheartened when their best efforts are undermined by "bought" or frightened procurators, and even more when the government's laws are unclear or suddenly changed. Konstantinov (1996, 255) cites one policeman's view of the future as follows:

> The question goes back to property. While the property owners are still undefined, strictly speaking we police are needed neither by the mafia nor by the state. What is going on is grabbing and division of everything that belongs to no one. Law will only be needed when the property-owners have sucked it all dry and say: "Enough!" Then we'll play by the rules.

Gangsters therefore may even have some public sympathy for their own sentiments about the racket, such as:

> I consider that people will require my services a hundred years from now; and a hundred years ago they needed them too. I'll have work and money independent of what political regime is in power. It may be necessary to break some law or other—that is in the blood. But it can be done either on the industrial plane or on the criminal one. Yes, I receive money from Petia, but Petia will never tell anyone and the police do not know. So on the criminal plane my activities do not exist. (Marzeeva 1996)

What is significant about this is the matter-of-fact slippage from one plane to another, from the criminal to the curiously expressed idea that the racket is industrial (or productive of a living). This is similar to the switching between discursive planes noted earlier, when the criminal brigade conceptualized in terms of humdrum Soviet labor is alternatively seen as a force of trained and rapacious violence. These planes refer to the variability of attitudes, which is part of the floating cynicism that enables protection to appear as a choice between various equivalent roofs. In fact, the roof itself is a concept which, by its applicability to one and another context, constructs the mental "stacking up" of homologous socio-political categories. It is not that the security firms, the criminal groups, and the police sections are in fact identical, though they may fulfill some of the same functions; but the wider socio-cultural attitudes toward the state, and particular enveloping concepts such as the roof, encourage the view that they are, and this, of course, promotes their actual likeness.

Conclusion

When a state establishes, or transforms, itself primarily in terms of an economic rationale, before a constitutional or a legal one, it may happen that the law becomes something that is up for definition and appropriation. In this situation, the "law" of the bandits enters the arena alongside that of the state, and it acquires a greater significance than the familiar notion of "honor among thieves." On one hand, it becomes a technique or an instrument. On the other, it is socially objectified, so it comes to stand for a way of life and an ethical stance; it becomes a "culture" to which others may be attracted or repelled. As a result, the mafias have something to sell. They sell not only their techniques of order and negotiation, as the rational choice theorists have argued, but also the whole social notion of themselves as the kind of people who are disciplined, orderly, and subject to law.

However, given that everyone knows that the bandits' "law" is not *the* law, why does it nevertheless have such a wide sphere of operation in Russia? Why is the enormous security industry closer in its practices to the gangsters than it is to the police? After all, in the United States there has also been a huge growth of private police in recent years, but practically all of them operate as approved complements to the police. In this comparison we can perhaps see what an answer for Russia might look like. In the United States, arguably, the rise of private policing is not the result of rising crime and the failure of the federal police but of wider changes in society and the growth of "mass private property," such as shopping malls or gated communities. The state police remain responsible for public space and "keeping the peace," but private policing has grown to provide crime deterrence for the new mass private properties.[36] In Russia the legal equivalent of mass private property is much wider. Many people think it amounts to all commercial property, and furthermore that commerce as such is clouded by illegitimacy ("The police should not guard private business! Do taxpayers pay the police so they should guard some stall or other?": Krom 1996). Thus Russian businessmen are placed by the popular imagination in a position resembling less that of the American mall owner than that of a casino owner or bookmaker, potentially vulnerable to police raids and hence also to bandit threats and extortions. Recall the Azerbaijani flower seller: it was because he was also a drug dealer that the bandit brigadier had such a hold over him. My argument here is in part a historical one. It is because Russian gangsters took hold of "dubious" activities long ago, because they honed their techniques in the late Soviet ambiance of patronage of the illegal shadow economy, and because ordinary business is still popularly regarded with suspicion, that the private security firms emerging later were forced to compromise with the rackets in a landscape that was mostly already carved up.

Pejovich (1997, 22–23) is right to see that the security firms and the mafias are essentially similar, in that they are both profit seekers who have incentives to enforce rules that encourage the production of goods that people want (while the police must make do with enforcing state laws that strengthen the government's political power). However, as I have shown, the mafias paradoxically also have a punitive, predatory aspect to their "law," deriving from their historical traditions as thieves as well as from requirements of internal control and external conflict. This predation can extend to "irrationally" denying growth to firms. Gangs differ in this respect, just as they differ in the extent to which they adhere to the old thieves' "understandings" or whether they have worked out new conventions for themselves. In either case, mafiosi may (and do) infiltrate the state and elected institutions. But if they are to take part in what Volkov (1998) calls the reconstruction of the state, the regaining by the state of full control over the means of violence, they must acquire a new sense of law. For the bandits' "law" is really aimed at regulating themselves, and fails utterly in imagination when faced with tasks such as general taxation and state services.[37] When people swear to adhere to the "understandings" they are swearing to something that is quite limited ethically, but that nevertheless affects their whole life. This is why the gangsters themselves can never be simply vendors of protection. As Marzeeva observes (1996), the bandit ethos taken out into the ordinary world seems in the end to be built on fear, fear that others will treat you as you treat them, that your friends will betray you, women will deceive you, your money will be stolen. Such fear is very catching. What is so regrettable is that so many people now hold what started as the outlaws' view of life:

> I do not want my children to live in a lawless country. I myself do not like to break the law. But today in Russia you have to choose: if you try to make some money, you either have to defend yourself or you have to ask someone to protect you. If you are sure you are protected, you can be happy, but if not, then your life is on borrowed time. Each new day may be your last. (Konstantinov 1996, 282)

CHAPTER 6
RETHINKING BRIBERY IN CONTEMPORARY RUSSIA

Bribery is commonly merged with more general "corruption" in studies of Russian society.[1] Statements such as the following are commonplace: "Less than six years after it began, the second great Russian revolution of this century is awash in corruption, opportunism, and crime. The government not only has failed to pursue the evidence of its predecessors' venality; it has been unable to hold in check the greed of its own ministers" (Handelman 1995, 3). This chapter attempts a more nuanced account of the specificity of bribery and its relations to certain other types of payments. It is not possible to document the incidence of bribery.[2] But, with the modesty appropriate to analysis of such a volatile epoch, we can try to explain what people think of bribery and whether this is changing.

I suggest that recent massive commercialization, together with lack of clear legal sanctions, has produced a myriad of new transactional "gray areas," but that, nevertheless, ordinary people do discriminate in how they ethically evaluate particular types of action. Bribery remains a morally condemned idea in Russian popular culture. However, it has been rethought in two ways since Soviet times: the scope of application of the idea of the bribe has shrunk, and the grounds for disapproval of bribery are changing and are sometimes challenged by different ethics. *Vziatka* (the bribe) as a representational category is applied unequivocally only to the public state sphere, and it is used with much less certainty with regard to unorthodox payments in private commercial life, which tend to be described in other ways, as "additional fees," "tariffs," "subsidies," "gratuities," "discounts," "premiums," and the like. Since 1991, as the formerly pervasive branches of the Soviet state have retreated, while private firms, cartels, crony networks, and mafialike organizations have burgeoned, the incidence of bribery may have increased numerically, but it has also retreated to a smaller arena of socio-economic life. Meanwhile, with regard to bribery itself, attitudes seem to be diverging. We can begin to see links between different views and the economic situation of various categories of people. For the economically disadvantaged, bribery is abhorred even though it is an essential survival strategy; for the radically impoverished, it is mostly out of reach and condemned as an unfair tactic of the better-off; and finally, among a small powerful elite, moral disapproval of bribery is swept aside in favor of a new ethic of commercial necessity.

The point here is that the torrent of analyses of "corruption" in the Western press, mirrored often in the Russian press, does not correspond to the differentiated practice and discourse of the people themselves. Journalistic harangues about generalized corruption cannot be helpful when they assume that all extralegal transactions are equally condemned and condemnable. Indeed, they risk a new orientalism whereby Russians appear as a thoroughly corrupted people. In my experience this is not at all the case. Certain transactions, like the bribe, are generally understood to be reprehensible, frequently even by the people practicing them, while others, equally extralegal or even illegal, are thought to be morally good, and yet others are regarded as ethically neutral because they are forced by circumstances. It is this tangle that this chapter seeks to elucidate.

If we pay attention to Russian concepts it is possible to define the bribe by three features: it is a payment improperly accepted to influence public duties that are meant to be performed for free; it is intentionally and voluntarily taken/offered; and it creates a particular, usually short-lived, "negative" social relation between the giver and the taker. The last feature is perhaps the most unfamiliar, but its social importance begins to be evident when one considers a statement made to me by several Russians, "It is impossible to bribe a kinsman or a friend." The statement brings to the fore three points made by Noonan (1984, xii–xiii): that what counts as bribery differs in different cultures, that a tension often exists between laws on bribery and the actually applied moral views of a community, and that the seriousness with which bribery is condemned varies from society to society and historically within one country. The statement that one cannot bribe a relative or a friend means in effect that, in Russia today, inducements paid to such closely related people do not count as bribes but as something else.[3]

The Russian idea of the bribe focuses on the taking (*vziat'*, to take), as opposed to the corrupting offer implied by the English word.[4] If the English abstract noun "bribery" can connote generalized improper persuasion, the

Russian *vziatochnichestvo* seems to refer simply to the presence of acts of bribing. However, in both languages, the definite noun (bribe or *vziatka*) refers an exchange in a single time span. Thus, although someone may repeatedly accept bribes, in each case the illegal favor is due for a particular payment taken. It is this feature of the *vziatka*, that it is essentially a one-time transaction, that serves to distinguish it sociologically from the reciprocal exchanges of favors within social networks of people in ongoing long-term relationships (*vzaimopomoshch'*) or the backdoor version of this, *blat* ("pull," connections). The "present nature" of the return for the bribe lays bare the transactional quality of the act and removes the possibility of seeing it in the warm light of "giving" relationships. Unlike the gift or the favor, the act of bribing cannot be seen as generous if its return is integral to the definition of the act. In part, the bribe's existence beyond the boundary of generosity also has to do with who can be bribed, because that person is always someone who has something specific to give. A warmly regarded relationship, on the other hand, seems to imply a richness of potential interactions, such that if you give something in that relationship you will not be sure of either when a return may be made or what precisely that return may consist of. Analytically, if *vzaimopomoshch'* or *blat* consists of multiple illicit favors given over time within such personal networks, *vziatka*, by contrast, sets up specific, immediate deals outside them.

People prefer mutual reciprocity, as I shall show later. It follows from this that bribery is something people *resort* to; in other words, bribery is practiced when people do not have the necessary networks of friends. Thus in everyday life for ordinary people bribery is something akin to other unpleasant economic necessities which are supposed to have disappeared with the previous regime (like queuing) and which are stigmatized partly because people with good connections do not have to engage in them.[5] Because of its relative impersonality and uncertainty, bribing often necessitates involving a mediator. The mediator provides information (for example, about who is dishonest enough to accept the bribe and yet reliable enough to perform the deed, how much should be paid, or when is the right moment) and becomes both a bridge and a buffer in what I suggest is the *essentially negative relation* of the briber and the bribed. Sometimes, as I show in a case study in the next section of this chapter, mediators can form part of an ongoing structure, which persists while the individuals offering and taking bribes change.

The specificity of the bribe can be seen if Russian practice is set against the types of bribery analyzed by Reisman (1979, 69–94). Reisman, referring mainly to the United States, suggests that there are three kinds of bribe: *transactional bribes* (payments to an official to expedite matters in one's favor, but not involving any illegal activity), *variance bribes* (payments made to secure deviance from the norm or the law), and *outright purchase* (when what is bought is not a particular service but a servant, an employee who appears to give full loyalty as an official while actually favoring the interests of the briber). In Russia the transactional type—the box of chocolates, flowers, bottle of vodka, or the envelope with a few rubles, for the nurse, accountant, teacher, and so forth—is too much part of everyday necessity to be seen as a full-fledged bribe. Like a tip, which is paid after rather than before a service, the transactional type of payment is seen as fundamentally innocuous, since after all no norm has been broken. The terms commonly used, *podmazat'* (to undergrease), and *dat' na lapu* (give to the paw), nevertheless suggest something slightly underhanded, and the convention certainly is to be discreet about such matters. A telling point is that in this kind of minor payment, if money is handed over it is pocketed but not "rudely" and openly counted. This practice indicates the existence of an unspoken convention that exactly how much is paid does not matter, though in fact this almost invariably masks what one man describes to me as "well-established local tariffs." In such a situation uncertainty about how much to give can be a source of considerable anxiety and irritation. If someone is new to a place or lacks local knowledge they can never be sure that they have given "enough" for the official actually to perform the service. In this respect, people sometimes say they are glad about the rise of commercialism, because at least the new "fees" are out in the open.[6] In contrast to the common "undergreasing," when a payment merits the more serious term "bribe" the amount paid matters explicitly, is agreed by negotiation, and the transaction is definitely secret. There must be some overlap with "giving to the paw," but in general the payment corresponds to what Reisman calls the "variance bribe": when specific payments are made for definite violations of rules.

I would also suggest that the Russian idea of the "bribe" does not extend to Reisman's third, "most noxious" type, the outright purchase (1979, 88–93). Such a case turns a public officeholder into someone who is also a secret employee. The maintenance of the organization has precedence over particular acts, so the sporadic nature of the bribe is replaced by the regularity of wages. As the case study shows, there are ambiguous cases here, too—for example, when a customs officer is regularly paid bribes for each consignment he allows through. But the fully bought person, who cannot refuse a trick and who remains a member of the illicit organization even after being dismissed from the official post, is no longer seen as taking bribes but as "kept." Particularly prevalent in mafia-organized activity, the relation is often underpinned by the threat of violence, so the bought person is more afraid of reprisals from underworld bosses than of discovery by the police (Konstantinov 1997, 235). This situation removes an essential aspect of the bribe, that it is generally understood to be a voluntary act which might in principle be refused. Thus regular payments made to police or racketeers, for example by traders and kiosk holders, are also not counted as bribes but as "tribute" (*dan'*), given under duress.

In some ways, attitudes toward bribery today continue those of Soviet times, but in others they diverge from them. The Soviet state created countless situations in which services were "free" and "equal," and yet could hardly be obtained without paying bribes. Whatever they actually did, people on the whole admired the communist ethic of honesty and accepted the public socialist ideology of unpaid, egalitarian distribution. The idea that housing, social services, transport, education, and so forth might be paid for at the cost of producing them never entered people's heads, if only because there was no way to know how much this cost was. Bribery therefore was doubly illegitimate, not only because it went against the public rules of probity and honesty, but also because the very idea that there might be a financial cost to the state's provisions (for example, the idea that "time equals money") was absent. So persons offering and taking bribes could not see themselves as employing money to pay for something, only as personally and duplicitously depriving others of their due. People might well feel that "stealing" (usually known by some other term) from the state at the workplace was almost their right, because they were badly paid and it was the state's duty to supply its workforce. But I have been told of a different feeling about bribery. Unlike "lifting," bribery could not be seen just as a relation between yourself and publicly owned objects lying around; first, to bribe was to provoke the veniality of *someone,* and second, it was a degrading use of money to divert the just allocation of resources away from its due recipients, one's comrades.[7] And from the point of view of the official, "taking" can be like stealing from an individual.[8] Bribery was practiced but was rhetorically repudiated by both ordinary people and high officials. A woman, describing a bribe she had given, said to me, "I hated myself for 'buying' Valia, and I hated the regime for putting me in the situation where I had to do it." Soviet officials accused of bribery, even while sitting in prison as a result of their own confessions—

like Usmankhodzhaev, former first secretary of the Uzbekistan (Karaulov 1993, 116–132), or Churbanov, former first deputy in the Ministry of Internal Affairs of the USSR and son-in-law of Brezhnev (Karaulov 1990, 372)—resolutely refused to admit that they had taken bribes, insisting that the accusations and confessions were fabricated.

Of course, it must be admitted that there were other, more cynical ways of talking, where the officials of the state were pictured as an anonymous "they." Inquiring about whether a friend's son was accepted into an institute, someone might ask, "*Dal?*" (Did you give?) to which the laconic reply would be "*Dal*" (I gave). In such discourse, assuming a rotten regime, reference to bribery could take on the overtones almost of resistance, that is, refusing the whole oily, sanctimonious, spuriously "personal" relations between officialdom and the people and treating "them" as no more than obstacles to be paid off. Today it seems that such late Soviet attitudes are diverging into two uncertain streams. On one hand, bribery is pictured tiredly and cynically as an inevitable aspect of commerce and capitalism. On the other, there are new perceptions that state and city officials, like everyone else in a commercial world, should be accountable. Either they should not take bribes, or they should give a receipt (!)—and in the latter case, the representation begins to shift, so the payment ceases to be a bribe and becomes a tariff or an additional charge. "Everything and everyone has a price," people now say, but with a hint of uncertainty, as if they are aware that in the new circumstances things should not be like this. Outflanked by tariffs and discounts, the bribe has almost become an insult from the past. But nevertheless it lurks still, being applicable to hidden, illicit agreements in those spheres where public probity continues to be expected. This is not entirely a survival from Soviet times and the situation now is complex and multilayered. Radical income differentiation has raised the stakes, creating both more reliance on bribery for survival as well as louder condemnation of it. To earlier moral bases for such judgments, such as Christian ethics or the ideal of the just, allocatory state and one's role as a deserving citizen in it, is added a new post-Soviet one: the idea that people exercising cold cash, rather than their common humanity, are taking advantage of the weakness of the state.

An important aspect of the new situation is that bribery can now be talked and written about openly. Accusations fly around concerning other people, and the press is likewise eager to publish stories concerning named businessmen and officials. This suggests a heated moral temperature around the subject akin to that of witchcraft accusations in other societies, a comparison discussed at length in Noonan (1984). The topic of the personal and political vendettas pursued by bribery accusations is an important one, but in this short chapter I confine myself to involvement in bribery itself. The fact is that people rarely use the term *vziatka* about their own activities.

There are two aspects to misconstruing one's own bribes, which overlap although they can be analytically distinguished. The overt disguising of an act as "not a bribe" is to be expected when it contravenes public norms and is no different from the various masking tactics intended to deceive the outside world that may accompany any illegal act. However, in the case of bribery there may also be self-deception. It is suggested here that this relates to the personal nature of the negative emotions most frequently associated with the bribe: shame and humiliation. As Simmel has argued (1978, 384), in all European cultures even small bribery is abhorred as the purchase of a person ("purchase" being used here not in the sense of hiring an employee, as in Reisman, but to suggest the idea of buying something which should not be bought, a personality). Indeed, the small bribe is somehow more shameful than a very large one, suggesting as it does that the person is willing to sell themselves for a paltry amount. Simmel argues that a huge transaction, just like an expensively "kept" person such as a millionaire's mistress, escapes entirely from the slur of bribery. The person in question may even be admired, as worthy of the expenditure of tremendous sums (1978, 388). As we shall see, this applies also in contemporary Russian, where *vziatka* tends not to be used in such cases and the word is somehow confined to smallish amounts handed over in person.

Specific emotions spring to life in the bribe encounter, when the domination and "hold" of one side over another is negotiated by subtle signs. So the disguise which cloaks the act of bribery is not just an issue of the extent to which people accept public norms, but is also tied to the equivocal quality of *facing the accomplice*. The act itself, of "handing over" and "taking," has the potential of putting out on the table, as it were, the price of the persons of the participants. As the case study shows, even in criminal circles the discomfort this engenders gives rise to characteristic approach tactics, displacements, "non-meetings," and evasions. So in discussing bribery we are not dealing simply with a moralizing public discourse about declining social standards that floats separately over cynical private habits. The arena of the bribe itself is a space full of ethical discrimination, and it is in the physical actions and etiquettes of displacement that we can see the evidence that moralizing and practice meet.

Anthropology has paid attention mostly to positive relations in society, especially those that are ongoing and self-reproducing. Negative, disavowed relations have received relatively little comment. Bribery is one type of such relations. Although, as pointed out earlier, the bribe sets up what is in principle a short-lived, even instantaneous, relation, in fact its negative charge lives on. Each side has entrusted to the other the possibility of disclosure and shame. I suggest that in Russia the potential scenarios in which such feelings might arise have diminished drastically, having been overtaken and swamped by relations conceived in other ways and with other ethics. However, they still exist, as documented below.

In what follows I provide a case study of bribery to illustrate some of the points just made. The argument then broadens out to indicate how the bribe is distinguished from other types of relation now current in everyday life.

A Case Study of Bribery

The case concerns bribery of customs officials on the Russian borders with Lithuania and Latvia in the mid-1990s, based on the work of Konstantinov (1997). Starting around 1992, various firms in St. Petersburg realized they could make huge profits by buying up metals cheaply from ailing state factories and selling them abroad. To do this, they had to pass through the customs at the border with the Baltic states, whence the goods were exported by other firms to Poland, Sweden, Holland, or Germany.

To exit from Russia each container of metals had to be accompanied by a Goods Customs Declaration, which was filled out at the customs office in St. Petersburg and then confirmed by inspection officers at the border itself. This set of circumstances gave ample opportunity for bribery.[9]

The best-laid plans are liable to failure. In September 1992, five lorries carrying nickel and copper belonging to the firm Trans-Oktavian were stopped at the Brusnichnoe post near Vyborg and turned back. They had been delayed en route and therefore missed the rota of bribed officials waiting for them. Forced to improvise, the firm attempted to rush the customs into letting them through: the trucks lurched out of the forest fifteen minutes before the post was due to close, and the armed guards with the convey threatened to report the inspectors if they did not "perform their duties in working time" and make a double-quick check. But an official spotted an irregularity in the documents, phoned the St. Petersburg customs office, and discovered another thicket of bribery there—at the truck inspection workshop called "the pit." Here there was huge pressure of work and a constantly changing staff, yet in such a place an officer could learn the secrets of preparing false documents. The unsuccessful venture of Trans-Oktavian provides us with two significant incidents that shed light on bribery more generally.

The customs man had spotted that there was something wrong with the stamp used on the documents.[10] Now this stamp (number 181) belonged to a girl called Lena working in the St. Petersburg office, and she had carelessly left it lying around. While she was away for a few days, her brother Sergei, who worked in "the pit," had filched the stamp in order to use it "to pay back a large loan" he had obtained from Artem, an employee of Trans-Oktavian. Artem asked for the customs stamp for one day, telling Sergei that he would use it to formalize a customs declaration for some dollars he intended to export. Sergei, having accepted the "loan," gave him the stamp, knowing really that it would be used for something far greater than a few dollars. Meanwhile, Sergei was too ashamed to admit to his sister Lena that he had taken the stamp. He encouraged her to think that it was "lost" and that he had had a new one made for her, exactly the same as the old one, so that she would not get into trouble. He gave her the "new" stamp, but when she looked carefully she understood that it was the old one and that her brother was deceiving her (Konstantinov 1997, 309–313).

In this episode we can see the characteristic misconstrual and displacement of the bribe. Evidently Sergei was bribed by Artem, but neither of them admitted it. What is interesting is that their disguises were not addressed to the public (to put the law off the scent) but were addressed to themselves and their close kin. Artem and Sergei pretended that the money paid was a loan and that the handover of the stamp was for a small personal transaction, thus avoiding ever having to use the word bribe. Sergei meanwhile elaborated a story to try to convince his sister that he had not taken a bribe and had not filched the stamp.

This is an example of what we can see as the dual mechanism of the denial of the bribe by the people concerned. On one hand, Konstantinov documents negative moments such as the tearing-up of a written bribe agreement (1997, 154), the nonmeeting when the bribe is left on the back seat of a parked car to be collected later by the accomplice (1997, 137), or the silent offer, when a policeman hands a note to a girl reporting a theft, "All that interests me is *baksy* (dollars)," a note she tore into tiny pieces, having handed over $100 (1997, 202), all of which can be seen as cover-ups to hinder investigation. But at the same time, all these acts are also more phenomenal repudiations of bribery itself, acts of destruction and deflection that cancel out what is denied by the honest self. Even bribed customs officials at the border behave in the same way: they keep two seals, a false one for goods they know to be contraband and a genuine one for ordinary work, and Konstantinov remarks that they *avoid even looking* at the counterfeit documents they stamp (1997, 317).

Now the second incident connected with Trans-Oktavian is the history of how Artem came to work for the firm. It turns out that he, too, had previously been a customs official in "the pit" but had been dismissed for refusing to name mates involved in a drunken brawl. Former customs officials are hot property in smuggling circles, because they know the changing formulae whereby counterfeit documents can be made to look genuine. All the same, Artem might have remained without a job were it not that he was helped to find work "according to his profession" by Oleg, a customs worker who "took" from Trans-Oktavian. Oleg suggested to the firm that they employ Artem to prepare false documents. Here we can begin to perceive the structure surrounding bribery along the "channel" leading from Russia to Europe.

Most common was for a particular customs official on the rota to be bribed to pass a given load at a particular date and time. Konstantinov describes an example: on November 30, 1993, the chief inspector at the tiny post of Torfianovka, Vladimir Ivanovich, took $2,000 for passing two containers of copper, and he subsequently took money for two further loads on December 12 and 28. Then he refused to take any further bribes, but the smugglers persuaded the head of the executive department, Sergei Evgen'evich, to take $1,500 for two further loads. He then also gave up, and it became the turn of a third official, Iurii Vasil'evich, to take the bribes, this time for only $1,000. There are two sides to the pattern thus revealed. On the customs side, one must realize that the officials came from a small, desolate village, which did not even have its own school and where the customs zone was an area of wealth, movement, and excitement, with its own glittering shop. All the villagers were insiders (*svoi*) and mostly related by kinship. The chance to "earn" by bribery was passed among them. Seniority was respected in the amounts demanded, and individuals moved in and out of the system (Konstantinov 1997, 420–421).

On the smugglers' side, it is evident that correctly arranging the bribe was a matter of considerable organizational complexity. They had to calculate the speed of the convoy and align it with the coming on duty of the bought team, as well as ensuring that vigilant overseers and extraneous trucks were out of the way. Konstantinov estimates that around 20 percent of the customs officials took bribes, and then perhaps only for a time (1997, 301). Smuggling firms tried to have a permanent employee on the customs staff (like Oleg, mentioned above in the Trans-Oktavian case, who was based in St. Petersburg), but at the border itself they always operated with someone called a "controller," who lived near the post and could monitor movements. The controller was an independent operator, who informed the firm of "windows," the times when bribed officials came on duty. The firm would attempt to use each of the windows, paying the controller a percentage of the profit on each successful transit (Konstantinov 1997, 412–414). The bribed officials were paid a lump sum by the controller for each load, while an "employee," who was a full member of the firm, was paid $3,000–$4,000 a month (1997, 415). The structure thus comprised the smugglers themselves, an employee who worked "on both sides of the barricade," some private entrepreneurs of information like the controllers, and a changing array of bribed officers on duty.

The controller in this scenario is the classic mediator, who negotiates the potentially awkward matter of the actual bribing. Konstantinov writes that the most successful controller on the Vyborg border, Arkadii Degurevich, achieved his numerous "windows" by means of his café. Once upon a time, he had persuaded the customs administration that their officers had "difficult material conditions," and he was thus able to open a café right inside the customs zone. Providing dinners and drinks at absurdly low prices, Arkadii was able to be present in the zone at any time he liked, while luring whole teams of customs men to his tables. He began by asking for a "friend's" truck to be examined "out of turn" (*vne ocheredi*). Soon many criminal bosses frequented the café, and Arkadii became the main controller for gangs all over North Russia, until an attempt was made on his life and he was forced out of business (Konstantinov 1997, 418–419).

Arkadii's café may suggest a certain sociality to this whole operation, but it should be remembered that most customs officials did not take bribes, that others refused offers after a few tricks, and that the ambience in this case was clearly one of danger and violence. Below I argue that the relations understood as bribery are essentially different from relations understood as reciprocity.

Bribery and Networks of Reciprocity

Personalized relations of reciprocity and rendering of favors have been and are extraordinarily widespread in Russia and other formerly state-planned countries (Firlit and Chlopecki 1992; Pawlik 1992; Bruno 1997;

Ledeneva 1997; Lonkila 1997). The use of personal connections to bypass the regulations and obtain benefits (*blat*) was so common that we must agree with all those writers who have argued that it was integral to state-planned economies, being a mechanism by which they could be made to work (more or less). Although perestroika saw the condemnation of *blat* by higher authorities,[11] the system was deeply embedded in social relations, including kinship, neighborhood, ethnicity, and common religion. Sometimes, as reported for the Polish *srodowisko*, (Pawlik 1992), reciprocity was experienced as a negative pressure—for example, when an unwanted, costly gift required the recipient to make a return at great expense. But more commonly the web of mutuality was felt as a welcome and supportive communality. Maternal networks are an example of this. Shchepanskaia (1996, 266) writes,

> The maternal tradition is not only an informational network for pregnant women, it also has a well developed set of customs, in particular of mutual help . . . The majority of things for my first child were donated by friends, close relatives, and even distant acquaintances. Indeed, this has a ritual significance. There is a popular belief that a pregnant woman should not sew or knit or buy the baby things herself: if she does, the baby may be stillborn or not live long. Buying baby things in a shop, therefore, is treated almost as a lack of respect for the custom.

Bribery, it is argued, was excluded from this morality. Like buying the baby clothes in a shop, it was rather a step out of "community" and into an asocial, monetized world.

It is a legitimate question to ask whether the distinction between bribery and networks of reciprocity has been eroded by the dramatic commercialization of the 1990s. Recent evidence suggests that the cultural systems of networks remain in place, and that bribery continues to be excluded from them. This can be seen from a recent study comparing informal exchange relations in St. Petersburg and Helsinki (Lonkila 1997). Data collected in 1993–94 among groups of teachers in both cities indicate a far greater prevalence of informal reciprocities in St. Petersburg and monetary purchases in Helsinki. The Russian teachers' diaries include such items as a loan of money, roughly equivalent to one week's wages, to Anton, "a neighbor whom we often meet; we help one another," or meeting "an old childhood friend who asks for help in placing her child in Alla's school" (Lonkila 1997, 4.2–5.2). It is significant that the services offered give the teachers access not only to the personal resources of their exchange partners but also to the resources of their work organizations (for example, an employee of a shoe factory who offers boots that are either better or cheaper than those obtainable in a department store; Lonkila 1997, 6.2). Illicit access to products through an employee is in principle a characteristic site of the bribe, but the St. Petersburg teachers operate instead entirely with the notion of *vzaimopomoshch'* among friends, in which "instrumental and altruistic aspects of social relations are intertwined to the extent that they seem impossible to separate" (Lonkila 1997, 6.3). The teachers devote much care to these friendships, for which ritual and sentimental occasions, such as birthdays, are important times of sociality.[12]

Similar attitudes are present also in the world of commerce. This can be seen from Bruno's perceptive work (1997) on gender and the culture of entrepreneurship in Moscow. Bruno finds the emergence of a strong counterculture of resistance to market relations, which are seen as "fraudulent" because the prices asked for goods are no longer set according to a consensual notion of fairness but according to monetary market laws.[13] This reactive culture is based mostly among women, including traders, who try to do everything through and for the sake of acquaintance (Bruno 1997). Increasingly, Bruno writes, money's buying power is seen as wiping out individuals' reliance on personal interaction and the ability to construct networks (1997, 69–70). In this situation, bribery is associated with market culture and the huge, disturbing shift it seems to presage: the notion that value may be expressed through monetary prices. As Bruno notes (1997, 68), this "threatens to undermine all the intricate webs of personal relations by offering the option of paying for something."

Bribery is condemned not just among the general public but by market traders themselves, and here it is linked to a self-perception of weakness and lack of knowledge. Traders at the huge Gariunai market in Lithuania (Hohnen 1997) are ashamed of having to trade at all, as street trading is still regarded as a makeshift strategy for those who do not have proper employment. They pay bribes of at least two kinds: to policemen at the market, who might pick them up for not having the necessary permits; and to custom officials at the Polish border to avoid having to pay large, erratic sums in VAT. Collective payment somewhat assuages the awkwardness and shame of bribing. One trader said, "So money is collected from all traders in the bus to bribe the custom officials in order to avoid problems. But if I was sure that I could pay the same or less by going by the rules, of course I would rather pay the government, but I don't know. I have nowhere to phone and ask about the rules and tell about the corruption at the borders" (Hohnen 1997, 80).

Better-connected traders, this man implied, would have friends among the police and be able to make some stable arrangement at the border.

There may be some inclination to convert a bribery relation into a longer-term one of mutual help. One could conceive of this happening where the bribe itself takes the form of a rather long-lasting service. In one such case, in Ulan-Ude in Siberia, work on a doctor's vegetable plot was offered to obtain an operation for a child. However, this arrangement did not lead to an ongoing friendship. The man who did the gardening had agreed to work for one season only, for a single benefit (the operation), and he did not conceive of carrying on digging in the future for the open-ended possible benefit of future medical services. The doctor, for his part, might have appreciated having a worker on tap, but the fact was that he did not want to enter into a relation of sociality and equality with the person who did the gardening. In short, this was a bribe, and sociality between the two would have had to have been far broader for it to transform itself into a friendship. Indeed, the understanding that this was a bribe, even if it was never openly stated, would work against the development of friendship. People said to me that if, in some case, a long-term relationship had in fact been initiated by a payment, that payment or service not only would never be called a bribe, it would not even be thought of as a bribe. For that would be to insult one's own friendship. Here what is at issue is not only the intention of the act but also the social capacity in which the participants are acting. We are dealing here with multiple aspects of the person. Precisely because a bribe does evoke the professional person of "the doctor," the doctor must separate acting as a friend, a positive ethical act, from the equivocal matter of selling his services, which was justified by him in this case by his low salary and overburden of work.

It is therefore interesting that the presence of such discrimination is recognized in the practice, if not the letter, of the Russian law. People prosecuted for taking bribes may successfully use the defense that the payment was not a bribe but was bound up in close personal reciprocities. In 1994, a certain Colonel Bukaev, a policeman, was prosecuted in St. Petersburg for obtaining bribes in the form of apartments for his wife and mistress in return for casting a blind eye to the affairs of a huge building firm he had been assigned to monitor on a regular basis. Though elaborate subterfuge was certainly going on in order to give the impression that the flat was an above-board transfer to an employee—Bukaev had divorced his wife, while continuing to live with her, and she had registered as a cleaner with the building firm, though never once appearing with mop and pail—Bukaev was vindicated at his trial. He was set free by the court, on the grounds that the flats received could not be called bribes, because a series of familial links, including those with the wife and mistress, tied Bukaev to the head of the building firm, and Bukaev himself "had acted in the capacity of a private person, not as a policeman" (Konstantinov 1997, 207–223).

The journalist Konstantinov clearly implies that the court judge had been influenced by the firm. Nevertheless, he asks, "Can we regard the mutual 'indebtedness' of officials and entrepreneurs as corruption? If in society such 'indebtedness' is the only method for the normal conduct of business, and for the overcoming of the obstacles of an incomplete law and tax system, then there is a real possibility of their becoming a basic part of the national mentality . . . People practicing such mutual debts will be very surprised if they are accused of dishonesty." Here we see the tendency of the rhetoric, even the practice, of mutual help to wipe out that of bribery.[14] Bukaev may have recognized that what he was doing was taking bribes, as is suggested by his subterfuges, but it was in the interests of both himself and the building firm to represent their activities as a different kind of relation—because "helping a friend" continues to have great positive resonance.

Bribery and the New Commercialism

Cultural representations regarding transactions for profit may differ markedly from one region of Russia to another, and they may also change with new economic conditions.[15] How, therefore, are we to understand the following report recently sent to me by an anthropologist from the city of Derbent in Dagestan?

> Pervasive venality has become increasingly clear. There seems to be almost no access to public services without a kind of extra payment or present. For example, admission to the kindergarten requires flowers, a box of chocolates, and U.S. $20 for the kindergarten director, in addition to the regular monthly fee. Although every employee pays monthly into an obligatory health insurance, every single service in the hospital has to be paid separately. Private and public institutions of education require substantial payments (several thousands dollars) for admission. For employment, the applicant requires a close relationship with the decision maker and/or a large payment. If the applicant cannot pay in advance, he usually agrees that the decision maker keeps the first year's salary. Many of these practices are not particularly new for local people, although they seem to have inflated since perestroika. (Leonhardt 1998)

The situation described might be one of ubiquitous bribery, or the pervasive use of personal connections, or the appearance of a new kind of "tribute," or a mixture of all three. Clearly the report indicates a massive monetization of public life, but we cannot understand what is going on in such situations unless we can penetrate the cultural context of local judgments.

Let me turn briefly to Ulan-Ude, where I know more of the context. Although not as pervasively as in Derbent, here, too, extra payments are made for access on a range of fronts (higher education, trading licenses, hospital beds, desirable jobs, and so forth). The operative moral distinction people try to apply here is between public and private institutions. An extra payment made to someone in charge of a public service is far more likely to be called a bribe than one made in the private sphere. The issue is not one of ownership, because in many cases ownership is unclear or has a mixed or collective form. The matter seems to have more to do with traditions of public (formerly state) allocation, in contrast to services that people now understand to be "bought." Thus an extra payment for a university place made when the institution has been established for generations is more condemned than an extra "fee" paid to a newly set-up school.

However, the whole situation is obscured by the fact that all institutions these days, including state ones, are expected to balance their budgets, and almost all are disastrously lacking in money. This means that now, unlike in Soviet times, some people see that their "extra payments" may be necessary. Parents often willingly pay odd sums (or food, clothing, and so forth) to schools, and they sympathize with teachers whose wages are delayed for months. The "extra payments" can enter organized systems for upkeep of the institution itself. This includes the distribution of incoming sums to teachers for their personal use. At the same time, some people at least are beginning to think that extra payments to ensure admission are justifiable "in this commercial world." In other words, we are seeing here a situation where *"bribery" is being institutionalized.* Reisman notes (1979, 85) that variance bribes become institutionalized when (a) they enjoy overt or tacit support at the pinnacle of power; (b) the volume of variance business is large; and (c) a bureaucracy develops to process the volume. These conditions may be in the making in parts of Russia for certain types of variance bribes, which now are coming to be regarded as more or less legitimate fees. As a result, the bribe per se is left to other, more limited, fields. It is difficult at this stage to be precise about what these are, but my impression from talking to people in Ulan-Ude is that the term "bribe" is restricted to individually pocketed sums paid for variance services to public officials who actually receive reasonable salaries.

Meanwhile the Derbent account raises several questions not yet addressed. What about the large payments made to get employment? Let us recall that the entire first year's salary is forgone if the applicant cannot pay in advance. Here we must turn to the relation between the bribe and the "tribute" (tribute being understood here as a payment made in respect of power subordination and political protection, rather than for any economic return).

Bribery and "Tribute"/Racket Payments

Russians might comment that the world of business is the wrong place to look for bribery. "Where do you find bribery? Where the state is, there will be bribes," several people have said to me. Here again, however, we must do some clarifying work. Bribes given to officials, it will be argued, are not the same as regular illicit payments (tribute) made to them.

In the Soviet period, it is well documented that in certain regions money and presents flowed upward to state officials, a process known as *vykolachivat' dan'*. How did this work? Zemtsov (1976), who worked as a sociologist for the first secretary of the Azerbaijan Communist Party, describes the machinations in great detail. Briefly, the state-owned company produced more than stated in the plan, sold the extra products on the side, and used the illicit profits to line the pockets of the managers as well as to pay higher authorities.[16] Bribery was used along the way, for example a paint-producing firm would use a small bribe to obtain from a supply company cheaper or poorer-quality components but in twice the planned amount. However, the distribution of the profits to all those involved in the subterfuge—the head of the paint workshop, the store manager, the accountant, the manager and salespeople of the paint shop, and the director of the firm himself—was not thought of as a matter of bribery (Zemtsov 1976, 22–23). One cannot bribe oneself, and all these people were in it together.[17]

The crucial payments upward through the Party and administration were also not seen as bribes. The rationale holding this vertical system together was quite simply the threat of losing one's own privileges at whatever level these were held. The honest director, who did not sell on the side and made no payments, would be called up and threatened, though no reference would be made to the real reason. Precisely because these illicit payments were expected and the whole system was protected from above, official posts were sold. In Azerbaijan in 1969, a police chief inspector's job cost 50,000 rubles, and a district procurator's cost 30,000 (Zemtsov 1976, 26).

The issue here is the distinction between the illegitimate selling of access, which is acknowledged to be bribery, and payments made under threat for little other reason than that the payee is in a position of power and wants to be paid. A lowly, but extremely widespread, example of the latter is the activities of GAI (the State Automobile Inspection Agency). In Almaty today, I am informed, the classic sequence is as follows: the motorist is flagged down, he comes over to the traffic policeman, bows and offers a cigarette, the policeman invents some minor infringement, states what the "fine" is, and the motorist pays up.[18] This is often loosely called a bribe by foreigners, but it is more often known as *dan'* by locals.[19] It would only be a bribe if the motorist were really infringing a rule for which he or she could expect prosecution, in which case the motorist would be getting something back from the deal. Usually, however, the payment is just "tribute," an acknowledgment of who rules the streets.

The same distinction holds for the payments made by stallholders to racketeers controlling markets or to police for ostensibly protecting them from rackets. Sometimes racketeers and/or the police provide a real service of protection, but often they are simply engaged in extortion. The latter, being a regular payment under explicit threat of physical retribution, is tribute in naked form. The distinction between extortion and bribery is recognized in Russian law and is often used in defense by people accused of offering bribes.[20]

Tribute paying, even the erratic street variety, seems to involve a different kind of sociality from that of the bribe. A prostitute, for example, when asked about rackets and whether everyone around was not "bought" (bribed) by them, replied, "No, they are not bought, but paid on a regular basis. It's the same everywhere. Their own girls, their own waitresses . . . they prefer to have dealings with people they know and not strangers" (Karaulov 1993, 181). This sociality is, however, not an affair of equal friends or relations, as in the networks of reciprocity, but skewed by the underlying threat. The prostitute said she was terribly afraid of the racket. In this situation, people play on gender, ethnicity, their humble poverty, and any links they might have to mask and humanize the situation (Humphrey 1999). Bruno, for example, writes of how women traders in Moscow try to appeal to the racketeers' gallantry in order to limit their dues to the mafia (1997, 72).

This need to present a front to counteract the underlying threat differentiates the tribute relation from ordinary reciprocity. At the same time, it is the absence of any specific return that differentiates tribute from bribery.

Finally, it should be noted that there is one important scenario where "tribute" turns mass bribery to its own purpose. The privatization of state assets by bureaucrats has created enormous opportunities for bribery. Rather than condemning this, certain reformers sometimes *justify* it by what looks like the tribute rationale masked as economic realism. For example, Gavriil Popov, then mayor of Moscow and engaged in privatizing city real estate, was asked in 1991 to explain why he had written that bureaucrats have a right to take bribes. He replied,

> The situation is as follows. Here is a bureaucrat. He has under his command, let's say, various shops and firms. What should we ask of him? That he organizes privatization by giving out everything he has and leaving himself naked as a bird, so he has to go out to work himself as a hired man in one of his own shops? . . . You should understand, as long as there are departments allocating [privatized flats] for free, there will always be the danger that someone will do it for a suitable reward. Everything that happens today is covert participation in this system. Ideally it would be different, and Ivan Ivanovich would simply give the contract to the best project. But we are realists. I know one thing: in our country these days, any privatization is a step ahead—at any price! Do you expect us to acquire capital and protect our virginity at the same time? (Karaulov 1993, 406–407, 410)

This is large-scale bribery that looks much like tribute, and for this reason it, too, may become accustomed, embedded, and part of the scenery, though no one who is not himself a top bureaucrat is likely to justify it quite like this. Yet words seem to fail before the huge sums acquired by figures of national importance, which no one knows how to describe; in these cases "*vziatka*" seems inadequate, almost irrelevant, as Simmel predicted.

Conclusion

The short account of bribery on the Baltic frontier showed in camera some processes that I attempted to describe in more general terms at the beginning of the chapter. Bribery is surrounded on all sides by other kinds of relations, which it partially overlaps, but it is sufficiently distinct to generate characteristic behaviors. On one hand, we saw how the customs men of the village of Torfianovka distinguished the taking of bribes, which they did for a time, from the handing on of the bribe opportunity to their co-villagers, which was part of "mutual help." Thus, both inside the microarena of the bribe itself, and in society more generally, bribery tends to be distinguished from personal reciprocity. On the other hand, the case study showed that *vziatki* are also differentiated from either regular wages paid by smuggling firms or from payment for information given to a privateer. Arkadii, the "controller" was not thought of as bribed because he was not in a public post. He was the archetypal mediator (between criminal firms and bribed officials), and with his café he created a border space—inside the zone and yet penetrable, a space where bribery could be hinted at, prepared, and set in train. As this chapter has also tried to show, bribery is differentiated from commercial payments in a double sense: it is both illegal and ethically negative. The new ethical distinctions people are beginning to make indicate that, although the Russian economy has undergone an immense upheaval and consequently the sites for bribery have shifted, the social requirement for moral evaluation has not been eroded. Bribery and the public discussions that surround it is a social phenomenon that indicates how people are coming to rethink concepts such as "the state," "public duty," or "commercial probity." I have argued that at the same time bribery is a personal and individual matter that creates peculiarly negatively charged relations between people, as we saw in the complex forms of denial employed by Artem, Sergei, and Lena, all involved in the Trans-Oktavian scam. Mediators like Arkadii are often employed precisely because of the combination of secrecy, cunning, and moral discomfort involved in bribing.

The chapter has shown how, despite commercialization, which has pushed people into rethinking bribery in some spheres, the concept remains alive in its classic arena—the gateways of the state. Here Konstantinov made a highly significant observation. He noticed that among the customs officials the sum demanded varied strictly according to the rank of the officer. The higher the official, the larger the bribe, even though the task to be accomplished through the "window" was exactly the same in each case, he comments (1997, 429–431). In other words, the bribe is not in essence just a payment for a commodity or service but is also a recognition of a person's socio-political, nonmarket status. This idea may provide a start for us to rethink bribery too, seeing it not so much as "corruption" and more as providing insight into the articulation of socio-political hierarchies of the people who make up "the state." Such a socio-political perspective also reveals how the process of privatization is resulting in the institutionalization of bribery in some spheres. Nevertheless, although bribery may be socially systemic, we should not forget that it can be pushed this way or that by the consciences of individual people.

PART III
RETHINKING PERSONHOOD

INTRODUCTION TO PART III

In the volatility of everyday life since perestroika, everywhere one finds sensational accounts of ordinary people turning to extraordinary ends to maintain their livelihoods or merely to stay afloat. Here the possibility of any actor proceeding from an essential rationality or cultivated human decency is cast into question by stereotypes that conjure for us the moral maw of the formerly socialist world. Yet, as we learned in Part II, what it means to be a moral person with conscience, as in the manifold examples of bribery, or what it means more simply to "become a person," in the case of Russian racketeers, is often far from what one might expect.

Chapter 7, "Avgai Khad," introduces this theme of the moral landscape by exploring powers seen in a widely perceived sacred site outside Ulaanbaatar. Taking its sacred origins not from antiquity but from the more pedestrian early 1970s, when a tremor dislodged a large boulder from the height of a rock formation, Avgai Khad "came alive" to its supplicants when some local residents restored the stone's "head," and good fortune ensued. Since then, visitors have come to seek favors, relieve sufferings, atone for misdeeds, and even borrow from the cache of rock offerings and valuables left on the open steppe. For the many Mongolians who observe how Avgai Khad roughly resembles a seated woman, the Mother Rock itself acts as a knowing subject, where human fortunes go in step under nature's gaze. Surely this would be an extra-communist realm if there ever was one. Yet as this chapter so effectively demonstrates, to know what counts as "ownerless property" at Avgai Khad comes only from a detailed grasp of the very fluid registers of "property" in another world without owners, where "interiorized conscience" found quite different intellectual ancestors—under Mongolian state socialism.

Chapter 8, "The Domestic Mode of Production," is a brisk but deceptively rich excursion further into powerfully local trajectories of Soviet and post-Soviet economic life. As in "Avgai Khad," however, the goal is not simply to underscore cultural context but to rethink the widely persuasive image of "naturally" autonomous actors, households, and kin groups, whose interactions with others are guided by a conscious understanding of reciprocity. This approach found one of its most erudite proponents in the anthropologist Marshall Sahlins and his theory of the "domestic mode of production," but it continues to hold broad sway more generally among many anthropological studies of the gift, rational choice theory in political science, and, of course, Keynesian economics. In eastern Siberia, however, we find that nature, spirit masters, Soviet-era politics, and the *oikos* (Greek for household, from which we take the term economics) were never entirely separable for the Buriat farmers who drive everyday economies. Freed from the bonds of collectivization and the "state reciprocities" of the USSR once lionized by Georges Bataille (1998), the greater majority of post-Soviet Buriat rural households have been operating according to a principle of "hierarchical shareholding." Here, shares (*khubi*) are "rights," in the Soviet sense of being adjudicated by collectives, and not unlike "state dues." But they are found rather than taken and encoded by scales of seniority, labor, honor, fate, and destiny. As with the Russian peasant commune (*mir*), Humphrey reminds us that for Buriats, the Soviet collective farms "did not come from Mars" but drew, however indirectly, on deeply held social forms. The challenge is not simply to ask how we can best understand post-Soviet micro-economies but to rethink our very assumptions about the protean natures and functions of Soviet collectivism itself.

Chapter 9, "Villas of the 'New Russians,'" takes on one of the post-Soviet age's best known symbolic Leviathans, the high profile, curiously propertied new rich. Here we move from the economics of reciprocity, exchange, barter, and bribery into, quite literally, construction. But again things are not quite what they seem: for even the newly super-rich have trouble achieving the kinds of social recognition they expect and desire. Humphrey gives us a kindly measured, if all too recognizable, portrait of a moneyed class that strains everywhere to distinguish itself from the gray Soviet masses before them. "Perhaps never before have style magazines been taken so literally to heart," she writes, in a world where "physically new bodies are . . . pummeled and cosseted into shape" at salons and gyms, and where private villas mushroom skyward in tightly guarded suburban settings. Yet not unlike Avgai

Khad, here is a stage where the morally and spiritually challenged inscribe their hopes and selves onto a material landscape, only to find their public displays so actively judged by others. Paradoxically, it is not only among the "dispossessed," as we saw in Chapter 2, but in some of Russia's most empowered elites that Humphrey finds actors suffering their "nonchoices"—from the reprobation of the underclass workmen who sabotage the trophy houses they are hired to build, to the envy and malice of Soviet-educated observers who see this particular rendition of the American Dream as being founded on the lucre of the unjust. Among these eminently entitled New Russians, paradoxically, the always shifting ground of cultural identities is at its least stable.

Whereas New Russians may be the antiheroes of the post-Soviet age, Siberian shamans have long labored under a burdensome heroism that many shamans themselves might like to shed. Chapter 10, "Shamans in the City," unravels much of this romanticism by showing how cultural concepts of morality and personhood can find their own enchantment in the seemingly impenetrable urban setting of the Soviet city, the industrial Bauhaus landscape in tatters. In a new age, Humphrey writes, as the Soviet master narrative of modernist cities serving its proletarian workers is vitiated, two prominent female shamans in Ulan-Ude find a certain re-enchantment: recalibrating the city in space and time, and conjuring new worlds for clients whose lives have been ravaged by the collapse of networks in city and country alike. This is not simply a return to long revered pasts, but a different sense of time, flattened, "horizontalized," made plastic by its very willingness to upend the historical record. Unlike their straining New Russian (or New Buriat) neighbors, whom teams of stylists press into new bodies and new lifestyles, here we find an urban class of Buriats who take hope in distinctly post-Soviet conceptual freedoms, as "reterritorialized" urbanites with a sacred tie to the wilds and "deterritorialized" citizens of a contemporary global community.

B. G. AND N. R.

CHAPTER 7
AVGAI KHAD
THEFT AND SOCIAL TRUST IN POSTCOMMUNIST MONGOLIA

In the 1970s, a new object of worship appeared in the steppes outside the capital city, Ulaanbaatar.[1] This is a large stone, said to be shaped like a sitting human being, called *avgai khad* ("married woman rock") or *eej khad* ("mother rock"). I write "said to be" because, for reasons shortly to be explained, I have not actually been able to see Avgai Khad. However, the events of my abortive visit to this sacred rock revealed a strange configuration of social fear and trust in a society half turned away from its recent communist past.

Sodnom-Teacher and his wife, Dulma, old friends with whom I was staying in the city, had told me about the stone years ago when it was still a clandestine object of worship (Sodnom is a lecturer at the university, though he grew up in eastern Mongolia in a herding family; Dulma is a housewife with a city background). Dulma had gone to Avgai Khad to make offerings in the hope of relief from her migraines. More recently, the stone has become a publicly acknowledged shrine and enormously popular. In September 1993, the headaches still persisting, she wanted to visit again. As we made preparations for the journey, my friends ran through what they knew about the cult.

The stone had not been worshiped until, sometime in the early 1970s, a round boulder at the top was pitched off by some natural event like an earth tremor. Local people replaced the *tolgoi* ("head"), and thereafter the rock began to grant boons to worshipers. After some years, the cult, though undercover, had become so popular that the district communist leader decided he must put a stop to such superstitious activities. He sent a large tractor to pull down the rock and raze the heaps of offerings. But as the tractor set out on its destructive journey something terrible happened: a child suddenly died— whether that of the leader or the tractor driver no one quite knows. Thereafter worship at the stone only intensified and no leaders dared challenge it.

When seen from the south, Avgai Khad looks like a mature woman sitting facing toward the rising sun. People say they can see large breasts and a rounded belly as though she is pregnant. There is a crevice between her breasts and her belly where offerings were first placed, but they reached such amounts that an altar was provided and soon the entire area around the stone was taken up with them. People offer compressed bricks of tea, and

8. *The sacred stone of Avgai Khad in 1992. Offerings are laid in front, and there is a rounded wall made of donations of "brick tea" (green tea pressed into rectangular blocks and wrapped in cloth). Photograph by Jasper Becker.*

9. *Another version of the sacred stone of Avgai Khad in 1992. Photograph by Jasper Becker.*

thousands of these now form a semicircular protective enclosure around the stone. The rock itself is swathed in yards of silk, and bottles of vodka, cheese and other dairy products, fruit, cakes, toys, children's clothes, and incense lie heaped around. People even give their jewels, gold, and other valuables. "It looks very beautiful," said Dulma. Worshippers make little rock heaps by placing stones on the boulders which lie in the steppe nearby. Going up to the main rock, they lean their foreheads against it and tell the Mother in a whisper about what is wrong and what they want. Then they should walk three times clockwise round the rock. The main offering in the mid-1990s was money. Because of inflation, money is often offered in packets of thousands of tugriks, and countless packets lie untouched at the shrine (as of 1993, 350 tugriks equalled U.S. $1, and the average monthly pay was around 2,000 tugriks). A single brick of tea is worth 800 tugriks. A trucker who once took some tea and sold it was punished by a calamity in his family.

It is, however, possible for desperate people to borrow from Avgai Khad. This should be done only in cases of dire need. Vodka should be taken only

10. *Avgai Khad in 1996. The wrappings of the bricks of tea have disintegrated. Blue silk offering scarves are laid out. The crutches of people cured by the spirit form a neat pile. A worshiper bows before the stone, which has now acquired a hat. Photograph by David Sneath.*

by alcoholics. When borrowing from Avgai Khad, people must make a vow to return the item at a certain date, and if they do not do this, misfortune is certain to befall them. Most people will not take the risk. Thus, in this country where herders are desperately poor, are paid low prices for their milk and meat, and have to struggle to get money even to obtain basic foods such as flour, rice, or sugar, Avgai Khad remains as an open treasury, her vast wealth simply waiting to be tossed by the wind or destroyed by rain and snow. Sodnom-Teacher told me that he had seen a newspaper article by some city rationalist that suggested gathering up the money and paying it into a bank to create an "Avgai Khad Fund" to be used for orphans. Needless to say, nothing had been done about this. As it was quite uncertain whether the Mother Rock would be pleased by the idea, prudence suggested it might be better to leave the money where it was.

The day for our visit dawned bright and cold, with a first smattering of snow on the slopes of Bogd Uul, the sacred mountain to the south of the city. We were to drive the 150 or so kilometers in Luvsandorzh's jeep, with his young son as driver. We locked the two doors of Sodnom's flat to the sound of hammering from downstairs, where his neighbor was also installing a second front door to deter thieves. Our offerings for the shrine were carefully hidden in the jeep; we remembered a previous journey on the steppes when a drunken gang had galloped up, stopped the car, brandished rocks, and peering inside had shouted for vodka or any Western goods. "I'll pay any thousands; I even offer my horse," one young man had yelled.

We drove out of the city and at the first mountain pass stopped to make an offering at the sacred cairn (*oboo*) for the success of our journey. There was now a strong wind with driving snow, and Sodnom frowned as I hastily laid some incense on the cairn rather than replenishing the cairn with stones and walking round it first, as custom dictates. Such wayside *oboo*s are important to travelers but are considered less powerful than the sacrificial cairns (*takhidag oboo*) on the summits of the four high mountains which surround Ulaanbaatar. These now have annual public ceremonies with officiating lamas, though people also climb up at other times to make offerings for their own purposes. Generally, these four mountains are constantly remembered, as Mongols, wherever they happen to be, offer them the first, best (*deej*) bit of any notable food or drink, flicking tiny amounts into the air in the direction of the mountains. Many people have the idea that these mountains have, or in some way "are," ruling spirits of the surrounding land. Each mountain has its own likes: Baian Zurkh accepts all kinds of food and alcohol, but Chingeltei likes sweet things, Songino takes alcohol, and Bogd Uul will only accept products made of milk. Avgai Khad seems to fit in some ways with this general idea, but there are no seasonal or communal rituals at this shrine. The Mother Rock alone has amassed an open treasury of offerings and welcomes women (the *oboo*s are traditionally an entirely male affair). Avgai Khad now surpasses the ancient mountain sites in the immediacy and personal nature of her attention to human problems. She grants children to the infertile, cures disease, and ensures the success of marriages, but she can also cause misfortunes to those who offend her. However, the fact that people had put crutches even on the wayside *oboo* ("laid there in gratitude at recovery," Sodnom said) suggests that there is some continuity between petitions made to the *oboo* and the new cult of Avgai Khad.

As we jolted along the tracks further into the hills the snowstorm turned into a blizzard. Visibility was reduced to a few yards. A Russian Volga lurched into view, crammed with people. We discovered with relief that they were also going to Avgai Khad and followed them lightheartedly, laughing unsympathetically as children's heads appeared one by one out of the back window to be sick. After a while, it became apparent that we were going in circles. The driver of the Volga ran over to our car and said the weather was too dangerous and he was turning back. "He's just lost his head," was the reaction in our jeep as we pressed on into the howling wind. Some miles further on, a small river suddenly appeared. Here were clustered two Volgas which had not dared make the crossing and a jeep stranded in the stream. Another jeep and two lorries shortly arrived. All were going to Avgai Khad, which everyone agreed must be not far away. Several hours now passed in which a car would be hauled out of the river only for another to get bogged down in it. Several of the cars were full of officials who sat tight inside in the warm, leaving the truckers, Sodnom-Teacher, and Luvsandorzh struggling to fix icy ropes and wedge stones under wheels in the driving snow. Then we looked round to see the trucks disappearing into the whiteness. There was now a heated discussion of good behavior: the officials should have given some appreciation to the truckers, but on the other hand no one should leave another human being stranded in a crisis. At this point, two jeeps were stuck in the river, the two Volgas were beached alongside, and our jeep was the only vehicle capable of crossing the stream and pulling anyone out. It was getting late, the river was covered with ice, and the storm was increasing in ferocity.

Sodnom-Teacher now told us that he had discovered the reason for this communal misfortune. In one of the jeeps was a high official with his son, whom we had seen ineffectually flapping round, tightly zipped into a modish anorak so that only his dark unhappy eyes were visible. Earlier in the summer, this boy had stolen a car, got drunk, and had a road accident in which a young girl was killed. Ever since, the boy had been in a deep depression, which was the reason the family was now going to Avgai Khad. "The sins of the boy are the cause of all this," Sodnom said, waving his arm at the blackening sky.

Furthermore, Avgai Khad, it seemed, had days on which "she did not like to receive people." This was one of these days. It was now generally decided to give up. We made our propitiation to Mother Rock, throwing generous bowls of vodka in what we guessed might be the right direction. But it was still required that we stay to help the stranded jeeps, though one of the Volgas now slipped away. We drove across the river and made numerous fruitless attempts to drag out the jeeps. I thought about freezing to death overnight. "Why don't we take the people to the nearest settlement? At least we could save them, and the jeeps could be collected when the storm dies down." I made this suggestion expecting it would have no effect, and sure enough, Sodnom brushed aside this Western thinking. The fact was no one would leave their cars, even if being frozen was a distinct possibility. They could not trust the first passerby, let alone a rescue team, not to steal every movable part. In the end, it was decided to send the remaining Volga in search of a nearby camp, which might have a tractor to pull out the jeeps.

To my surprise, since the likelihood of finding such a camp seemed remote, this plan was a sign for Luvsandorzh immediately to decide that we should leave the scene. He explained, "If they find a tractor it will use diesel. The Volga driver will certainly tell them our jeep also runs on diesel and the tractor driver will not come out unless we provide the fuel. Let's beat it now, otherwise we will not have enough to get back to Ulaanbaatar." Thus assuming the hardheartedness of the unknown tractor driver, we made an elaborate excuse and set off. "At least we are now free of the influence of that evil boy," said Sodnom-Teacher. But matters did not improve. After some thirty kilometers our engine failed. After a tense hour or two, and long prayers in Tibetan, the engine came haltingly to life. Soon, virtually in the dark, we came across a green Lada, almost buried in snow. The people inside were marmot hunters, and they had run out of gas. The driver stumbled over to us, his hair covered in frost to the scalp and icicles dangling from his ears. He was shaking so hard he could barely speak. We offered a ride, but these people also refused to leave their car. They sent a young boy with us to call out a relative from the city to rescue them. Waiting, even overnight, and the probability of frostbite were preferable to the *certainty*, assumed by everyone, that their car would be robbed of all removable parts and rendered useless if they left it.

As we approached the city and safety, Luvsandorzh leaned out of his window to throw a bowl of vodka to the *oboo*. He said:

Oboony ikh n'tand
Ölznii ikh n'nadad,
Öndöriin ikh n'tand
Öglögiin ikh n'nadad

The greatest of the *oboos* to you
The majority of the luck to me,
The highest mountain to you,
Most of the offerings to me.

Arriving home we discussed this ill-fated expedition and why the people so obstinately stuck to their cars. Sodnom said, "First of all, they knew they would not actually die. All Mongolians know that if you have gasoline or diesel, all you have to do is find a clump of *ders* grass. With fuel you can make it burn slowly down to the root ball; you can sit on the heated earth and survive for some hours." I said I had not seen a bit of *ders* in the entire journey, and I was very glad we had not been forced to try this method. He laughed and said, "Well, it is true that when I was young, no one would have behaved like this. We used to leave our tents unlocked and all our property unguarded for days. The only danger was from professional horse thieves, who made raids from a long way away. Otherwise there was complete trust." I asked when this idyllic state of affairs had ended, expecting him to blame the new relaxation of public control brought by democracy. However, his reply was more interesting. He said, "Oh, this mistrust started with collectivization in the early 1960s. As you know, virtually all our property, all our herds, all things like buildings, cars, and machinery, were taken over by the state. And that was all right to steal. It was 'ownerless property,' as we used to say. Even religious people somehow did not blame a person who took things from the state. In fact, almost everyone did it if they could get away with it."

Socialist property was "ownerless" but at the same time each bit of it was always the responsibility of some state-defined post or status. I began to understand that people got used both to theft and to endless precautions against theft, and to a concept of property that was depersonalized because the relation between people and things was conditional. It was refracted by an abstract idea to which people gave only partial acknowledgment. State property "for the benefit of all" was detached; it was detached both from the producers, who rarely used their own products, and from the consumers, who had little knowledge of the source of goods.

In the precollectivized past, there had been little factory-made or "unmarked" property in Mongolia. Virtually all things were made by someone specific, in their own way. During the social life of things, they were further marked by the patina of use, by the grime and scratches and worn patches made by particular owners. People knew who made bridles or wooden bowls or tent poles, and they knew the patterns of different regions, often even those of particular makers. Even livestock was marked in a somewhat similar way, since herders recognized the characteristics of flocks bred by neighbors, and where the animals were too numerous there was a system of brands and earmarks which both linked and differentiated the animals of each family. Theft was socially virtually impossible because all things were so closely associated with recognized owners. This is why Sodnom-Teacher stressed that the horse rustlers had been both professional and from distant parts: they had to be specialists to be able to mount lightning raids from sufficiently far away for the brands not to be recognized. The victims had to be socially distant enough from the rustlers to be constituted as "people from whom one could steal."

Collectivized property and industrially produced goods were a new category, anonymous, easily appropriated and relinquished. The idea of state property for the benefit of all was always in competition with individual desires and needs. The property that was "in my charge and yet not mine" was always subject to filching, as officials knew well. The system was maintained by means of a massive apparatus of police and interior ministry control, which encompassed thieving as part of regular practice and sometimes severely punished it.

During 1990–92 Mongolia turned toward the market economy. The state herds were virtually all distributed among private owners, and to a lesser extent so were buildings, tractors, cars, and so forth. However, this has not reconstituted the precollectivized relation between people and property. The legitimacy of how the items were distributed, who got what and why, is still a matter of tension, though it seems to be accepted as a fait accompli. It is true that people do not overtly distinguish between the few private animals they owned in the collective period and those they received later, but still we cannot speak of the inevitable closeness that Sodnom-Teacher described for the period of his youth. In fact, theft has increased in the 1990s. As elsewhere in the formerly socialist world, it is most evident in the towns and in district-center villages where underemployed young people gather and there are plenty of migrants. But even in the countryside, where everyone knows everyone else, people are robbed and many take part in theft, and there is no one who is not on their guard against it. If in socialist times theft from the state was part of general practice—you suddenly needed a new tire, or a sheep to kill to welcome a guest— theft is now from private householders with their equivocal, newly distributed property. It is perceived as part of the fight of each man for himself (which everyone was taught in school is intrinsic to capitalism), and it is all the easier now that the apparatus of control is no longer feared. The jealous guarding of cars epitomizes this situation. In Mongolia cars are extraordinarily expensive, and almost no one earns enough simply to buy one from their wages. Cars come to people by other routes. They are emblems of the kind of highly desirable property that is dotted infrequently over the social landscape, no doubt unfairly, as many people must think.

People are too poor for a robbery simply to be written off as of no account. For months afterward, people will search for a stolen item, calling unexpectedly at a suspect neighbor or going to lamas and fortune tellers to give them a clue. On the Mongolian-Tyvan border, where cattle theft is endemic, people have captured human hostages in order to get their animals back.

In this situation of social mistrust, Avgai Khad is a curious phenomenon. In England, such a place would have been robbed and wrecked almost before it got going. Why has this not happened in Mongolia? The idea is just as abstract as the concept of state property. Here people are reconstituting nature, in this case the rock, whose "head" was put back, and giving to it, with the idea that the personification of nature (the "wife" or "mother") will enable them to live successfully. Human misfortunes are aligned with perturbances of nature. I heard of one woman whose son had suddenly died. She went to consult a lama, who said that this tragedy was her responsibility.

"You disturbed the stones of Avgai Khad," he said.

"No, I didn't," she replied in surprise.

"Think more carefully," he replied. She thought hard and apparently remembered that as a child she had toppled some stones to the ground in the vicinity of Avgai Khad. The lama advised her that prayer and offering at the rock would bring back calm and harmony to her life.

It was this nameless concept of natural order that Luvsandorzh was addressing at the *oboo* on the way home (he refused to give it as definite an identity as a spirit of the land, *gazaryn ezen*). In this way of thinking, nature must be tended so that it may tend us. I do not think that this is seen as definitely as an exchange, but rather that items are given as signs of homage to Avgai Khad, or as pledges of good faith, in the hope that this will be reciprocated by a force that is greater than human activities and encompasses them. The processes of reciprocation in nature are mysterious and unpredictable as well as omnipresent (remember that our libation to Avgai Khad was made into the empty air when we had no real idea where the rock lay), but to make such an offering and a vow is to become part of these processes.

It is the idea of necessity that allows borrowing from Avgai Khad not to be considered as theft. Necessity, as I came to understand, is seen not just as a set of general conditions but also as something that includes desires, things that may be necessary for me but not for you, if our human lives are to be lived as they should be. People I spoke to agreed that a man who borrowed a large sum from Avgai Khad to pay for his son's college course was quite justified in doing so, as a good education in this case was a necessity. It corresponds with this attitude that the money "paid in" to the Mother Rock is also a matter of the individual conscience. Dulma never told me, nor even Sodnom, how much she was going to offer when she made her petition to be rid of the migraines.

Perhaps there is something distinctively postsocialist about the phenomenon of the Mother Rock. We could say from the outside that it has established a small area of economic mutuality in a world beset with lack of trust and that Avgai Khad is thus a social institution. But the people involved do not see it like this. For them it is a means of influencing the events in their own lives, a way of making wishes come true. Mother Rock, they say, has *real* power, like the power that brought about the sudden blizzard. Mongolians would absolutely refuse the idea that Avgai Khad is some kind of substitute for previous communal institutions. This is because its source is quite different. It is founded on an idea of interiorized conscience, in its own idiom of individual human relations with nature, rather than legal rules derived from an intellectualist theory about society. Avgai Khad has its own separate place alongside the emergence of small Buddhist monasteries and nunneries, the success of evangelist missions, and the enthusiasm for all sorts of cults which is present in Mongolia of late.

CHAPTER 8
THE DOMESTIC MODE OF PRODUCTION IN POST-SOVIET SIBERIA?

This chapter shows how Marshall Sahlins's concept of the Domestic Mode of Production (DMP) stimulated me to look at aspects of rural life in contemporary Russia in a way that I would not otherwise have done.[1] The idea of the DMP is that in many kinship-based societies, both production and consumption are restricted to the requirements of the household sphere. For Sahlins, therefore, domestic groups have a "natural autonomy." Where groups and households interact, Sahlins would argue that reciprocity is the guiding principle of the bargain. Although the concept of modes of production has lapsed in anthropology since the passing of Structural Marxism, and in spite of criticisms that economic anthropologists have made of the DMP model, the DMP remains part of our vocabulary as anthropologists. I use it here as a "countermodel."

Contemporary Russia seems far indeed from the tribal terrains of the Domestic Mode of Production. However, it is in categories remarkably like Sahlins's that many Russians have been trying to address problems of the decollectivization and privatization of agriculture. In the abstract, if a collective farm is disbanded, what is left are the hundreds of households that subsist on their so-called "private plots." The "private plot" is a shorthand for a small holding consisting usually of a house, a vegetable garden, a few livestock, pigs and chickens, and rights to a hay meadow where fodder can be cut to sustain the animals over the long winters. Suddenly, this begins to look like familiar DMP territory, and reform-minded Russians are asking themselves questions like Sahlins's (1972, 130–131): how can production be intensified on these individual plots, and what kinds of leadership structure will curb the tendency to self-oriented anarchy?

For an anthropologist, Sahlins's immensely stimulating essay provokes further thought on these matters, inspired to a great extent by his own later work on culture. It is argued here that to see contemporary Russia in terms of the DMP would be to neglect a predominantly indigenous understanding of post-Soviet political economy, which I term "hierarchical shareholding." At root, the DMP-like categories employed by Russian reformers are formed on the basis of theoretical individualism—influenced in their case not so much by Aleksandr V. Chaianov as by Boris Yeltsin's Euro-American advisors and rational choice theory.[2] The indigenous idea to which attention is drawn here, on the other hand, is one in which farmers are social beings right from the start, from their innermost inclinations, from their understanding of the person to their concepts of the state. In many important contexts, they see themselves as part of a socio-political "whole" (Sneath 1996). The idea is crucial to the explanation of why collective farms have been maintained in such wide areas of Russia, despite a string of presidential edicts to privatize from 1992 onward. This chapter briefly analyzes these ideas as they exist among Buriats, though in my opinion something not dissimilar is current also among other native people of Russian Asia and even—strengthened by the Soviet experience—among some of the Russians themselves.[3] This is an example of a "DMP-like situation," which may help us rethink the DMP itself.

I focus on Sahlins's discussion of how leaders and "tribal powers encroach on the domestic system to undermine its autonomy, curb its anarchy, and unleash its productivity" (1972, 130). The political negation of the centrifugal tendencies to which the DMP is naturally inclined is, according to Sahlins, negotiated by means of reciprocity. Where the political and kinship systems are not differentiated, leadership is a higher form of kinship and hence committed to generosity; but this liberality of the chiefs must ignore the flow of goods the other way (upward from the households), and it disguises what are actually relations of exchange, transaction, even exploitation (1972, 141), and ultimately contradiction (1972, 143). In this model, the households appear like little self-sufficient balls, linked by lines of "reciprocity" of one kind or another, to separate and larger balls, the chiefs. Later in *Stone Age Economics* Sahlins introduces the idea of "pooling" or redistribution, only to dissolve it, too, into "an organization of reciprocities, a system of reciprocities" (1972, 188).

But what if the domestic groups and chiefs were not imagined as separate but as one whole "society"? The tribal leaders then do not "encroach," as

Sahlins put it, but are no less integrated than anyone else. If we accept Maurice Bloch's argument (1989) that "society" is a model, distinct from the messier arrangements of practical life and sustained by ritualized enactments, then it can be seen that such a model could base itself on kinship or on some other social form. In Inner Asia, kinship is not the only idiom in which "society" is imagined, for there is also a concept of the ruled domain which sometimes coincides with patrilineal structures and sometimes exists without them.[4] In my view, hierarchical shareholding is a cultural principle which can obtain in either case, but I shall focus here on the Buriat example where political leadership and kinship seniority tend to coincide, as in the cases discussed by Sahlins. We are dealing here with very "ancient" ideas, which nevertheless have been transmitted and reenacted periodically over centuries—and have legitimacy today partly because of the ancientness people attribute to them.

Buriat culture, as distinct from the Mongolian, imagines the family only as a temporally specific part of the wider patrikin, which includes the leaders as well as the ancestors of the past and those descendants yet unborn. The household is due a share in the whole, as represented ritually in meat division at sacrifices, just as lineage divisions also receive a share at a higher level. This way of seeing oneself, defined genealogically within groups that are at once political and kinship-structured, is analogous to, and sometimes even directly mapped onto, the positioning of oneself in collectives on the basis of notional shares of collective resources.[5] The collective here appears as a stage in a series of nested hierarchies, from the household, through production teams, brigades, collectives, the subdistrict, the district, and the republic itself. Such a vision of society has been encouraged recently by the practice of publishing the budgets of districts and so on with the distribution of resources among their parts, and by the allocation of land shares among individuals at district level. No matter that the budgeted sums seem to disappear almost without trace and the land shares are no more than an idea for the great majority of people: these public pronouncements reinforce indigenous ideas of belonging to a whole within which there is a process of *allocation*.

Of course, actual allocations (pensions, loans, subsidies, handouts by enterprise managers, distributions at sacrifices, etc.) are not the only economic activities present. But they have had a relative invisibility in the literature and require more attention if we are to understand life in large parts of Russia today.

In brief, this material suggests five ways in which the DMP model can be rethought:

1. The "natural" tendency of domestic groups to autonomous subsistence is placed in doubt by cultures in which there is a "social" tendency for households to see themselves as economically and spiritually incomplete.

2. The centrifugal nature and anarchy of domestic groups founded on separate rights to resources may be encompassed in such situations by higher communal rights, in the Buriat case manifest in ritual and ideas of ancestral spirit masters of the land.

3. Strong and successful leadership does organize communal activities that increase production; however, this is not a consequence of reciprocity but of command, duty, obligation, and example.

4. Shareholding transcends the domestic group. Unlike the notion of "pooling" (Sahlins 1972, 94, 188) it is a highly articulated form of redistribution which registers differentiation and hierarchy as well as belonging.

5. Relations are personalized and political, more than law-governed or economically motivated. This creates a register of culturally specific enactments of appeasement, anger, and fate that are not reducible to reciprocity.

In the Buriat situation, far from the domestic groups being economically autonomous, there is resistance to the idea of independence. The economy is set up in such a way that the "private plots" can hardly be self-reproducing: the livestock require cultivated fodder[6] and the people need flour,[7] and both fodder and food grains are produced on huge, distant fields with large tractors, drilling machines, combine harvesters, and so forth. In other words, these essentials are produced collectively, and there is very little inclination on the part of householders to take over this work and do it themselves on a small scale.[8]

By the late 1990s, almost all collective farms in Buriatia were bankrupt, but this did not put them out of business. One result is that public work and dividends for shares are not paid in money, but precisely in those items that the members have decided not to, or cannot, produce for themselves (flour, fodder, firewood, vodka, tea, sugar, and occasional allotments of clothing). The domestic group is thus economically incomplete. It is suggested here, however, that this is not just a "fallout" of the socialist economy but is also a reflection of an indigenous view of how things are or should be. In a wider perspective, people see themselves as part of, and hence dependent on, "nature" (*baidal*, the way things are "out there"), which includes the weather, the state of the grasses, the fertility of people and livestock, the presence or absence of disease, wolves, hailstorms, and so forth. Since the domestic group depends so greatly on natural processes and enacts regular communal rituals to call down the blessings of the spirit masters[9] of the land, waters, and skies, the idea of domestic "autonomy" is in any case an impossibility. The designation of some part of narrowly human economic activity to the collectivity is in a sense neither here nor there—things could be organized this way (in Buriatia they are; in Mongolia today, on the whole, they are not)—in any case, the domestic group is located within and sustained in its efforts by a providing, or alternatively "punishing," world governed by masters both spiritual and temporal. The anthropological issue in relation to Sahlins, then, is whether this provision is to be seen as obtained through "reciprocity" or by means of another idiom. The interesting thing about the Buriats is the remarkable extent to which they support the shareholding idea: in other words, they give accord to the principle of the lot rather than that of the bargain.

The irony of agriculture in provincial Russia is that the very idea that was supposed to introduce privatization and capitalism, "shares," which could be bought and sold in the open market, has been turned on its head (or rather, outside in) to reproduce and actualize the indigenous notion of shareholding. What has happened is that local authorities have forbidden the free sale of shares.[10] The villagers strongly support this prohibition, since otherwise they say "foreigners" might get hold of "our ancestral lands." Americans are often agitatedly imagined in the strange role of the grabbers of shares in bankrupt collectives, but the actual practice is that neighbors from the next village are debarred. The result is "insiders' collectives" (Konstantinov 1997), in which kinship and indigenous notions of landownership and sharing have more or less full sway.

Under post-Soviet collectivism, shareholding works as follows: all land and other assets are theoretically divided up and allotted to the population on the basis of length and quality of work contributed by 1991 (when the Soviet Union collapsed).[11] Most people have never even seen the documents entitling them to shares. All the land and assets are given "back" to the collective (in fact, they were never removed from it). Benefits ("dividends") such as fodder are then given to the populace in proportion to the size of their shares, while workers in the collective are paid by a variety of methods (for further details on this situation, see Humphrey 1998).

Sahlins's formula of the natural autonomy of subsistence-oriented house-holds would look good on the desks of reformist planners, who are waiting for the collectives to collapse and disappear. Indeed I have met young administrators, graduates of Management Training Centers, who would love this natural propensity to reveal itself. They encourage people to "take out" their shares in real land and livestock and set up independent farms. But the villagers say (misunderstanding their own history which was never so impoverished): what mad person would want to "go back" to the far past of bare subsistence, and who would want all the trouble of independence, when we are all "our people" anyway?

One uncomfortable fact for reformers is that collective farms did not come from Mars and were not solely state instruments to expropriate surplus from the peasants. The fact that Russians created collective farms in their own land reminds us that, for them to work, ruling ideas must incorporate (even if they horribly distort them) a number of features in which the subject people can recognize their authentic longings.[12] Collective farms were born amid fierce resistance and suffering in the 1930s. But it is arguable that what was resisted was their absolute egalitarianism and the cruelty with which it was imposed, not their collectivism. What was hated was the way they annihilated everything families and groups had built up over generations and instead created the undifferentiated kolkhozniks, who were all constituted as "the same," even ironing out gender differences. Collectives soon ended most of their pretensions to egalitarianism. Thereafter they were lived in and their rankings became the operative hierarchy of rural life. In the late 1990s, a curtain has been drawn over memories of repression, at least among people like the Buriats who had never known private property in land and prefer to see themselves as beneficiaries of the education, medicine, and technologies of the Soviet state. The collectives became a fact of social nature, and this is because they corresponded in many ways to indigenous and deeply felt concepts of the social unity. That is, they constituted a manifested version of such a unity which, over the generations, took over from memories of earlier versions.[13]

Of course, people bent the rules and thieved from collectives, and the dense entanglements of relations of survival were an essential aspect of life within them (Humphrey 1983). Equivalent facts were noted by Sahlins in his discussion of popular relations with the chiefly domain. His observation that the economically failing domain (read collective) is also the one in which dues (labor) are not paid in and stealing becomes almost barefaced, the process he called "negative reciprocity" (1972, 143), is also pertinent to the current Russian situation. Conversely, the wealth created by successful organization of communal activities allows the chief (read chairman) to be generous to the people (1972, 140). However, what I would like to query about this is the idea that *reciprocity*, positive or negative, even redistribution seen as the "organization of reciprocities" (1972, 188), is the right way to analyze these internal relations.

Let me first step back to explain the fundaments of the indigenous ideas of "hierarchical shareholding" which have reappeared in the collective farms. The share (Mongolian *xubi*, Buriat *khubi*) has the connotations of portion, lot, and destiny. It appears in the distribution of the product of the whole (Sneath 1996) to members by virtue of their social position, represented by "shares," in the whole. Shares are most evident in distribution of sacred, fortune-imbued meat at sacrifices to the ancestral spirit owners of the land, a ritual that became enormously popular in Buriatia in the 1990s (Humphrey 1998). In this context shares are used both to indicate the kinship equivalence of the "men of a clan" and to mark distinction/hierarchy.[14] The totality of the meat contributed is divided into the same number of shares as the number of male heads of household in the "society." However, although in some Buriat communities the shares received are "equal,"[15] so that each family receives the good fortune bestowed by the ancestor, even in these cases the order in which the trays of meat are laid out spatially establishes a clear hierarchy of genealogical seniority.[16] Furthermore, the "share" implies not only what is received but also what is put in, and here, though each family gets one ritual share and eats their fill, the richer people contribute many shares, the middling ones fewer, and the really poor none. In this way, the notion of *khubi* allows a general redistribution of meat while also encoding a scale of seniority.

The idea of shares has been reproduced through the centuries in many different contexts: in the allocation of appanages (*xubi*) by Chinggis Khan to his sons and wives; in the division of lay offerings among lamas in Mongolian and Buriat Buddhist monasteries; in the allocation of hay meadows among Buriat households in the early twentieth century; in the cutting up of the carcass of a hunted animal, and today even in the simple shares of meat at a family meal. In these examples, which are no longer concerned with the ritual equivalence of the male clan members as in the ancestral sacrifice, the shares are allocated only on the basis of differential status. The clearest case is the family meal, in which each person receives their portion. "Pooling" (1972,

94) does not describe this well. The people are as differentiated from one another as the neck, ribs, and haunches are symbolically distinct.

The share implies a part of the whole that is pertinent to the self (in Buddhist contexts a *xubitai xün* is someone with good karma from a previous life; in the context of privatization in Mongolian *xubiin mal* are "private" livestock). In a public, more overtly political context, there is a similarly relational term, *alba*, which denotes imperial state duty and feudal obligations. Even today in Mongolia, livestock kept by a herder but belonging to a collective are called *alban mal* (Sneath 1996).[17] The significant fact is that personal shares and state dues are closely related ideas for the Buriats and both are somehow given and fated. This can be seen in their characterization of smallpox. In the late nineteenth century, someone who fell ill with this disease was said to have "got their share" (*khubiia aba*) or to "be lying down in obligation" (*albanda khebte*), because the Eastern Skies were thought to send smallpox to each family as their share/duty. The Buriat writer Khangalov (1958, I, 457) adds bleakly that the Skies send smallpox so that people should die in the numbers prescribed (for the world to go on as it should do). The fated quality implied in shares appears in how Mongolian people talk about it today: to "take" one's share implies a presumptuous grasping; a more appropriate expression is to "find" one's share (*khubi olo*). If inexplicable misfortunes occur —the cow has died, the son is ill—this is often attributed to inadvertent angering of the land spirit which is reversible by performing one's duty (making an offering). The contemporary Buriat shamanic ritual of a household to appease an evidently angry spirit is called *alban*—"duty" (Zhukovskaia 1997).

It is true that Buriats today use Russian terms (*pai, dolia*) when talking about the collectives, land shares, and so forth, but it seems to me that the older ideas often influence the way they actually go about things. These have been reinforced and set in new idioms by Soviet political culture. The main input of Soviet culture, apart from the massive repressive power of the state,[18] has been the introduction of the hierarchy of labor in place of genealogy as the legitimating principle of social differentiation. Not only is it on this basis that shares (*pai*) are allocated, but the practice of handouts works this way too: above a minimum for survival (the hay, firewood, and fodder that all members receive)[19] the bestowals of sugar, vodka, clothing, and so forth are distributed broadly in terms of labor status. Veterans, stalwarts, and worthies get more, while layabouts get much less. This might look like reciprocity—"You work and I'll make sure to distribute some vodka"—but reciprocity does not explain the underlying motivations that commonly operate, nor the totality of transfers that take place.

The leaders feel a broad responsibility for all "their" people, including those who cannot work, the sick, and the alcoholics. The people expect this to be honored (I have seen the constant stream of petitioners in the chairman's office; a share is a right). The householders, for their part, do not think of themselves as working in order to reciprocate so much as *obliged to obey*, so they work quite largely to try to make sure the official is not angered.[20] It is thought that a leader not only has a right but also a duty to give orders, and if they are wrongheaded nothing will be done because that is just how things are. Anger also falls on one's head and is not really predictable. The householder has the obligation to *otchityvat'sia*, an almost untranslatable expression, which means to account to the leader for what he/she has been doing in relation to these orders. The very existence of this expression indicates, of course, that orders might not be carried out. But what we have here is a variety of relations (rhetorical demonstration of power, "paternal care," or rage, on one hand, and evasiveness, demonstrative obedience, or "gratitude," on the other). This is in a quite different register from the quid pro quo of reciprocity, however that notion is expanded.

I am not trying to argue here that the workers and householders are not self-interested. Rather, in this mode of relations the self-interest appears in "political" as much as in economic forms—it appears in unwillingness, disobligingness, neglect, or simply failure to fulfill the duty (Scott 1990). It is arguable also that even apparently economic forms, like the "contracts" that many collectives have introduced instead of orders, in fact operate politically. As there is no legal system to enforce contracts, it is left to the vagaries of exigency and obligation on either side as to whether the conditions are fulfilled (Humphrey and Sneath 1999).

It is interesting, then, to think about the cast that the notion of duty throws over many transactions, even those of overtly bargaining kinds. People are trading with one another, doing bits of work on the side, making and selling handicrafts, thieving, using collective property to their own profit, exchanging gifts—in short, anything that will help them survive. A great deal of this has to be seen in terms of exchange, but it is also arguable that, where kin networks are used, the relations are conceived in terms of obligation and can sustain imbalances between households over an indefinite period (Sneath in Humphrey and Sneath 1999). Inside the collectives, even when workers bargain directly with the management, "reciprocity" as a dualistic relation (Sahlins 1972, 188) does not quite sum up what is going on.

In the summer of 1996, I was present at a collective farm on the day seven haymaking teams were supposed to come out to mow. Not a single person appeared. The same was true the next day. The chairman was in distraction: the grass was beginning to wilt. On the fourth day the teams presented an united offer: they would come out if each person was given ten boxes of cigarettes. The chairman somehow obtained the cigarettes, and haymaking started next day. There are several points that can be made about this. First, everyone knew that the haymaking would happen. Kin had come from the city specially to take part in it, and it was known that the collective hay was relied on by other dependent households who could not mow themselves (the aged, ill, single mothers, and so forth). Furthermore, the collective cattle, reliant on the collective hay, were the source of the butter and meat which were the only salable items at that time of year, insuring that the farm could continue to provide transport and fuel that everyone used and feed the school boardinghouse on which at least seventy families relied. Thus the encompassing social element and systemic distribution to the whole was in fact the background raison d'être for what looked on the surface like a straightforward transaction. Furthermore, the collective haymaking fell due at exactly the same time that individual haymaking on household plots could best take place, yet people did not use the crucial few days to their own advantage. They just sat at home and waited. They were *not obeying*, rather than acting "economically." Finally, in a Mongolian context, cigarettes are not just ordinary payment but have honorific connotations. They are "gifts," and consequently their presentation elevated the situation from a work-for-pay confrontation to one colored by the ancient imperial light of duty and bestowal.[21]

The succession of ritualized and nonritual times is highly relevant here. Nonritual time is a kind of blank for "society" in its collective form, and conversely at ritualized occasions joint behavior and hierarchy are obligatory. For example, it is the height of impoliteness to take even a sip of drink by oneself rather than after a toast (when all drink together), and toasts are offered in order of status and always with some honorific words. Ritual occasions are extremely frequent, especially in the summer and autumn, when weddings, hospitable dinners for visitors, sacrifices, public holidays, and so forth happen almost every day. Now the allocations of goods by the collective always take place at such special festivities. The director of a farm *has to* get luxuries to distribute on International Women's Day, has to give a substantial gift at weddings, and must make a general handout of provisions for the New Year celebrations. One might imagine that the first thing bankrupt collectives would drop would be their own celebrations. However, this is not the case: the Milkmaids' Ball, the Day of the Livestock Worker, and so forth happen as before. It would be quite wrong to imagine that the milkmaids demand a ball, or that the collective holds a ball to reward them. There is an intense life precisely "in society," when the asocial, incomplete existence of any group is elevated by ritual to the plane of incorporation and appropriate status.

To conclude, the DMP model envisages "naturally" independent households which are encouraged into greater productivity by a collection of reciprocity ties with the leadership. The Buriat example, in contrast, shows a case where, even when independent smallholdings are encouraged by the government to become private and collective farms are weak, the households "naturally" imagine themselves as hierarchically situated parts in a whole. The genealogical definition of "society" enacted in sacrifices (in which, let us remember, leaders take part) is replaced in the collective-farm scenario by a hierarchy of quality of labor. The DMP envisages the leader's power as a function of the services and goods owed to him by domestic groups.[22] But the Buriat case, in either genealogical or labor scenarios, shows that another principle of power must be at work. Of course, both economic competence and technical ability are helpful. As regards labor, domestic production with its manual methods is at the bottom of the scale, and technological expertise is always found at the nodes of collective leadership.[23] But leadership in fact rests on mastery of the organization, rather than flows of goods as such. Mastery in the end, though it is a socially recognized idea, seems to be a quality of individual personality (a quasi-magical, quasi-sacred power), and it transcends both genealogy and knowledge/expertise. The householders, who look as though they are engaged in reciprocity with leaders, are really, at a deeper level, receiving their lots in the domain of the fortune-channeling master.

The importance of such ideas is not that they sum up all of what is happening, but that they serve, especially in ritual, to "make" the social ties which are a cause for the appearance of things.

CHAPTER 9
THE VILLAS OF THE "NEW RUSSIANS"
A SKETCH OF CONSUMPTION AND CULTURAL IDENTITY IN POST-SOVIET LANDSCAPES

Since the early 1990s, developments of spectacular villas designed for the habitation of the rich have appeared on the outskirts of Russian cities.[1] For the first time since the Revolution, we see the construction of large, individually owned houses for single families. The villas are interesting in two ways, for they represent not only a new form of real estate but also a new and evolving architectural style. Their raw, red brick facades give them quite a different appearance from the apartment blocks and weather-beaten log cottages of the Soviet era. What can be discovered from the villas about the cultural identity of the people who commission them, the business elites who are called the New Russians? The story I tell reveals the deep ambiguity of "readings" of the material object, not only in general but more particularly when cultural identity is so contested as to be hardly achievable.

The New Russians can be imagined as a cultural entity with a shining, spectacular face and a shadowy side. There is a certain circularity in their relation with the villas, since if people are asked who the New Russians are they will often reply that they are the ones who own that kind of conspicuous house. These new kinds of people are known to others by appearances, that is, when material signs of their presence are perceived in the post-Soviet landscape. "We often see his shining automobile racing through the city at high speed. Sometimes his slightly plump figure in an expensive cashmere coat is glimpsed as he passes from his car to a restaurant or bank or through the mysteriously glittering doors of a luxurious office" (Kryshtanovskaia 1997). I suggest that we are faced here, more starkly than in most cases, with the two-sidedness of "identity," that is, the relation between identity as conferred by others and identity as felt and expressed from inside.[2]

This chapter underlines the difficulty involved in achieving cultural identity amid the contested values of contemporary Russia. In the context of consumption, it is useful to distinguish between mytho-historical self-images (interpretations of one's material objects that provide a placement of the self in the world) and what is said about these same objects when no such mythic work has been achieved. The villas of the New Russians are the ground for two specific self-images, that of an haute bourgeoisie within an imagined "historical" empire and that of sleek, efficient Europeans within a globalized vista of modern business elites. I follow Miller (1994a, 313–316) in arguing that this contradiction of myths is neither inauthentic nor a cause of anxiety to the New Russians themselves. Indeed, there is a third villa style which is hyped as the most prestigious and popular, namely the combination of the two styles mentioned above (*Business in Russia* 1995, xxiv). The point, however, is that it is very often the case that none of these styles can be achieved. There is a slippage between the mental image and the physical fact of the building, often indeed a ludicrous gap. This reveals the unintended aspects of identity creation, the heaps and bits and pieces that have somehow ended up on the site, which of course are at the same time visible and "readable" by everyone else. The slippage may be unintended but is no accident, since it reflects the general post-Soviet condition, which is characterized by uncertainty or irony toward any grand mythic projects.

Furthermore, the very materiality of the villas, which are built for a widely detested social category, the New Russians, becomes a fertile ground for acts of demonstrative negligence, even sabotage. Building teams are often drawn from the rural poor on temporary contracts, in other words from people who have no liking whatsoever for the rich in Russia's divided society. The New Russian client buys, let us say, "a Jacuzzi," which indeed appears in the bathroom, only to find that it is fatally cracked, somehow built in with insoluble plumbing problems, and surrounded by tiles that clatter from the wall at a touch.

Consumption is central to the creation of culture, since it involves a process of objectification which enables material things and their discourses to become forms through which people have consciousness of themselves. Miller (1994b, 66) has written of the fundamental contradiction inherent in this process, of culture's tendency towards reification, whereby "forces which were developed to enhance human understanding may become instead the reified goal of life and obfuscate and oppress their own creators." The case I am considering should be located perhaps "before" this stage, at the beginning of culture's work. The New Russians are struggling not so much with an already completed reification as with the conditions of achieving meaning, and here the contradiction of objectification is not just a question of alienation or appropriation but also the very basic problem of achieving the intended wholeness and coherence of the objects themselves. What kind of sign, even to oneself, is the villa that does not function as a house, or the Jacuzzi which is broken? Before addressing this question, it is necessary first to deal with the category of the New Russians and the people denoted by the term.

The New Russians in the Public Landscape

The term "New Russian" has its place among a host of epithets of difference, labels for people marked in some way as somehow alien from the unmarked, "ordinary" Russian crowd. Gypsies, Caucasians, Tajik refugees, and many others are subject to intense stereotyping in the shifting matrix of economic-political competition, where images of shady deals intersect with broader categories of "race" and nation (Lemon 1996; Humphrey 1997). But the New Russian idea engenders a further anxious ambiguity, as these new people are understood not to be intrinsically other but indeed to have derived and spun away from "us," the unmarked mainstream. Furthermore, it is felt that they may indeed represent Russia's future.

The term "New Russian" has acquired a definite and transferable meaning. It refers to an image of people with a new and alien mentality, people who are rapacious, materialist, and shockingly economically successful. In short, New Russians are "new" because they do not give precedence to various hoary Soviet values, which are still mostly seen in a rosy hue by everyone else: the value of honest labor, of supporting the *kollektiv*, of respect for the working masses, of high-minded personal frugality, and above all the value of production of goods for the benefit of society as a whole. In this mode of talking, New Russians are presumed to be "corrupt." I have often been told that no one could become so rich in an honest way. This can imply a general moral condemnation, not simply an accusation of illegality. New Russian "faults" may sometimes mean only acting autonomously for one's own economic benefit, which was virtually prohibited one way or another in Soviet times, and leaping to riches by financial astuteness (in other words, as if by magic) rather than by the time-honored methods of patronage and *blat* (Humphrey 1995).[3] Business people do not share these values, but the term "New Russian" is rarely used as a self-appellation, unless with an ironic smile as an explanation to outsiders.[4]

Recently, the term has become omnipresent in the media as a description which can be applied in spreading contexts. So New Russian can apply to Georgians, Buriats, and so forth,[5] and even to Gypsy children who skip school to set up their own money-spinning businesses, in this case described by their teacher with some admiration for their initiative (*Izvestiia* August 6, 1997, 5). By the late 1990s, the term no longer necessarily implied condemnation, and the tone in which it was used indicated much about the speaker. Nevertheless, the intelligentsia still contrasts the New with Eternal Russians. For example, a theater critic accuses a production of a play by Dostoevsky of conjuring up luxury both on the stage and off (the unbelievably large bouquet from the mayor of Moscow, Iurii Luzhkov, the audience of political and commercial personalities, the noisy actors depicting "foreign Russians with their mad and light money, who are unable to create a form for themselves"), and all this is incompatible with the "wild, nervous, thirsty condition of the Russian soul" (Maksimova 1997). At the same time, there are many young people for whom "lack of form" creates no anxiety at all. For them, it is enough of a goal to become rich. "New Russians, ah, there are so many wannabes," as one businessman said to me.

In sum, we have a term which refers to a new mentality and an aspirational status rather than to a defined social group, a term, furthermore, which is primarily used from outside. In many ways the category is not unlike *Homo Sovieticus,* the New Soviet Man, which was similarly an aimed-for goal for some, a rhetorical image, and an object of endless ironic musings from the intelligentsia. Interestingly, both categories are structured by gender, though in different ways. The New Soviet Man was accompanied by the New Soviet Woman, who stood at his shoulder as a "lesser equal" in the same heroic mold.[6] The New Russian, on the other hand, is also pictured as a man, but with glamorous female dependents. Advertising directed at New Russians supposes a penumbra of "feminine" wives, mistresses, and high-class prostitutes, who emphatically do not engage in work or business and whose time is pictured as being spent in consumption, homemaking, manicures, self-improvement, and so forth. One even finds a rhetorical flourish dimly reminiscent of earlier inspirational efforts. For example, the glossy magazine *Domovoi* (*Home Spirit*) for March 1997 has a cover with a trailing flower and the words:

> Life is a pure flame,
> and we live
> with an invisible sun,
> shining in us

Perhaps because consumption plays such a large part in the presumed activity of the New Russians and because it is the women who do much of the buying, the whole category appears as an uneasy world, ferociously male on its leading edge and yet feminized inside by gendered objects designed to appeal to women. As will be discussed below, the villa itself has this same structure.

In short, I am suggesting here that "New Russian" is a cultural category and that it is this changing cultural entity, rather than a presumed social reality lying beneath it, which should be used to explain the relation between the villas and the identity formation of the owners. Rather than visualizing the issue as a dualistic opposition between "people" and "things" (for discussion, see Miller 1994b) this chapter asks: what kinds of culturally defined persons engage in the making of the villas? And we should be aware of these houses in the same cultural medium, that is, by the term widely used to refer to them, *kottedzhi* (a word resonant of refined repose, deriving from the English "cottage").

However, a cultural account is not in the end adequate unless there is some knowledge of the social, economic, and political circumstances in which the cultural phenomena arise. This is fundamental when the achievement of culture is in doubt. Anthropologists often assume, perhaps because this is their experience of fieldwork, that culture is unproblematically in existence (whatever is there, is "culture"). But the case of the New Russians shows clearly that culture—in this instance, the convincing coincidence of the desired images with the material objects—has to be *achieved* and may be a process fraught with difficulty. To explain the construction of New Russian culture requires that an account be given of economic and social conflicts, though I confine myself to an extremely brief summary here.

The business, service, and financial elite of Russia exists in a complex world peopled also by government officials, elected politicians, the managers of former state (now "privatized") enterprises, industrial workers and miners, state employees (such as teachers or doctors), state dependents (such as pensioners), petty traders, the armed services, and agricultural workers. The most notable fact about this elite is that it has money at its disposal but pays very little tax,[7] whereas virtually all other people are subject to late payment of miserable wages, payment in kind, or no wages at all, while the enterprises for which they work are subject to high taxation. During the 1990s, the Russian economy, especially outside the metropolis, became substantially demonetized. There was a mass turn to subsistence agriculture, even by city dwellers, and to barter. In circumstances where there is a general lack of money (when even unemployment benefits might be paid in fur coats[8] or an electricity bill in saplings; Humphrey 1997), when poverty exists on a vast scale,[9] and street prices are the same as those in Western Europe, it is not surprising that business elites are the object of intense envy and dislike.

The "New Russians" can be broadly described in terms of wealth (rich),[10] generation (young and early middle-aged), occupation (finance, business, services, crime),[11] and lifestyle (innovative, Western). They are thus culturally somewhat distinct from the old Soviet *nomenklatura*,[12] those managers and officials who have retained influence while also generally clinging to previous methods and values. The distinction holds even though many of the *nomenklatura* have become managers of privatized enterprises and in some cases very rich,[13] and even though many of the New Russians are people who "rose out of production," having gained experience (trading, negotiating, making contacts) in the previous Soviet enterprises and then turned this to good account in their new life as entrepreneurs. Now, very few New Russians make their money from manufacturing. Rather, they are importers, exporters, retailers, wholesalers, bankers, financial consultants, racketeers, and so forth, and in these activities they both cooperate and compete with the other main economic players on the scene, the directors of enterprises, the aspiring petty traders, and the government officials.

It is difficult to be more precise than this in mapping cultural categories, such as New Russian and *nomenklatura*, onto the shifting and complex occupational categories of a diversifying economy.[14] The children of the old Soviet elite have had an advantageous position from which to start up new businesses; the pervasive network of protection-patronage "roofs" ties many a disparate institution together; while young, flexible, and commercially astute people can try their hands in a number of contexts, moving from illegal to legitimate business, from employee to entrepreneur, or from government official to banker, and back again. Nevertheless, a certain consolidation is becoming apparent. In the 1990s, difficulty in obtaining loans from banks and high taxation created obstacles to setting up new firms, and the number of small businesses seemed to decline (Nelson and Kuzes 1995, 124). In particular locations, however, banks, government agencies, and successful firms often maintained tightly linked and mutually beneficial relations (Clarke, Ashwin, and Borisov 1997). Still, close as these ties may be, the villas are a mark of cultural change: the old *nomenklatura* tends to be content with its already highly privileged apartments and country homes (dachas), while it is the business people, wielding wealth rather than power, who put much of their money into building villas.

The New Russians bear an ideological weight on all sides: they are the great hope for a new bourgeois transition to capitalist prosperity for the whole country and at the same time they are the reviled carriers of the erstwhile crime of speculation.[15] This situation promotes an anxiety more acute than that created by the previous gulf between New Soviet Man/Woman and the realities of life. The New Russians ponder the pages of *Vogue* and feel they should fashion themselves as better than their Western equivalents, because after all they are Russians, and in the vanguard. Hence the importance of styling salons and gyms, where physically new bodies are being pummeled and cosseted into shape. Perhaps never before have style magazines been taken so literally to heart, by people who missed out on generations of advertising: New Russians scrutinize *Vogue* because they think they should really look like that. Bearing the results in their newly thin (to the point of emaciation) bodies, the current wives produce themselves to excel over their lumpier sisters, the former wives, wannabes, and no-hopers.

The spread of visualization in the Russian culture industry has given birth to a new social institution, the *prezentatsiia,* a media party for the celebration of new cultural events (a film or album release, an exhibition, a new journal) which normally takes place in the vacated halls of high culture, such as the Central House of Artists. Condee and Padunov (1995, 159–160) have remarked that the ritual of *prezentatsiia* "serves high culture with an eviction notice," replacing it if only for a night with the culture of titillation and spectacle. Here, and in the newspaper reports next day, New Russians become the visible emblems for the flashy ebullience of a new cultural wave. Yet there is an undertow of anxious relations, heard in the bitter accusations of heartless vulgarity from outside and the rumors of depression, anorexia, or desperation from inside (the last perhaps not unconnected with the insecurity of economic life and the dangerous ties with racketeers which virtually all businesses are forced to maintain).[16]

The sociologist Kryshtanovskaia has written, "We call him the 'New Russian' and we suspect him of all possible vices. But to be honest, we know almost nothing of his life" (Kryshtanovskaia 1997).[17] However, this "ignorance" is no barrier to the construction of categories, and does not mean it is impossible to identify actual people as New Russians (people will say, for example, "My nephew is a New Russian"), but it does raise a problem of the cultural self-identity of people so described. How does one see oneself through a category that has been created largely out of negation?[18]

Material Culture and Identity in a Political Context

This chapter takes into account the theoretical critiques of a transparent notion of identity which sees it as integral and originating, as the unmediated emanation of a centered author of social practice. The concept of identity used here is not essentialist[19] but positional and strategic. The example of the New Russians is a good one to illustrate the point that identity does not signal some inner cultural "self" underlying superficial differences and more genuine than the artificially imposed "selves" given from outside. The New Russians have no shared history, or if they do, it is an extremely short one. We should accept that such an identity can never be unified and that in our times it is increasingly constructed through contradictory and contested discourses.

Stuart Hall (1996, 2) points out that what is needed to theorize identity is "not a theory of the knowing subject, but rather a theory of discursive practice." However, this should not so much entail abandoning the subject as reconceptualizing it in a displaced or decentered position. This rethinking stresses the concept of "identification," which is the process by which subjects relate to discursive practices, and the politics of exclusion that appears to entail. Identification operates by the "binding and marking of symbolic boundaries, the production of 'frontier-effects'"(Hall 1996, 3), which requires that what is left outside, its constitutive outside, in fact consolidates the process itself. In this case we are dealing with a most complex process, however, whereby those left outside may not only consolidate but may also undermine the meanings given by the New Russians themselves, thus creating fractured, never-quite-achieved images. The construction of a public exterior (the villas, the Mercedes cars, the designer clothes) that excludes others is also the shining face on which the excluded inscribe their envy, jealousy, admiration, and so forth, thereby establishing certain socially current meanings that even the New Russians cannot ignore.

This chapter thus points to the difficulty and contingency of identification as a process. This is particularly the case with identification through the medium of large material objects like houses, which are subject to economic, political, and other constraints and always sit in a landscape created by other interests and histories. The projection of cultural identity in such a situation is always "too much" or "too little," an overdetermination or a lack (Hall 1996, 3), and in this case the misfit is especially interesting in relation to Russian history. It is argued here that the New Russians are engaging in a process of self-identification, using the resources of history and European culture to represent themselves to themselves. But essentially the success of this process is dependent on the relation of New Russians to political powers that can sustain them. The further one moves from a political metropolis, the weaker and more incoherent this self-identity becomes, contested and laughed at from outside and incapable of containing and subsuming the objects to its own interpretations. Here another process takes place, a default consumption, whereby the material objects, appropriated one by one, themselves appear as sufficient, as almost "un-reinterpreted" things, to be appropriated for "what they are." This second process I call "content consumption," that is, content as distinguished from form. With this process, rather than cultural identity being created through reinterpreting objects, the goods themselves confer their identity on the people ("the man with the Mercedes," "I am the sort of person who has a *kottedzh*").

The attitude this latter process reveals is founded partly on the inability of a particular group to remythicize objects culturally,[20] and partly on a more pervasive post-Soviet eclecticism, an anti-utopian signaling that subverts any grand myth (Boym 1994, 250). Now it is true that in a few of the most sophisticated metropolitan villas, where the owners may be financial "sponsors" of conceptual artists or filmmakers, there is a radical eclecticism which is a consciously postmodern statement. But in the provinces something quite different seems to be going on, a plainly acquisitive "content consumption" that is more like a fallout of Soviet-era socialist realism, the anti-aesthetic which lingered into the 1970s and 1980s as the naturalist depiction of "reality," but now bereft of the Stalinist myth which had inspired it (Groys 1993). In this case, "content consumption" cannot be regarded as a culturally creative gesture, insofar as it cannot attain style and ignores form.

The above implies that it would be wrong to suppose that our task is to discover what New Russian cultural identity is, as if "it" were a whole "thing" waiting in limbo, ready for analysis. Rather, we should be looking at the historically formed contexts where affirmations of identity appear or are made evident. The building of new houses is evidently a quite specific context. Consumption here, instead of being constituted as entirely separate from production (as an activity only of choosing or receiving already constituted objects, as in Soviet times) is promoted by real-estate agents as a wonderfully creative matter. The client is encouraged to intervene in the production of the villa as a whole object. Villas are constructed and marketed in Russia as repertoires of parts, such as "S. P. Poras staircases, heating systems, Saunatec saunas, and winter gardens with Forsan Metalityo equipment" (*Business in*

Russia 1995, xxvii), which are built into whole houses along with locally made foundations, bricklaying, roofing, and so forth. Architects are notably absent from this process. The clients are thus, at least in the agents' rhetoric, enabled to create their "own individual comfort and luxury" (often an illusion, as discussed below). To help them, a host of lifestyle magazines, real-estate agents, interior designers, landscapers, floral consultants, and so forth have appeared in the metropolis. These agencies are staffed by candidate New Russians, the cutting edge of the aspirational class, the interpreters who take the most active part in concocting the mytho-historical stories that give sense to the whole idea of the *kottedzh*. In the provinces these "cultural translators" (Bredin 1996) hardly exist, and this is another factor that encourages the piecemeal activity of "content consumption."

Superficially, the villas might be seen as a quite unproblematic arena for identity construction, simply as Veblenesque conspicuous consumption aimed to convey messages and make an impression. Furthermore, because the New Russians suddenly emerged only after 1990, their villas escape the condition of the socially formed habitus which structures most forms of dwelling everywhere. Carsten and Hugh-Jones (1996, 64) have written, "A ready-made environment fashioned by a previous generation and lived in long before it becomes an object of thought, the house is a prime agent of socialization." Clearly the villas are not like this, as many of them are not lived in at all, as will be explained below. However, I argue that even in the most inventive scenario the villas are involved with existing cultural categories if not with a traditional habitus. Perhaps more generally one could say that there is a contradiction between "conspicuous consumption" and the idea of inventing an utterly new house style, since material objects cannot denote any meanings unless they are part of some kind of semantic convention. What is significant in the case of the villas is that the value attached to such conventions is disputed. For example, high fences may denote privacy, but is privacy a "bad" or a "good" thing? In various parts of Russia there are different outcomes of the shifting "battle of the sign" (Voloshinov 1973). Furthermore, the battle-grounds of pervasive social disagreements uncover further layers of discord and lack of conviction, so a villa glowingly viewed by some as a "palace in the Baroque style" may, by other people (or at another time), be seen only in terms of its brand-name German components and compared unfavorably with Swedish varieties, or it may simply be summed up by price, and again this may be done sourly or with admiration. Such piercing of the cocoons of cultural agreements about what things mean are fiercest in the provinces, perhaps, but even in the great cities there are other, more practical, ways to undermine pretensions.

For all the elimination of architects, the consumption of housing in Russia is not a free arena for bricolage according to whim. On the contrary, the clients have to contend not only with the financial transaction (how to get hold of and transfer money in order actually to receive an inhabitable building)[21] but also with Russian planning laws, the politics of urban space, the problems of transportation, struggles over supply of electricity, water, or telephone lines and the slapdash habits of builders. Then there are the neighbors. We should be asking ourselves why construction companies advertise bulletproof glass windows and almost always refer to security in one way or another. It is not that we can see consumption as in principle free, but hemmed in by such limitations. Rather, such conditions are intrinsic to the process of consumption of housing from the outset (Herzfeld 1991). They are social conditions informing not only "choices," but also "nonchoices"—the outcomes that no one really wanted or consciously planned for. There is perhaps always an underside to identity, namely, the unselfconscious practices which are nevertheless perceived sharply from the outside.

The rest of the chapter discusses the socio-political conditions of the existence of villas and then comments on the aesthetics of these new houses. I use Revzin's (1993) discussion of architectural meaning, in particular his distinction between stylistic and iconographic analyses of architecture as art, to provide the means for describing the semiotic connotations of the villa. I conclude with some implications of Boris Groys's radical argument (1992, 1993) about the aesthetic power acquired by the political leader in Stalinist Soviet society to make an argument for the implicit politicization of the aesthetics of Russian housing.

Housing as Property: The Dacha and Villa Compared

To understand the impact of the villas, we have to think ourselves into a situation where for seventy years housing was deliberately divorced from wealth, and wealth to a great extent from power and status. This long-standing Soviet arrangement has not changed overnight. Even in the summer of 1996, Russian government leaders, including Yeltsin, were all allotted housing in the same, externally unremarkable apartment block in Moscow, a block also inhabited by a due percentage of "the people" in archetypal Soviet style.[22] Politicians who lost their posts had to leave the apartment block (Rykovtseva 1996).[23] Villas on the other hand embody a new relationship with the dwelling: the villa is private property and a demonstration of wealth rather than political position. This involves a nexus of relations to property and regulations which can best be understood by comparing the villa with the dacha.

In what follows I am heading toward the idea that the appearance of the villa is not just a matter of chosen style, but rather that its whole existence in the landscape is a function first of all of its economic-political status. Let us examine first the idea of "property." The origin of the word dacha, from *dat'* (to give) lies with seventeenth century bestowals from the tsar, an idea followed also in the Stalinist period when comfortable wooden summer houses in the Russian style were allotted to officials and elite intellectuals. Another type of dacha appeared from the 1950s onward, when land for vegetable plots was given out to institutions. This was then divided among favored workers, and the recipients often built tiny houses on their plots which they called dachas. Commonly they had no electricity, running water, or central heating. By the late 1970s, plots were being given out by city district administrations to worthy and needy citizens, now further and further away from the city and ever smaller in size.[24] It was only in the 1990s that dachas began to be bought and sold. Thus the historically established idea of the dacha is of something given to worthy citizens by the state, and a dacha likewise could in principle be taken away, for example, on dismissal from a post.

The modern villa, in contrast, exists only as a private purchase, and it came into being when the building of private houses in urban areas was legalized in 1991. Describing the advent of a new villa development near his dacha at Firsanovka, between Moscow and St. Petersburg, Shevelev has written:

> Traditionally, Soviet dacha owners could be separated into the possessors of village houses with six *sotok*[25] of land, and the masters of prewar dachas with larger grounds. There is no need to explain the fact that between the two there was some dislike and reciprocal disdain, because all of that is a matter of the past. These antagonisms were forgotten as soon as the three-story red brick newcomers appeared. Compared with them, the constructions on six *sotok* and the dachas of the *nomenklatura* look equally poverty-stricken. (Shevelev 1996, 26)

There is another aspect to the dacha which contrasts with the villa, its personalized domesticity. Aleksandr Vysokovskii (1993, 271–308) has argued convincingly that although neither Soviet apartments nor dachas were their occupants' private property, people developed a "false sense of ownership" in reference to the spaces they inhabited, particularly the dacha, which they usually built with their own hands: "Pseudo-ownership is a very real cultural phenomenon in this society, which for more than seventy years has declared and waged unceasing war on private property.... People tend to 'acquire' what they use, without considering who really owns it" (Vysokovskii 1993, 277).

With its hammock under the apple trees, its veranda crammed with jars of salted cabbage, its privy under nodding sunflowers, the dacha as a building was the result of ceaseless tactics to create a sense of privacy and individuality by outwitting the norms and building regulations of the state. The built area of the dacha was predetermined, as was its site on the plot, the materials, and the number of stories (only one). It was forbidden to enlarge it by adding a shed, and so forth. Yet any guest at a dacha settlement will notice that virtually all of them have a bulging second story, almost like a mushroom cap on a stalk: this is the mansard roof, an excellent way to get more space while remaining within the one-story rule. The dacha-with-mansard looks like a chosen architectural style, but in fact it was a functional strategy in the politics of construction.

11. *A splendid new villa at Nikolina Gora near Moscow, architects Velichkin and Golovanov. Photograph by Project Russia, 1999, no. 9.*

12. A 90-percent finished "cottage" near Ulan-Ude, Buriatia, in the winter of 2000. Photograph by Balzhan Zhimbiev.

The villa has a quite different appearance, for the owners do not see themselves as engaged in creating domesticity in the face of state-dictated homogeneity. The rationale is quite different. The purchaser of a villa is a master who signals the social position of the independent operator. His prominent gates and walls connote withdrawal from the mass of the people, his turrets evoke an "I'll look after myself" defiance. In Russia, as suggested above, one cannot assume personal identification to be stronger with private property than with state-owned dachas. Rather, private property connotes independent operation in the market, and identity is marked here by signs of success in this dangerous arena, not by domesticity. Having said this, we note that advertisements addressed to New Russians try constantly to overcome the presumed alienness of the market by appealing to reassuring emotions: "Windows of Rehau plastic: windows for your loved one," "Furniture from the firm *Furniture:* a magical door into the world of your daydreams," or "Cactuses for the home: love them, pamper them: they will not deceive you" (*Domovoi*, February 1997).

Villa settlements are so numerous as to alter the urban environs substantially,[26] and they are not just found on the outskirts of the metropolitan cities

13. *A team of Buriat builders hired on a contract basis for new private housing, Ulan-Ude, Buriatia, in the summer of 2000. Photograph by Balzhan Zhimbiev.*

of Moscow and St. Petersburg. They appear around cities and towns at each level in the administrative hierarchy. Republican capitals like Ulan-Ude, center of the Buriat Republic in Siberia, provincial (*oblast*) centers such as Yaroslavl, and even district-level (*raion*) towns such as Gusinoozersk, center of Selenga Raion in the Buriat Republic, all have their areas of villa development. It is true that villas in the most distant regions are relatively small and few. Nevertheless, they bear the same relation to the standard Soviet housing stock as do the metropolitan villas, namely, that they are detached houses built as the private property of "the rich," and they therefore arouse the same furious question: why is there money to build those palaces (*dvortsy*) when we can hardly feed our children?

Reading Expense

It is far from certain that the more specific images of owners and estate agents ("a Finnish *kottedzh*," "a unique atmosphere reminiscent of Rococo palaces") are readable by many people from the house in front of them. What is clear is that people these days have a good idea of how much villas cost, because prices have become an obsession in general. Even small provincial towns have at least one supermarket selling costly foreign goods, which most people will have visited even if they have never bought anything there. From such luxuries downward, through counterfeited brand-name goods, solid home manufactures and utensils, to bricks, concrete blocks, tiles or nails, people scrutinize the goods and carefully note the prices. In one respect, Russians can judge one another's consumption according to a commonly accepted scale—by the cost. This is the first step in the semiotics of the villa, the reading of price.

The new villas are, of course, expensive. It would be more accurate to say they are glaringly expensive, since they are almost invariably constructed with decorative façades of brick, a material which is both new-looking and costly in the Russian context.[27] Bright bricks are so much the norm for *kottedzhi* than a glance over the landscape singles out these developments from any other buildings. It is inconceivable that a villa would be constructed of Russian concrete panels like the gaunt apartment houses, and Western details and prefabricated kits are common. Wooden villas are extremely rare, perhaps because they might connote associations with the lowly log cabin, even though wooden houses are several times cheaper and retain the heat through the winter better than brick ones.[28] In Ulan-Ude in the summer of 1996 to build a small version of such a villa, with three bedrooms, cost between 350 and 370 million rubles, about $70,000, when the median wage, for those lucky enough to have one, was around $75 a month. Significantly, villas are often sold for dollars by the square meter (one near Moscow cost $3,000 per square meter in 1997). This economic practice confutes the rhetoric of individuality and taste, and it is at one with the obsession with price among the people in general.

Villas in the Politics of the Locality

In July 1996, I visited a few villa development sites on the outskirts of the city of Ulan-Ude, a puzzling experience. In one case, the site was located in an open steppe, but the villas were all built cheek by jowl. There was hardly enough space for each house to have a small garden. The site was about half a mile from a rural road which perhaps had a bus service, but clearly it would be difficult to live there without a car.[29] At another site, tall, impressive houses jostled side by side, but a closer look revealed roughly finished walls and uneven windows everywhere. The houses had electricity but no water or drainage. In both places residents were curiously absent, but guards leapt out aggressively as soon as we approached. "Why have you come here?" they inquired suspiciously. When we said we were interested in new architecture, a look of disbelief crossed their faces.

These few observations: the close-packed building site, the distance from basic city services, the low quality of the construction, the absence of residents, and the suspicion of visitors seem to be characteristic of villa settlements elsewhere.

> The construction is striking in its prodigality and absurdity. It is clearly being put up by one firm with the aim of selling the houses. But to whom? What kind of person would one have to be to buy such a thing? Both in pocket and in intelligence, because all this luxury is crammed onto miserable plots, wall to wall, window to window. Either the attraction to the six-*sotok* plot has become a genetic endowment, or someone is getting ready for all-round defense. (Shevelev 1996, 26)

Here we touch upon the "nonchoices" which I suggest are inherent in the processes of consumption as far as private housing is concerned. How can they be explained?

Shevelev's ironic suggestions about genetic endowment and all-round defense are not so far off the mark, as I discuss below, but the villas are also embedded in the post-Soviet politics of land development. In Soviet times all cities had forward-looking general plans prescribing where building developments of various types could take place. These plans were worked out centrally, and so the plan of Ulan-Ude, for example, was designed thousands of miles away in Leningrad. Today, these plans are still in theory operational, though in many cases they are approaching the date of renewal.[30] More important is the fact that the mentality of the plan, which still exists for many city officials, is being turned to the pursuit of profit, and hence it battles with new forces engendered by privatization. As well as conforming with the general plan, villa builders have to negotiate a great number of other *spravki* (permits), each of which might be refused and may have to be paid for.[31]

In Ulan-Ude in 1996, there were just three plots designated for villa development within the city boundaries. It is evident that the politics leading to such an outcome are complex: in some cases land is obtained from the province-level forestry commission, in others from local state farms, in yet others "from Russia herself" (the administration in Moscow). The coordination of land use and its allocation—to the city, to private building firms, to industrial enterprises, or to individuals—is done by land committees at the district level,[32] but such arrangements do not prevent conflicts. For example, the enlargement of city boundaries may be resisted by agricultural settlements on the fringes, themselves eager to take advantage of the possible sale of construction land (Ruble 1995, 126), or powerful industrial firms may use their influence to lean on local authorities to allow the construction of *kottedzh* housing in desirable spots to sell to their managers (Ruble 1995, 125–126). The result of such negotiations is an odd disposition of development sites, here crammed uncomfortably beneath looming public housing, there located miles from the city in a waterless wasteland.

With all this, the chief planner of Ulan-Ude spoke to me with accustomed authority of the "norms" of land allowed for housing of various types: one *sotka* for central city plots, four *sotok* for vegetable plot-type dachas near the city, eight *sotok* for more distant dachas, and twelve *sotok* for the new private villas on the outskirts. It is a curious fact that despite the great expanses of land available in Russia by European standards, the planner-architect spoke almost disapprovingly of twelve *sotok* (less than one-third of an acre) as a "very large plot," and he implied that he had been driven to allow so much mainly because the boundaries of the city had recently been expanded to take in former agricultural land. Here the city regulations encountered the rural norms of twelve *sotok* for villagers living by subsistence farming, and therefore the city planners had been forced to allow villa developers the same amount. It seems that two factors combine to reduce the size of development plots: the desire of the possessors of land to maximize their returns; and the Soviet principle of the "norm," which is tied somehow to a moralizing "no more than anyone else" and "only what they deserve." The idea of the land "norm" is indeed far older than the Soviet version of it and is deeply embedded in the attitudes of many Russians, so it is significant that even among potential owners of such villas I did not encounter objections to the small size of plots. On the contrary, some people praised the houses for being sufficiently far apart to conform with sanitary and fire regulations.

Once I was returning with some Buriat friends to Ulan-Ude and reached a pleasant bluff overlooking a river; before us there stretched several empty wooded valleys threaded with winding tributaries, and just beyond there lay the city. Imagining how such hillsides would be scattered with private housing were this in Europe, I asked my friend why the New Russians had not built villas here. "Who would want to live out here all on their own?" was the response. "Anyway, a house on its own would be robbed within days." It is virtually impossible to get urban services extended to distant lone houses, whereas a whole settlement of *kottedzhi* stands a chance. But security is just as important: virtually every villa for sale in *Mir i Dom Nedvizhimost'*, a Moscow-based real-estate journal, is advertised with some such phrase as: "sited in an elite *kottedzh* development with its own defense." The idea of security pertains not only to the housing scheme as a whole but to the individual dwelling too. Shevelev comments:

> A new wave of owners appeared in 1995. The most vivid of them, in local views, was Konstantin Natanovich Borovoi, who built a house in Firsanovka which left no one in any doubt that it was his fortress. A fence suited for an atomic base, embrasures rather than windows, and walls like those of Butyrki [a prison in Moscow]. "That is not a house, it's a military objective," said Firsanovka, and they did not envy Borovoi. They felt only pity for him, just as one always feels compassion for people living under the conditions of a regime. (Shevelev 1996, 26)

The "building in" of defense into the villa raises interesting questions about conspicuous consumption. Signals of luxury in contemporary Russia are almost metonymically related to security, and the explanation for this may be that the symbolic function of conspicuous consumption is first of all pared down to index pure wealth, and wealth is assumed to attract crime. The distinctiveness of the Russian situation can be seen if it is compared with the houses built by successful business people in the Andes.

The Otavalenos build splendid houses in their villages with the proceeds of textile trading done in the cities. They are too busy to spend much time at these houses, which are described by Colloredo-Mansfield (1994) as prime examples of conspicuous consumption. The Andean villas legitimate the economic status of the family and its descendants in relation to the social world of the owners, which remains that of the kin in the village. People hold conflicting standards for appraising displays of wealth, and the meaning of wealth is not self-evident. So along with creating a new flat-topped house style to communicate and legitimize a modern type of urban wealth, some rich people have also turned to the enhancement of traditional forms, and in both cases they use local materials and village work parties. This practice reaffirms local, reciprocal economic relationships (Colloredo-Mansfield 1994, 861–862).

By contrast, the New Russians create social enclaves fenced off from the ordinary dacha dwellers and villagers. Local materials are abhorred. To the extent they have to be used, they are the source of the most annoying "ineptitude," such as concrete stairs in which every step is a different height. Villas are never built by neighborly work parties but by ill-trained teams assembled by contractors. "How to avoid choosing the wrong contractor" is a theme of real-estate publications. The advice is to make sure the same firm handles all stages of building and finishing, "otherwise various contractors may pass the blame for various flaws to their fellow workers, the outcome of which will be the infamous collective irresponsibility" (*Business in Russia* 1995, xxv). Such magazines also advocate getting rid of Russian labor altogether ("No More Plumbers," *Business in Russia* 1995: xxiv),[33] and employing foreign teams instead. As one might expect, the social exclusivity of the development is a selling point. "Not just anyone can get a *kottedzh* there," I was told, and developers advertise "neighbors worthy of you" as part of the deal. Thus reciprocal economic relations, along with exchange of homegrown vegetables, spades, and all the rest of the dacha ambience, is the last thing the New Russians want to be involved with. It is therefore not surprising that the villa is not conceptualized as a wealth-enhanced version of the dacha. Instead, it refers to the deeper imperial past, in the form of the *kottedzh*.

The Aesthetics of the *Kottedzh*

Builders and estate agents make efforts to provide "styles," which are marketed to dovetail with, or evoke, the emerging cultural tastes of New Russians. In this context we can now discuss the villas in semiotic terms, though such conscious semantic representation is only part of the villas' social significance. In discussing architectural meaning, Revzin (1993) distinguished between two distinct semantic structures, one of style and another of iconography. "The semantics of style," he wrote, "does not emerge from the sum of meanings produced by separate elements but rather as a result of prescribing meaning to stylistic categories and establishing their connections with general cultural categories." He continues, "Everything is different in iconographic language. A distinct element—a motif, a stable compositional scheme—carries meaning that is defined and quite autonomous. For instance, a temple cupola usually signifies a heavenly dome, regardless of period or style" (1993, 220). We may not agree with some of the assumptions here (Revzin writes of wholes and elements carrying meaning, as if no one gave such meanings and no one ever misunderstood them). But Revzin's distinction between style (in the particular sense outlined above) and icon is useful, as it enables us to discuss the mythic meaning of the stylistic category of the *kottedzh* in general and to distinguish it from the meanings attributed to types and elements within villas as specific houses.

Any villa, however grandiose and elaborate, can be referred to as a *kottedzh*. The term refers to leisure dwellings scattered in the parks of princely estates of the eighteenth-century Russian aristocracy. An example is the "Cottage Palace" in the grounds of the magnificent Versailles-inspired Peterhof Palace. The architect, Adam Menelaws, designed the Kottedzh to resemble an English cottage, where the tsar would be able to feel himself a private individual in a light and graceful setting. The building is not in any particular architectural style: it combines Neo-Gothic tracery with features of an Italian villa and medieval vernacular (Shvidkovskii 1996, 234–235).

In post-Soviet Russia, the establishing of the eclectic *kottedzh* as a "stylistic category" in Revzin's sense is performed by taste-forming magazines. *Mir i Dom Nedvizhimost'* (1997, 3), for example, carries an article on the imperial park of Il'inskoe, in which there were several pavilions, artful ruins, a dairy, outhouses, and cottages. All were set in a "delightful rural composition, linked by peaceful alleys." Allowed to fall into ruin in Soviet times, Il'inskoe has since been acquired by a commercial firm, which has built in the grounds a number of standardized silicate-brick *kottedzhi*. The owners are encouraged to see themselves mythically, as descendants of the most outstanding people of the time, the elite of Moscow society, who were favorites and guests of the tsars at Il'inskoe. The journal enthuses: "The reconstruction of the demolished outhouses and cottages in the previous proportions, the return to the historical style given to each of them, carries in itself the secret of the transformation of an immemorial historical ensemble into a residence complex, in which its own architectural and artistic qualities and comfort will answer the highest demands of contemporary European standards" (*Mir i Dom Nedvizhimost'* 1997, 3) The overall "style," in Revzin's sense, of the modern *kottedzh* is so eclectic as almost to reject style, and as far as I know the actual copying of earlier aristocratic pavilions is rare in the extreme. What the "style" does do is to establish an imaginative link between contemporary individual villas and the notion of the eighteenth-century *kottedzh* in its regal setting.

The *kottedzh* "style" leaps over various other existing types of Russian housing, which the New Russians have not embraced, notably the classically proportioned eighteenth- and nineteenth-century country estate or the solid *izba* (peasant farmhouse), not to mention the houses of the non-Russian peoples of the empire. Even the Art Nouveau *style moderne* (Brumfield 1993) and pseudo-Russian Byzantine Revival architecture (Boym 1994, 266), both popular among pre–First World War merchants of Moscow, have not reappeared in any significant numbers. It is significant, in this context, that the villa clients normally do not engage architects but use building firms with their own draughtsmen instead.[34] Architects are producing albums of designs to attract clients, sometimes incorporating features of the local and native traditions, but evidently they often misjudge the New Russians.[35] Even in Buriatia, few if any clients have come forward to build a *kottedzh* incorporating an interesting transformation of a *yurta* (the indigenous Buriat dwelling). The villas that are actually built somehow have to be able to reconcile the vaguely historical with foreign-modern, not indigenous or native components. However, this "style" which is not a style is not divorced from Russian architectural traditions. The original aristocratic *kottedzh* itself was an amalgam of elements or a pastiche alluding to European models of various dates.

Shvidkovskii (1997) reports, nevertheless, that the most recent New Russian villas in Moscow are starting to be architect-designed, mainly because clients are beginning to demand more specific historical styles which are difficult to achieve without a professional. This trend is associated with the grand building projects of the metropolis. Moscow's popular and active mayor, Iurii Luzhkov, has embarked on a transformation of the city, the development of expensive shops and vast malls together with the grandiose reconstruction of symbolically important historical buildings.[36] The mayor demands the creation of a distinctive "Moscow style," and although no one is quite sure what this is, it is definitely not Soviet—not Constructivist or "Bolshevik" (Shvidkovskii 1997). Showpiece shopping complexes are not banished to the outskirts but consciously constructed to make harmonious ensembles with potent architectural symbols of Russian history in the center. It is significant that it is not architects but the Moscow city government, backed by Yeltsin, that is at the forefront in creating a distinctive architecture for the capital. As Shvidkovskii (1997) points out, this merging of the new and ancient city represents the ideology of the present power structure, in which business has an important part. The modern commercial block, with its turrets as references to adjacent monuments, is intended to demonstrate the profitability and stability of the regime.

This politicized architecture rejects the specific emblems of Soviet architecture, but it is continuous with the Soviet idea, embodied above all by Stalin, of the leader as wielder of aesthetic power (Groys 1993). In my view, it supports the New Russians' self-identification via their buildings by providing a context in which historical and European images can make sense. This can be seen more clearly if we examine the interior design elements incorporated in villas. Revzin's idea of iconography (1993) is useful for discussing this, as it draws attention to architectural elements transposed into the villa for the very reason that they have independent, nonlocal meanings. The state's Moscow style is the context within which these items can be reincorporated as statements of specifically Russian identity.

Business in Russia (May 1995) tells us there are three basic types of interior. The first is the "so-called European style, which presupposes a range of light colors, simple and rational use of space, plenty of light, air, and modern, built-in light sources. Such interior designs are similar to those of offices." The second is the Napoleon III style, which is "essentially a blend of the Classical Baroque and Renaissance and creates the feeling of a sumptuous palace. It calls for intricate modeling on ceilings and walls, tapestry, rich fireplace design, inlaid parquet floor in seven or eight varieties of wood, sculptured archways, [and] chandeliers." The third and most popular style is a combination of the first two. "The rationality, functionality, and simplicity of the basic interior design are more or less harmoniously merged with single elements from the distant past. For example, arched openings look good with columns or half-columns made of modern imitation marble." (*Business in Russia,* May 1995)

The curiously eclectic *kottedzh,* the overall "style," in Revzin's sense, can incorporate and Russify what otherwise would seem like architectural oxymorons (for example, the European functional aristocratic retreat). Nor is a masculinized fortified exterior with a feminized, sleek, or luxurious interior at odds with New Russian social culture, as mentioned earlier. Under the headline "A Woman at Home Should Know Her Place," the magazine *Domovoi* (1997, 3) runs a piece on the boudoir. Accompanied by eighteenth-century French engravings, the article illustrates some boudoirs suitable for active, modern Russian women ("in the boudoir it is absolutely necessary to have a little divan for beauty sleep"), where she can seclude herself for feminine, yet influential pursuits. All this makes a certain sense in relation to the mythical background notion of the *kottedzh* as the leisure dwelling of favorites in the exclusive park of the ruler, but it only attains viability because it is being advertised and constructed in the context of the government's projected change of political culture and the actual reconstruction of Moscow's great tsarist monuments.[37]

To some extent this set of notional references is reproduced in the provinces, in the domains of the regional prefectures. But the greater the influence of the conservatively Soviet *nomenklatura,* the weaker are the historical-aristocratic connotations of the villa. In distant towns the power of restrictive planners is greater, the animosity of local workmen more evident, the foreign design parts more difficult to acquire, and the purchase of "Moscow style," indeed of any named style, less. This is the realm of what I call "content consumption," where items of the house are put together as barely planned conglomerates. A kitchen may be distant from other plumbing, a bathroom located on the ground floor when all the bedrooms are on the fourth floor, or a ceremonial hall may take most of the interior space. Function and security have priority (storerooms for business stock, iron grills over windows, and armor-plated doors). Here, where money is scarcer, villas take years to put together with whatever one can obtain: one may have a fitted kitchen, but not a bathroom, or electricity but no telephone. Furthermore, items may be present, but *ne rabotaiut* (they are "not working"). The aspirants to the status of New Russian may have to put up with the aspiration for a villa.

Thus, from the iconographic point of view, an item in a villa has its place in a three-tiered structure of potentiality. A Jacuzzi, let us say, may be successfully integrated in a design scheme like "Napoleon III" along with swagged curtains, gold-framed mirrors, and so forth. Or it may be simply a Jacuzzi set down in an otherwise unremarkable bathroom (the "content consumption" variant). Or the Jacuzzi may be broken or not working, a sign that indicates the beleaguered situation of the owner. The point is that people know that any one of these possibilities contains the potentiality for the other two. Villas are the architectural embodiment of New Russian cultural identity precisely in manifesting this shifting range of potentialities, and we should not make the mistake of thinking that successful reproduction of any one model design "represents identity."

The *Kottedzh* as a Place for Living (or Not)

The equivocal nature of self-identification is paralleled by the uncertain and probably changing role of villas in New Russians' lives. Whatever their mythic evocations, in practice villa developments are modeled on the Euro-American suburban house designed for year-round living by a single family. This might in principle imply substantial social changes, especially in contrast to the crowed multi-occupancy of the communal flat of Soviet times. The suburb, however, is at odds with the established Russian urban way of life, which is based on the city apartment, with the dacha as an occasional retreat. It is difficult for New Russians to overcome these established ways, not only because they form the familiar habitus of expected sociality, but also because the entire infrastructure is designed to support them and not the suburb. Several people have told me how they began to rethink the idea of actually living in the *kottedzh* after they broke the springs of their cars on the roads, shivered in inadequate private central heating, and found themselves marooned in a half-deserted building site.

All this makes the *kottedzh* quite unlike the dwelling of established societies. Bloch (1995) has described how the Zafimaniry house grows and literally hardens as the married couple live together and build their mutuality. "This house and this wood can be seen as material culture, but to an extent this is misleading in that such a phrase suggests something different from non-material culture. It would be quite misleading to see Zafimaniry houses as expressing Zafimaniry marriage and society and containing married pairs. The house is the marriage" (1995, 215). The New Russian *kottedzh,* in contrast, is objectified as material culture, and it has an existence that the owners may hardly incorporate into their everyday life. Shevelev (1996) describes what seems to be a common pattern of use. His New Russian neighbors at Firsanovka arrive at two o'clock on Saturdays, park their Volvos in their yards ("where they are the only living element—everything else is bare earth"), let out the Rottweilers, set up a table by the car, make shashlyk and drink vodka; by eight they are singing along to pop songs, and by ten they tie up the dogs and set off for home. They hardly enter the villa. The incomers do not visit the neighboring dachas and know nothing of the surroundings that make the place dear to the natives, the fact that Solzhenitsyn lived nearby, that Lermontov's grandmother's estate is not far away, or that Lenin went hunting in these forests.

This pattern, in which evidently the city apartment is still the basic home of the New Russian family, does not mean that they do not identify their status with the *kottedzh.* As people in the provinces have often told me, it is sufficient to let drop a phrase like "Last weekend at the *kottedzh,* we . . . " for listeners to be impressed. The role of the *kottedzh* in establishing what kind of person you are dealing with is also why it is often used as a backdrop for making business contracts. A lavish meal and a tour of the site, with explanations of all the improvements to be made and the fittings shortly to be introduced, declares the achievements and aspirations of the owner to the business colleague. To have a villa is a very fine thing, but to live year-round in it is another matter, and the large numbers of villas abandoned and for sale indicate that many people must have made an expensive mistake.

Conclusion

Generally, anthropological studies of identity concern small peripheral groups that bravely construct their culture amid the oppressive weight of homogenization and global economies. Here we have quite a different case: a massively wealthy elite whose consumption nevertheless has difficulty in achieving cultural coherence. What Miller (1994a) calls the "forging" of cultural identity cannot be easily achieved in contemporary Russia. "Forging" is a pun referring to the simultaneous "process by which intractable materials are, in the forge, turned into something new, both useful, solid, and fine" and to the act of forgery as an act of fakery (1994a, 321). I would agree with Miller that the authentic culture of modern urban people may be created out of faked or recycled images. But for this authenticity to happen there must be certain conditions, and these seem not to be present in Russia at the moment. There must be a resilience and energy given to image making itself, and this, Mayor Luzhkov notwithstanding, is undercut in Russia by postsocialist mistrust of all grandiose myths. Furthermore, there must be the possibility of rather direct appropriation of material objects to the process of identification. Clothing, food, and media presentations are quite easily turned to this task, but the house is a much more recalcitrant, and therefore in many ways a more interesting, object. The urban villa, as a physical object, cannot be directly created, even if the intermediary of the architect is removed. The house is irrevocably locked into the fact of its construction by culturally excluded others and its geographical positioning in their world. It thus bears the evidence in itself of the redoubts and battle scars of the Russian economy and society. The visibility of this evidence and its potential for multiple readings destabilizes the linking of mythic identifications with actual houses.

The above is perhaps putting it too mildly: the vast majority of villas are unrecognizable as examples of any specific image of the *kottedzh*. Even so, it has to be said that the villas have a characteristic appearance. Here we do not find the long, lazy horizontal lines surveying a verdant landscape of a Frank Lloyd Wright house. Most Russian villas rear upward in several stories, with sharply tilted roofs, pointed gables and porches, and they frequently have long thin windows running up through several floors. The turret or tower is a favorite feature. This remarkable verticality may be to some extent un-intended: if you want a very large house but have only been given a tiny plot, there is no other way to go. But surely a thrusting verticality is relevant to the question of cultural identity. Like a person's handwriting, it is the unconscious trace of the self. I cannot do otherwise than make an outsider's interpretation here: these villas seem at once ambitious and embattled, grandiose and unfinished. They look both foreign in their sharp facades and Russian as they huddle together. The owners may not have quite intended it this way, but then they, like anyone else, are not quite masters of their cultural identity.

CHAPTER 10
SHAMANS IN THE CITY

In many Siberian cities, it is now normal for anyone with a misfortune or a quandary to visit a shaman.[1] This chapter discusses Buriat shamans in the city of Ulan-Ude. It does not pretend to analyze shamanic activities in full but has a quite particular aim, to explore the idea of the city as a place for shamanic activity, that is, a place where magical events happen. Although "urban shamanism" is now a familiar term in the literature (Balzer 1993; Hoppal 1996; Kendall 1996), little attention has been paid to the meanings places in the city have for shamans and their clients,[2] nor to the way they imagine the relation between the city and surrounding lands.

Buriat shamans used to live dispersed in remote steppes and valleys. The shamanic landscape comprised numerous "natural" sites, such as sacred mountains, springs, trees or lakes, where ancestral and other spirits were said to dwell. From the 1930s onward, and more or less continuously through the Soviet period, shamans were repressed, sent to prison and camps, and even put to death, though shamanic practices continued in the countryside in secret (Zhukovskaia 1996). The shamans described here are those who appeared as if from nowhere in the late 1980s, the magicians of the city. Who are these shamans, and what feats do they accomplish in the post-Soviet city?

In brief, the most prominent urban shamans are city-born and bred, tend to emerge from the middle-class intelligentsia, and are women as often as men. Their self-designation as "shamans" indicates that they claim shamanic descent (*udha*) in either the father's or the mother's line, and they have created a professional association to differentiate themselves from the tide of diverse pretenders, "*ekstra-sensy*," and diviners whom they call charlatans. Nevertheless, their reputations derive from particular psychological and psychic help given to individuals, such as miraculous cures or predictions of future events. Group rituals are far fewer than in pre-Soviet times and mostly take place outside the city in honor of ancestors and deities.

Shamans see themselves as forced by powers outside their control (spirits) to serve needy and desperate people. These clients, mostly well educated and till recently instructed in atheism, are now beset with economic disaster and new uncertainties. They, and often the shamans too, experience a crisis of practice. As a Khakass shaman said, "Since the sources of true shamanism hardly survive, people who have shamanic abilities cannot really understand what they should be doing. We are pressured by civilization. It is difficult to combine an atheistic education and a shamanic calling . . . some people cannot bear it. People may lose their minds or commit suicide" (Korotkova 1999, 6). I heard the same from Buriat shamans. In these circumstances, the people who do become shamans have to be extraordinarily self-confident, resilient, and above all creative, since they must weave together whatever images will produce belief and trust from bewildered, disheartened clients. The situation produces what is called "postmodern shamanism" (Hoppal 1996).[3] The difficult-to-believe physical feats of the old stories (such as walking on water) have been largely jettisoned in favor of vastly expanded "historical" claims to inspirational power. One contemporary Buriat shaman declares that his roots include on his mother's side forty-two Khordut shamans going back to Burkhan Khan, king of the Torgut; and on his father's side a line to the twelfth Dalai Lama, Geser of Amdo, through the sky god Esege Malan to Khormuzda and the "three Zoroastrian fire-worshipers—the Syrian, the German, and the Central Asian," and through the Huns to Attila, all of these existing in a cosmic space which he called the "noosphere" (Khamgushkeev 1997, 148–149).

One curious fact emerged from conversations with shamans and rituals I observed in 1996: no shaman ever mentioned the one activity that anthropologists have conventionally used to define the shaman: flying to "the other world," that is, to the sky or the underworld or generally to distant cosmological realms. Rather, as was always the main tradition among Buriats, it is the spirit powers that come to the shamans. Meanwhile, the shamans travel in this world, the city and its surroundings.

Here I suggest that the city is not just a backdrop, nor simply an underlying structure. In a sense, of course, the city is a context for shamanic activity, but at the same time shamans themselves "actualize space" in De

Certeau's phrase and thereby create new contexts of the city. In talking about themselves, shamans describe their moments of occult triumph; and if we think about what they say, it turns out that the incidents of mastery take place in certain culturally highly salient places, such as a school, a rock concert, or a Buddhist monastery. This wizardly domination of place in narrative—a fabulous domination, one might say—contrasts with the shamans' lives and professional practices. These, as we shall see, are partly concealed and partly laid out for consumption. Different contexts are created by narrative and by practice. In both cases, I suggest, shamans vitalize urban places by transmogrification, re-envisioning them in relation to other spaces and times and turning them into sites of energy where social relations are refashioned.

Narratives of the City

A discussion of shamans' narratives involves juxtaposing their accounts with the everyday social activity of the city, viewed through ordinary people's talk, experience, and feelings about the urban environment. Talking about a place is a way to describe social relations going on both inside it and beyond it. Alaina Lemon (1997) developed this point in her work on images of the Moscow metro. "When it comes to social mediations of space, we need more levels of agency than that proposed in a dyadic relation of individual to built structure: such constructions cross media and genre, and involve many speakers even indirectly" (1997, 5). The point is that ordinary people too talk about the city poetically, and, as they mention an object, what they say reverberates with disjunctions between what is and what might be or ought to be. Their narratives become energized when they cross-cut from the familiar to its politically charged implications for authority, identity, or decency. I suggest that the shamans work in a multivalent way that almost unconsciously catches hold of these everyday "loaded" images and attaches them to yet another set of preoccupations, the unseen forces which shamans alone perceive.

Let me take the example of the city bus. A woman from Ulan-Ude wrote to the local newspaper:

A lot of people were waiting at the bus stop. At last the long-awaited communal transport arrived. There were amazingly few people inside, so it was even possible to get a seat by the window. Well, maybe this had been a window, but there was a sheet of iron instead of glass, with a couple of small holes in it. Looking round the bus, you saw a few of these holes, but they were mostly frozen up. Well, it's winter, so what can you expect. Maybe for this reason, it was dark and gloomy in the bus, not a smile, the faces preoccupied. It was quiet; the passengers were silent, and so was the driver. Everyone was thinking his own thoughts.

After a few stops I began to wonder: where are we going? I crouched to peer through a hole: "Aha, a known apartment block, I'll have to get out soon." Meanwhile, the bus had filled up; as usual people took up not only sitting and standing places but also crowded into any possible space for hanging.

At one stop the bus remained standing for ages. It seems one of the doors wouldn't shut. And over the intercom the driver yelled: "Where are you climbing, fuck your mother! Free the fucking door!" My heart grew sad, and I clambered out before my stop. The bus drove off, with its frozen windows, grim people and angry driver. (Perevalova 1994, 4)

Let us compare this to the narrative of one shaman, Nadia Stepanova, taken from a 1996 interview:

I took a job, I entered the Communist Party, but still I had visions and visions, appearances and appearances, from morning to night. I went in the tram and I saw through the people. In the bus, and I saw everything. I couldn't sit in public transport, I couldn't be with people. What people were thinking and were going to say, I knew it all. I had to go to work on the bus, but after two stops I couldn't take any more, because people have so many evil thoughts. I couldn't stand in a queue. God, I couldn't be any-where. Once I got off at a stop by a building site, and the spirits showed me a vision, "If you don't become a shaman a blue dump truck will come out and kill you." Vrrr! They showed me a vision of how a massive wheel crushes a human body. So then I decided to become a shaman.

Nadia Stepanova's narrative here, I think, achieves a forceful validity be-cause it intersects with the familiar image of the bus, which ordinary people can already conceive in a politically charged way as a microcosm of social ills. The first woman took the trouble to write to the paper because she saw her account as the "prose of life," the bus as the blinded ship of post-Soviet fools. The shaman claims not just to notice angry people but to "see" them—that is, to experience them—because she feels inside herself their "evil thoughts," and she then takes a momentous decision.

The Post-Soviet City

Some Russian writers have argued, in a fit of patriotic zeal, that Brezhnev-era towns were postmodern before postmodernism was invented, and that Russians were the first to live through the era of "fatal banality" and simulacra described by Baudrillard (Boym 1994, 223). Be this as it may with regard to the metropolis, I do not think it is true of the provincial Siberian city. In Ulan-Ude, for example, the capital of the Buriat Republic, modernism reigned and to a great extent still does so. That is, the idea of the city is a modernist one, planned for the purposes of administration, industrialization, education, and higher living standards. The city has a center for government, surveillance, parades, and high culture, a commercial area including preserved merchants' houses from the nineteenth century, and great expanses of communal apartment blocks, factories, and barracks. But in awkward terrain there are interfilations of higgledy-piggledy wooden cottages, known locally as "impudent houses" ("*nakhalovki,*" from *nakhal,* a cheeky person), because they were put up without permission. The city is extraordinarily spread out, partly because it embodies the modernist values of space, light, and grandness, and partly because new factories and institutes were repeatedly sited on the outskirts. The main Buddhist monastery is located some thirty kilometers away. In a Soviet city no one had a choice about where they lived: you were in the housing queue and you took what you got. For this reason, though a few people live near their work, large numbers have to travel for miles. The bus and the tram are not incidental to urban life; people spend hours on them every working day. Now, it is mainly commerce and religion that has overturned the accustomed journeys of Soviet times (the bread shop here, a kilometer away the meat shop, the post office another ten minutes on the bus). Teeming markets, wholesale depots, street traders, the odd department store, and private services have sprung up; swept away by the authorities, they reappear somewhere else. Defunct Soviet institutions, closed for lack of cash, are metamorphosed: an old swimming pool turns out to be a clothes market, a culture club houses an association for lay Buddhists.

The Siberian city, far more than the West European city, stands apart from its surrounding landscape. The suburb as an idea hardly exists. Unfenced pastures start right outside the walls of the apartments. The "countryside" in Siberia is wild, a forested realm where there really are elks and bears, and where if wolves come and eat your sheep, that is bad but only to be expected. With the tumultuous rivers that pour through it, the built city with its river banks, bridges, and paved areas could be seen as a bulwark against the wild. But in fact the city, especially the post-Soviet city, is not entirely a sheltering place.

Bachelard (1994, 6) wrote about the house that it "shelters daydreaming, the house protects the dreamer, the house allows one to dream in peace." He continued that "daydreaming has a privilege of autovalorization. It derives direct pleasure from its own being. Therefore the places in which we have experienced daydreaming reconstitute themselves in a new daydream, and it is because our memories of former dwelling-places are relived as daydreams that these dwelling-places are relived as daydreams." Bachelard aimed to show that the house considered poetically has the power to integrate the thoughts, memories, and dreams of humankind, this binding principle being the daydream. Now the city is unlike the house, in that it alternates violence with shelter, transit with the haven, and the alien and disturbing with the familiar. These days the Soviet master narrative that gave the city its structural sense and purpose has gone. Individual life, even family life, with its musings cannot construct an encompassing discourse of the city; or to put this another way, people's everyday experience underdetermines new constructions of the order of the city. I am not trying to argue that the imagination of shamans is somehow a kind of functional response, "reordering" the city by providing an integrative principle. Rather, the shamans seem to me to shift the plane on which the city is imagined, cross-cutting from the citizens' direct concerns to a vision in which the city is recalibrated in space and time. In this shamanic vision the wholeness and bulwarklike quality of the Soviet city is lost. The city is repartitioned and relinked with its hinterland and the wilderness beyond, and thus it is also rechronologized in relation to ancestral time. The city so imagined is dissolved outward and backward in a way that is deeply destabilizing to the public institutions of order, though these partial shamanic visions are comforting to individual people for a while. I say "for a while" because the shamanic rituals and explanations have to be constantly renewed.

"Personal Myths"

Nadia Stepanova's bus-stop episode is part of a life narrative, a genre for which Pluzhnikov (1996) has suggested the term "personal myth." This is the auto-account that gives validation to the claim to be a shaman: it describes extraordinary episodes really experienced by the person, magical events that happened in places everyone knows, yet it also conforms to the cultural standard of shamanic illness, struggles with spirits, and eventual acceptance of the role of shaman. I talked mainly to two well-known Buriat shamans, Nadia Stepanova and Eshin-Horloo Dashibalbarovna Tsybykzhapova [also called Zoia]. Both are women aged around fifty, Nadia perhaps more traditional and Zoia more exuberantly militant. Both described school as a crucial first site in the personal myth, the place where childish competitiveness revealed to each that they had extraordinary powers. In Zoia's case, it was abnormal physical strength, when she nearly killed another little girl on the playground. Nadia, when only a small girl, could "see" what would happen and what other people thought. When she was tested along with the class, she could stand up and before her eyes a whole page would be there, with all the blots and uneven letters, and she could effortlessly read it out to the teacher.

When she was a little older, Nadia was visited by frightening visions of a creature with striped, hairy arms constantly following her. Religious elders in the family said she would become a shaman. Nadia's mother refused this future for her daughter and set off for her ancestral village in Kabansk district to hold a ritual to cut off shamanic spirit links. She came back to the city and said the ritual had been done. Immediately Nadia had a huge flow of scarlet menstrual blood. This the mother interpreted as a cleansing of spirit powers. But still Nadia was tortured by visions, and still her mother would not even consider the possibility she should become a shaman. When Nadia reached the age of around thirty, her mother was struck paralyzed. They took her mother to the hospital, which now became the place of proof of the occult, for here the doctors measured the mother's blood pressure and it was completely normal. Nadia told me, "It was 120/80, and the doctors were amazed. I didn't really understand at the time. I thought she was somehow guilty, but now I know that this was proof the gods had punished her, because she was against me becoming a shaman."

The mother died, and soon Nadia herself become ill with terrible headaches and a burst eardrum. She went to the hospital, and now the doctors were unable to cope. They said she had appendicitis, "Go and get in the queue and have it out." Nadia laughed. "But my blood pressure was sky-high, over 200. They saw I was in a bad way and gave me injections, but it went even higher, 260, 280. 'Go home,' they said. 'Go home to die,' I thought. 'Go, go,' they said, 'we can't do anything for you.' So I went home, naturally, and there my husband invited a clear seer (*iasnovidaiushchii*). He said I must become a shaman."

In these incidents, the school and the hospital—two paradigmatic Sovietizing institutions—are set up as doubly validating places. On one hand, the teachers and doctors provide the evidence for shamanic power, which here bases itself on super-excellence, or confounding the grading provided by the normal authority of reading and measuring. On the other hand, the teachers and doctors are quite simply vanquished in the play of power.

The other shaman, Zoia, described to me her own stark shamanic battles. One took place in a basement, a hangout for a youth gang, at a rock concert, when Zoia was coming to terms with her visions and abilities before she formally became a shaman. She said:

> When I came in, there was a Russian lad, Volodia. He said he was a 'clear seer,' but he turned out to be just an ordinary black sorcerer. As soon as he saw me, he started to move his arms and twist, and I 'saw' he was sitting on my heart chakra and was pressing, choking me. . . . To my luck some friends of mine came in, and it got lighter in that basement, so they started the concert. As soon as the music started, something pulled me. I couldn't sit down. I moved to the music. At that, the sorcerer stood up. And all the rest of that crowd, a hundred or more, were sitting; and we two alone, we danced to the music. They started to pray, "*Om, Mani, Badme, Hum,*" and suddenly he tore off his shirt and stood before me, naked to the waist, threatening with his fists. And I, also in a trance, threw off my skirt, flung off my boots, and faced him! [Laughs.] The important thing is, I was standing in front of a group that had come in, Radi Yogis[4] visiting from Khabarovsk, ten of them, and I stood in front like their leader. And then it started, real oriental martial wrestling, my legs and arms moved I don't know how, and he did the same. It was fantastic, and those lads behind me smiled and silently prayed, and when they reached "*O Gospodi, s usti prosti menia greshnego*" (O God, forgive me, a sinner), he fell over on his knees on the floor, and he did not get up. That was fantastic!

After this defeat of the Russian sorcerer, Zoia traveled and performed with the Radi Yogis around Siberian towns. One day as she was sitting at home by her altar praying, three men appeared, two Buriats and a Mongol Buddhist lama. They had found her by consulting Buddhist astrological texts, which also predicted that she would be able remove evil spirits that had caused a son and daughter-in-law to be killed in an accident. Subsequently, Zoia traveled all over Russia with this Mongol lama, conducting prayers and cures. "Let's go to Moscow, you can be my interpreter," he said. Zoia laughed when she described this to me. "I was then the Party secretary of the Irrigation Department of Buriatia! It was like a fable—three traveling gnomes arrive by magic and force that sitting person to do something."

"But like it or not," she continued, "it was the time of perestroika, and they were closing down all sorts of Soviet institutions, so I took up work with that lama."

It would take many pages to describe Zoia's adventures as she traveled the length and breadth of Russia with the lama. The main point is that in these "personal myths" we see a constant shifting from the mundane to the occult—for example, from the Russian lad called Volodia to the black sorcerer, from the basement hangout to the site of a great magic victory. For Zoia, the shedding of the Soviet identity of Party secretary for that of traveling assistant exorcist is quite matter-of-fact (she could see the writing on the wall for her job with the Communist Party) but also mysterious, since it was by astrological divination that the three strangers had discovered Zoia's obscure dwelling.

Travels: Conquering Significant Spaces

Zoia eventually jettisoned the Mongol lama, who had become obsessively interested in her as a woman. One of her greatest moments, not by accident, I think, took place in the Buddhist monastery at Ivolga just outside the city of Ulan-Ude. From the eighteenth century onward, Buddhism largely swamped shamanism in many areas of Buriatia. Entirely destroyed in the late 1930s, Buddhism was established again in etiolated form by the Soviets after the Second World War. Thereafter it was subordinated to the state. Today the Buddhist establishment is divided, but the religion has expanded and is identified with Buriat national aspirations (Zhukovskaia 1992). The government still attempts to keep it under close control.

That Zoia's first public shamanic deed took place at the most important monastery of the Republic was therefore important. She told me:

> In 1991, when I was not yet a curing shaman and didn't understand myself, there were four of us, all Buriats, who went to the monastery to pray. We were in the large hall of the main temple, and suddenly I don't know what is happening to me, but I stand up and I raise my arm. And I see there is a great round drum hanging, and it draws me to it. I ask the old lama sitting there, "May I go up?" "You may," and he wipes his eyes and looks at me aghast. And I go up, though not with my own woman's steps but with a majestic male stride—it was Geser Khan, you see—and I take hold of the drum and make three booming strikes. My body was visited by Geser Khan, come down to earth!

Geser Khan, I should explain, is *not* a shamanic spirit, but a hero of oral epics widely known in Asia, especially in Tibet, and often depicted as an enemy of Buddhism. So here was a woman shaman, possessed by a male spirit, and not any male but a virile, militant hero, who dared strike the sacred drum of the dozing lamas.

Significantly, in several of the post-Soviet Asian republics, not only in Buriatia, but also in Tyva, Kyrgyzia, the Altai, Kalmykia, and Kazakhstan, it is this type of mythic hero who has been appropriated from epic narrative and turned into the spirit of the nation (Hamayon 1997). In Buriatia in the summer of 1995, some years after Zoia's adventure in the monastery, local authorities decided to hold a series of ceremonies in honor of Geser, and a banner embodying his spirit was ritually honored throughout the country, passing from district to district in a series of ceremonies.

Zoia was alert to such cultural currents of the times. Her homeland in eastern Buriatia is not one of the Buriat regions where the Geser epic is well known, and in fact she used not a native Buriat but a Russian pronunciation of his name. "Geser Khan" is therefore, like other deities called on by Zoia (the Goddess Green Tara, the Archangel Michael, Japanese samurai, and some beings she called "Autopilots of the Cosmos"), an image appropriated from public culture that has aroused people's curiosity.

Both Nadia and Zoia operate with a combination of individual shamanic spirits and international or universal "deities." With Nadia the construction seems more traditional, that is, ancestral clan spirits on one hand and a deity she calls Blue Eternal Sky on the other. In Zoia's more eclectic practice, the individual spirits are the clients' previous incarnations, hidden earlier selves which lie within the personality and haunt this life. Zoia "draws them out" and voices their songs or shrieks of pain, often to the shock of clients whose "past" is thus rudely revealed.

Shamanic Practice

I want now to turn from what shamans say about themselves to what I was able to observe about how they live and their activities. Perhaps Zoia was so impressed with her own boldness in the guise of Geser Khan because it contrasts with the general invisibility and secrecy of shamans' lives as people. It is true that there is an Association of Shamans in Ulan-Ude, founded by Nadia around 1992, with some forty members. The association has premises in a former student hostel. Here shamans each have a consulting room, and they hang notices on the door stating their names, hours of work, and divinatory techniques (for example, "seeing" in vodka, using playing cards, or arranging stones). The point of this is to let the clients know what items they should bring to the session. (In Tyva, I am informed, a similar association of shamans in the city of Kyzyl in 1993 was more commercial. The notices read: Shaman X, cleansing demons from the home, 20,000 rubles; Shaman Y, sending off the soul of the dead, 50,000 rubles; and so forth).[5] In Ulan-Ude in the early 1990s, long queues would form at the association from five or six in the morning, and a row of cars would be waiting outside in the hope of taking a shaman off to treat a patient at home. But by the summer of 1996, the association had fallen somewhat by the wayside, if it had not closed entirely. The shamans in it quarreled, and many well-known shamans never joined anyway. Nadia ceased to be the president. So to visit a shaman like Nadia or Zoia you have to seek them out; you have to know people who know them, who can lead you to where they are staying.

Shamans seem to live in the interstices of the city: Nadia's family has an "impudent" house in Nakhalovka, and both she and Zoia work professionally from transient borrowed flats or hired rooms in the great, gray expanse of apartments. Svetlana Boym (1994, 140) has written of how there was no mediating space in Soviet Russia between the public and the private, no space of conventional socialization; you were either in the space of official decorum or in the nooks of domesticity. Any other space, like the hallways or backyards of apartment blocks, was a space of alienation, belonging to everyone and no one, and often a hangout for drunks and strewn with rubbish and graffiti. Boym was writing about houses, but if we extend her idea to the city and post-Soviet times, then I think we can perceive several such alienated spaces. Of course, many public institutions have closed, such as kindergartens, swimming pools, or clubs, and these have been taken over by impermanent commercial enterprises. But in the outer dwelling zones, where most people live, a prime example of alienated space is the former student hostel. It is from a tiny third-floor flat in such a place that Nadia operates, in a huge, dusty, half-inhabited block, past a grim and silent guardian, along unlit corridors and beyond heaps of lumber and fallen plaster.

If the shaman's working place in the plan of the city is anonymous and difficult to find, the use of space within is a strange transformation of the domestic. Nadia's working flat is an ordinary one, with a kitchen/living room and a toilet. But in contrast to the turned-inward, curtained coziness of domesticity, here the kitchen window is flung open, because from it Nadia throws her libations of vodka and milk to the spirits. The gas stove is used for offerings of meat and fat to the fire god. The chair opposite the window is where the client sits in bowed, suppliant pose, while Nadia stalks the room loudly calling on the spirits. One woman came with pains in her legs and back. Like Lévi-Strauss's famous shaman-trickster, Nadia purified the patient's body with sacred smoke; and then, kneeling down, she went over the body sucking out the harmful "something." Suddenly, she leapt to her feet with dramatic retching noises and rushed to the toilet, and we heard her flushing whatever "it" was away.

In this transformation of the hostel flat into a professional workspace, we seem to see a new stripped-down privacy to the shaman's activities. Certainly, elaborate costumes, drumming, and above all the presence and participation of an audience—the "society," which according to some theories of shamanism is supposed to be so essential to validating the shaman's efforts—has all gone. Perhaps this can again be related to post-Soviet sensibilities. Years of enforced communality, living in hostels, barracks, and communal flats has left people hypersensitive to privacy, afraid of being spied on, embarrassed, or roughly judged or envied by the surrounding crowd. Boym perceptively suggested that what people seek nevertheless is often an alternative sociality, rather than complete solitude. "Secrecy in the communal apartment," she has written, "was a game of searching for alternative communalities." Boym described how in her own collective kindergarten the

14. The shaman Nadia in performance in a city apartment, Ulan-Ude, Buriatia, 1997. Photograph by Hürelbaatar.

15. *The shaman Batu-Dalai makes a libation of vodka to the ancestors; the woman client whose ancestors are being honored sits behind. Kizhinga village, 1997. Photograph by Hürelbaatar.*

children had a secret ritual of burying little fetish objects, and this was a shared knowledge, a bond between friends. It was designed against the teacher, who invariably found it out in the end. "This secrecy is not solitary," Boym writes (1994, 146). I think that the privacy of the visit to the shaman is somewhat similar, though here the alternative bond is not projected inward to buried fetishes but projected outward as a compact to counteract the evil perceived in the city and the wilderness beyond it.

Zoia described how an unknown woman who intruded into her home one evening turned out to be a "stalking vampire, like a vacuum cleaner who sucked up alien energies," and how as she was going out this women left behind "two dark blue eyes and a dark blue nose." There was a din as this being (*sushchestvo*) flew into Zoia and penetrated her: "*Gospodi, mama!* if you could only imagine what it was like—a burning light bulb, as though every atom within me was burning like light bulbs, a terrible pain. Inside me was such a color-music (*svetomuzyka*), even on television you cannot imagine such a thing."

Here, an urban imagination (vacuum cleaner, light bulb, atoms, television) heightens the image of intrusion and crystallizes a fear that seems to be more common than in the past, of sorcery or spells attributed to the evil intentions of living people rather than to ancestral spirits. Zoia said someone must have sent the woman to attack her. This seems to be a general dread, not limited to the city (see Lacaze 1996, writing about a remote region of Mongolia, who explains the increased fear of maledictions [xaraal] as the outcome of a "revenge perspective" among ordinary people [149–150]).

The urban shaman nevertheless mainly sees the causes for misfortune in ancestral beings; this opens up the alternative sociality of personal links between clients and spirits in the wilderness beyond the city. I was present when another woman patient came to Nadia's consulting room with a sad problem: her daughter had had a miscarriage and she had come to discover the cause. Having called her own spirits and made a libation, Nadia asked the woman for the name of her grandfathers on both sides, her grandmothers, great-grandparents, and the villages where they lived. The woman grew distraught, because she did not know. Nadia tried to visualize the ancestors, to provoke the woman's memory, but it did not work. In the end, the woman was dismissed and Nadia told her to come back only when she had the information. Other people told me that this woman must have been a fool, because everyone knows that you have to visit your relatives and find out about your ancestors before going to a shaman.

Taken together, the preoccupation with "evil thoughts" and ancestral causes provide interesting illumination of the social relations of the city. First, the people in the city are crowded together, but not with people they choose or want to live with. Those who do have individual flats, nowadays the majority, exchange barely a civil nod with the people who have been allocated to live next door. The city neighborhood is hardly an operative idea in 1990s Russia. It is true that the fall of Soviet power has seen a return of street life to the city (bazaar, hawkers, and sellers), but so far these have not created friendly conviviality—more the opposite conviction that one will be cheated by anonymous others, and a determination to find some other, private, and "reliable" way. Secondly, most Buriats came to live in the city from the 1960s onward, and therefore virtually all of the ancestors and ancestral places are located outside the city, at scattered villages and settlements miles away.

So by insisting that clients recall their ancestors, what the shamans are doing is relinking individual city people through half-forgotten familial ties with sacred-scary places in the countryside. This has to be done to discover the cause of misfortune, in shamanic idiom. The shamanic construction of causality is that otherwise inexplicable happenings are brought about by the vengeance of neglected spirits, these being the souls of dead humans transformed by ancient injustices into the touchy "masters" of mountains, rocks, trees, or springs. Nadia told me that a shaman needs to find out who a client's ancestors are, first, to know who that person is, an identity quite separate from the client's job, class, education, or personality as evidenced in the city. The naming of ancestral sites narrows the field for the shaman to discover which spirit of the wild may have caused the trouble. When the offended spirit has been revealed, the shaman commonly orders the client to go out to the mountain (tree, etc.) residence of the spirit and perform the ritual called *alban,* which means duty, service, or tribute. *Alban* is a sacrifice, usually conducted by another country shaman, with the aim of giving acknowledgment and respect to the neglected spirit (Zhukovskaia 1996). Even out on the mountainside, this ritual is not collective in the sense of gathering the whole local community together; it was described to me how a shaman in the Aga District performed five separate rites in a row, each for a different family.[6]

By insisting on these country links, the shamans reconceptualize and segment the city, so it is now composed of individuals belonging to familial or descent groups whose origins lie far away. The city becomes a place where the citizens' mysterious misfortunes are caused from outside and within a time frame that reaches far into the past.

All this is happening at a time when the balance of city-rural relations is deeply problematic. During most of the Soviet period, with its food shortages and queues, residents of the city used to rely on country relatives for meat, butter, flour, cheese, and so forth, all staples of diet. Rural people relied on city relatives for manufactures, favors with officials, and the chance to squeeze into the city as a family member. During the stable post-Khrushchev years, perhaps it would be true to say that the ties slackened, since city food supplies were adequate and residence permits were brought into force to prevent rural-urban migration. In post-Soviet times, the balance has tipped further in the favor of the city. The city is the only place where there is money, markets are full of goods and food, even if many people cannot afford them, and urban people all have vegetable plots for subsistence. Residence regulations have been tightened further, explicitly to keep the country cousins out. It is country people who are dependent now, desperate for the circulating lifeblood of the contemporary world: money, electricity, gasoline, and information, all of which come from the city.

The shamans, however, are insisting on something more than an urban-rural exchange, since the ancestral sites are shared with networks of kin (some of whom may live at the village while others are scattered all over the place), and the fortune of all of them depends on observance of the rituals. Appadurai (1996, 179) has written of how rites of passage "produce locality" in a world where the notion of neighborhood is threatened. Even in small-scale societies, he writes, locality cannot be taken for granted, for regular work is needed to maintain it (1996, 180). This insight is useful in discussing the post-Soviet case, where the locality being produced is the more fragile for having to unite spatially dispersed people and furthermore is entangled in city-countryside dependencies and enmities. It is significant that villagers now often invite city shamans to revivify spirit relations. Nadia told me, for example, how she was invited in 1995 to a village in Bichura District, where people had forgotten their ancestors, to help their local shaman with a ritual to "smooth over the fault." Three mountain spirits were called forth. "They arrived," said Nadia, "dirty, small. There was a taller white one, looking displeased. They all came in greasy clothes, in patches. And the place was dirty too, bottles, stuff thrown everywhere. I was sorry for them. I told the local shaman, 'You must clear up this place. The spirits are complaining.' Through my conversations with them I opened up cleanliness (*chistota*)—cleanliness of thought, of deeds, and of desires."

Both Nadia and Zoia were consecrated as shamans in rituals at their parents' villages, where their own ancestral spirits reside. But relations here are quite tense and ambiguous, as we saw when Nadia's mother tried to cut the link. When the citified shamans go uninvited without a special local tie to worship, say, at a famous sacred mountain, they are bound to fall foul of one of the innumerable rules for correct ritual behavior. This is pounced on by the local shamans, who say the city shamans are not genuine and blame them for all sorts of misfortunes. For example, a three-year drought in the distant Tunka Valley is said to have been caused by the dreadful ritual mistake of a self-declared Buriat shaman, formerly a professor of Marxist-Leninist philosophy, a woman who climbed up a sacred mountain prohibited to women.

It is possible that this professor was quite frightened by the torrent of hate unleashed by her act, as she now declares she is not a shaman, just someone who studies and appreciates shamanism. This recalls what Raymond Williams (1973, 128) wrote about the characteristic attitudes of people in the rapidly industrializing city. There is a confidence that humanity can remake the world but at the same time a new awe in the face of wild places. If we are justified in drawing a parallel with the Soviet city, which reinforced a confidence in refashioning the world with the ideology of communism, we should remember what Williams added: that the power to remake the world is always ambiguous, as is the choice whether to remake it or not, since it must always run up against the pieties and habitudes of previous generations.

In post-Soviet Russia, the days of modernizing, utopian dreams are definitively gone. Glasnost, as Boym remarks (1994, 228), was not an ideology of newness. Curiously, in the hands of urban shamans, I have observed, there is not much of a return to history either. Rather, the past is sucked up into the present, horizontalized, and unlinked from time. Thus, though the shamans of the city have to operate with the spirits of the wild, they tend to play down their precise ancestral historicity (for example, they do not often cite genealogies). In fact, going through my notes I noticed that it was mostly I who used the word "ancestors," while the shamans more often talked of a range of atemporal spirit beings ("gods," "powers," "masters"). Furthermore, there is a tendency when shamans talk to the anthropologist, as opposed to the client (for whom ancestry does matter), to downplay the spirits of the wild and to highlight other delocalized, international, or abstract powers. Zoia explained to me:

> I came to understand that a person born in a given place, like it or not, inevitably absorbs the energy of that place. So I am grateful to the ancestors, as you call them, because they awakened me, raised me up, pushed me, and made me. And so it happened that the more I rose up and grew from that energy, I also activated them and raised them up together with myself. And it turns out, whether they like it or not, that it is not I who am dependent on them, but they who are dependent on me. You see! It is not they, the dead, who command me, but I who command them. And you see, it is not just them, but all kinds of forces that go through me, *idaky* and *sakhiusy*[7] and shamanic spirits, all of them.

In what we might see as an echo of the city's preeminence in sources of energy, surrounded by the desperate country people, she continued:

> That growling dirty voice of mine, when I was singing, that was the dirty spirits, the shamanic ones, who don't want to go away and attach themselves to us living people, their own descendants, and destroy our energy.

This statement is quite clear, but in much of what the shamans said it was impossible to tell whether they were talking about traditional shamanic spirits or the unkind, cruel thoughts of living people, the evil powers that so oppressed Nadia on the bus. With both of these urban shamans, there was a kind of narrative in which wild spirits were conflated with human evil and thus were to be overcome in an internal spiritual battle. Perhaps this is a new departure in shamanism, and certainly it is at odds with the construction of the *alban* ritual in which clients are instructed to worship and respect the spirits in the mountains. For Zoia, in a turn that I think would have been quite foreign to the people of the village, the shaman ancestor spirits even became the enemies of shamanism (that is, the new shamanism as she conceived it). She described a battle with evil forces within her:

> And what do you know, one wonderful day, in the cloudy shadows, it was as if there were two Eshin-Horloo [her Buriat name], one in white clothing and one in black. And the one in white stretched her hand to set fire to the one in black, to annihilate her, and it turned out that I was neutralizing, with my own will, consciously all that was within me that was negative towards shamanism.

She continued that the shamanism of the dirty spirits is a terrible thing, which must be re-created and rethought, working together with the light forces of nature. She quoted to me a poem she had composed last summer, which was a strange thing, a shaman's poem as it were against shamanism:

> *Ne budut nad mirom zloveishchie bubny stuchat'*
> *A budet molitva sviataia,*
> *A budet v serdtse sila, kotoruiu nam nado znat'*
> *Chtoby istina stala siiaia.*

> (No longer will evil drums ring out over the world
> But there will be sacred prayer,
> And in the heart will be power, which we need to know,
> If the genuine truth is to shine through.)

If all this suggests a new energized shamanism purifying the old, its other face is a yearning toward powers of world significance. In the following account Zoia interestingly sees herself not in an active, mobile shamanic mode but as grounded, receptive, childlike. She said:

At six in the morning, I was just awake, you understand, lying there, and I began to see the face. A huge, dark blue face, nearly a meter [high], the face of Archangel Michael. I felt I could talk to him telepathically. I said, "Show me the world." I felt someone was turning me over on my back. I saw myself, as a one-year-old girl, a tiny girl, looking upward somewhere, and people in a whitish mist were swimming like fish, all naked, in a whitish fog; that's how the world appeared to me. I was not frightened, and I felt I knew that being. Oh, he had a handsome, bearded European face, and I knew it was the Archangel, no one else. From these meetings with him everything changed for me.

Perhaps the city itself as a pool of diverse, rather deracinated clients constitutes the wider neighborhood of interpretation that desires such images. Note that the poem was composed in Russian, and that three-quarters of the city population is Russian. I once asked a Buriat friend whether the Buriats accept as genuine such "deities" as Geser Khan, the Archangel Michael, or the Autopilots of the Cosmos. To my surprise, he replied that there was no question; Buriats would be disappointed if their shamans did not have such gods, because this demonstrates their breadth and capacity. Here we have to understand first, that after generations of Soviet schooling, many urban Buriats, especially the young, know extraordinarily little about their earlier culture and are easily convinced about what it may have contained; and second, that Buriat people, including shamans, see shamanism as a religion on a par with Christianity and Buddhism (Khagdaev 1998). They are proud that Russians and people of other nationalities consult Buriat shamans.

To conclude: it seems that people enjoy the shamans' magical incidents of destabilization of Soviet and Buddhist contexts (the school, the hospital, the monastery) and their revitalization as sites of spiritual vigor. By these narratives and events, the city is "actualized" as a new, occulted locale. But it is thereby also put into a wider context; perception of evil and misfortune in the city implies an awareness of relational flows of spirit power from outside. This seems to resonate with the economic-political relations of the city with the countryside. The tendency for general disintegration in post-Soviet society is very pervasive, and the notion of the city as a bulwark against outsiders has been reinforced by post-Soviet legislation (against migrants, foreign traders, refugees). Shamanic practice undermines this particular division. But the city shamans' perception, of their own cleansing and revivifying power in the villages, often runs up against the secret continuities of country people's practices. Here I have tried to give an impression of how these complex relations are actualized in both narrative and practice. Urban shamans create city people as reterritorialized subjects, attached by familial ties to sacred places in the wild outside, even as they dream up deterritorialized gods of the contemporary world, which exert benign power in international space.

NOTES

Introduction

1. Young-ho Nam, personal communication.
2. Galina Manzanova, economic advisor to the Buriat government, personal communication.

1. "Icebergs," Barter, and the Mafia in Provincial Russia

1. Originally published in *Anthropology Today* 7, 2 (1991): 8–13.
2. *Dialog* 1992 (2): 58.
3. The reader should not be confused by this. At present it has the character of a local coupon as described, but the expression *kartochnaia sistema* is used for the general rationing that some economists advocate introducing for the USSR as a whole in the future.
4. *Dialog* 1990 (2): 57.
5. *Dialog* 1990 (2): 58. Residence documents have therefore almost become a commodity.
6. *Dialog* 1990 (2): 58.
7. *Molodezh' Buriatii* (1990): 3.
8. *Dialog* 1990 (8): 81. This journal praises the initiative of one new commercial bank, the Vostok, based in Ufa. But it notes that such independence is anathema to the state. Commercial banks were formerly allowed to operate without paying taxes. Now the Vostok has been asked to pay a 60-percent tax.
9. *Dialog* 1990 (2): 73.
10. There is a rather disorganized movement called the Democratic International Movement of Tyva, headed by Dr. Kaadyr-Ool Alekseevich Bicheldey, a historian, but this is not what lies behind the attacks on Russians. He only wants to revive the culture of the Tyvinians.
11. The population of Tyva ASSR is 70 percent Tyvinian and 30 percent Russian. The disturbances have only affected regions where the two groups live side by side, not the remote Tyvinian-only regions.
12. Valery Sharov, Far Eastern correspondent of *Literaturnaia gazeta*, personal communication.

2. Mythmaking, Narratives, and the Dispossessed in Russia

1. Originally published in *Cambridge Anthropology* 19, no. 2 (1996/97): 70–92.
   This article is dedicated, with deep respect, to the memory of Ernest Gellner. It was written in 1993 while Ernest's own concern with the political events in Russia and Eastern Europe was at its most creative, influencing each member of our department in different ways. If themes from Ernest's contemporary work, especially "Notes on Atomization" and "From the Interstices of a Command-admin System" from his *Conditions of Liberty: Civil Society and Its Rivals* (1994) are evident here, perhaps no less important an influence was Ernest's own life as a person and a scholar. He never forgot the experience of being one of the dispossessed at the hands of the communist regime in Czechoslovakia, and much of his scholarly life was devoted to understanding the roots of that system of oppression. Although this article raises different theoretical issues from those pursued by Ernest, it reflects his presence, and the inspiration I have found in the characteristic intentness of his scrutiny of Russian society.

   I am most grateful to the following people whose discussions of this paper provided me with valued insights: Tone Bringa, Myriam Hivon, Graham MacCann, Sergei Panarin, Piers Vitebsky, Effie Voutira, and Balzhan Zhimbiev.

2. An acronym derived from the expression "without definite place of habitation" (*bez opredelennogo mesto zhitel'stva*).

3. This paper was written in 1993 and should be taken to reflect conditions in Russia in the early 1990s.

4. Benefits to the "unemployed" are paid partly by the state and partly by the organization dismissing the workers. Saving on such dues is one reason why many collectives prefer to keep workers on their books in part-time or very lowly paid positions.

5. Such state salaries were later (March 1993) raised to 30,000–40,000 rubles. Because of inflation and constant changes in salaries, these figures should be viewed comparatively, reflecting abrupt changes in the relative status and economic security of various categories of workers.

6. At the end of 1992, the FMS estimated that there were in Russia around 470,000 refugees from war zones and a further 800,000 "forced migrants" from the successor states, and they predicted altogether about 2,000,000 refugees by the end of 1993, the great majority of these being Russians returning to the homeland from the successor states of the CIS (Visens 1992). The Russian diaspora is huge; approximately 25 million live in the successor states. Interviews I conducted in 1993 with Russian repatriates from Central Asia suggested that further great inflows should be expected, with the return of virtually all Russians from Tajikistan and large numbers from the 6 million living in Kazakhstan.

7. In December 1992, Russia belatedly signed the 1951 International Convention on Refugees (Patrification). But the head of the FMS, which is responsible for enforcing the convention, said in a 1993 interview that Russian Federation could not possibly fulfill its obligations in this regard (Baiduzhii 1993).

8. This production-redistribution model spread over from such real productive enterprises as farms, factories, or mines to institutions in general, including, for example,

higher-educational institutes or rest homes. The Bobrynskii Rest Home in Vologda province is one such case. It has (1993) a staff of sixty, which is many more than the number of people usually taking a rest there. The rest home provides houses for the staff, fields and vegetable plots for their farms, and subsidized milk, piglets, and transport. Work in the rest home is minimal to nonexistent, since other enterprises can hardly afford to send their members for a vacation. Especially in winter the staff spend much of their time loafing around or drinking. Still, they have a legitimate context in which to exist (Myriam Hivon, personal communication).

9. A Russian peasant from Vologda province put this another way, "These days the state has completely retreated from the village, retreated without a glance at the peasantry" (Nikol'skii 1993b).

10. Far be it from me to decry the relevance of etymology. As Herzfeld (1986) has pointed out, "Far more than a mere pruning game, the search for an etymological history of reification serves to remind us of processes that are constantly at work through language and other semiotic systems and that principally serve in the interests of those political and ideological formations that have successfully established their respective legitimacies."

11. This has implications for common understandings of the locus and nature of political agency. Kavelin has argued that while Europe developed the idea of an individualism that became increasingly limited by public authorities, Russian thought moved from a different base. In Russia, an initially despotic state began the process of cultivating the idea of the autonomous individual with the sovereign. In particular, Peter the Great served as the model (Kavelin 1989, 164–165). Some have seen a re-emergence of such an idea in the Gorbachev era. A prominent Soviet politician declared in 1990 that the assumption of these [new] plenary powers (that is, Gorbachev's simultaneous assumption of the posts of President and General Secretary) demonstrated that it was just the very first step and that establishing a more efficient mechanism for fulfilling laws and presidential decrees is needed.

12. To quote the words of a Russian organizer of the 1989 miner's strike in the Kuzbas region: "If this [chaos] happens, only a strong figure could save us, someone not afraid of blood or of spilling blood, someone who could steer society onto a governable course, stay in power long enough to create order, and retire from the scene. When a society falls apart, it's no time for ethics. What's needed is a person who knows how to use power" (Bonet 1992).

13. This appeared not so much in questioning the principle of power as in debating the legitimate hold the goal of power might have over the personality. We have only to remember the questioning among leftists before 1917 of their own ideal of the revolutionary, who "has no interests of his own, no feeling, no belongings; he does not even have a name. Everything in him is absorbed by a single exclusive interest, a single passion—the revolution" (Sergei Nechaev, quoted in Kelly 1987, 195). The debate about how to live with the goal of an abstract and yet personalized power, led these writers to debate the relation between means and ends, the ethics of taking life in the revolutionary cause, and above all the "self-censorship" that buttressed the rigid revolutionary personality (Kelly 1987).

14. This nickname may derive from *golova* (head), used figuratively, as in English, to designate the leader.

15. From *hung-hu-tzu* (Chinese "Red Beards") a popular name for bandits in northeast China in the early part of the century.

16. From Chiang Kai-shek, the Chinese general and warlord who fought the Communists.

17. The "Bratva" came from the working-class district on the "other side" of the River Ude. They dressed in wadded jackets emblematic of "proletarianness" and, curiously, slippers. Alone among all the gangs in having a Russian name the Bratva were described to me as *chernaia massa* ("the masses"); this derives from the history of the city, which was a Jewish-dominated trading settlement in the nineteenth century, to which a Russian working class was introduced only in the early Soviet period. This "other side of the Ude" is their district, whereas the rest of the city has come to be settled by Buriats, Russians, Germans, etc., of the administrative and service classes.

18. The fights caused serious injuries and occasionally even death; it should be noted, however, that they were somewhat orchestrated, the numbers on either side taking part being agreed beforehand.

19. While I was in northern China in the summer of 1993 I and a Buriat colleague met a group of young Russian prostitutes from Ulan-Ude who were being run from a prison-like hotel by a Buriat madam. Hearing my colleague was also from Ulan-Ude, the girls brightened up and identified themselves, "We're Chiang-kai-she. Who are you?"

20. I am aware that the situation is different in metropolitan cities such as Moscow and St. Petersburg, where the way of life of the "hippies" and to a lesser extent the "punks" is intentionally designed to be emblematic of wandering and rootlessness (Bushnell 190).

21. Barthes (1985, 37) points out that the advertisement does not just give the message that the product is Italian; it evokes "Italianicity." The suffix *-icity* serves to produce an abstract substantive from an adjective. "Italianicity is not Italy; it is the condensed essence of all that can be Italian, from spaghetti to painting." A similar mythicizing effect is produced in Russian in political discourse by adding the suffix *-shchina* to a proper name. The suffix *-shchina* connotes a despotic regime, and together with the name of the power holder (Beria, Stalin, etc.) mythicizes an epoch of personalized power.

22. They say the station is dangerous and almost unbearable because of all the other "various people" who make their homes there.

3. Creating a Culture of Disillusionment

1. Originally published in *Worlds Apart: Modernity through the Prism of the Local,* ed. Daniel Miller (New York: Routledge, 1995): 43–68.
   I am grateful to Ira and Sergei Panarin, Tania Medvedeva, Marina Mongush, and Balzhan Zhimbiev for generously providing me with information. David Anderson and Daniel Miller gave valuable comments on an earlier draft of this paper, for which many thanks.

2. I refer here to production on the private plots (also herding, fishing, and hunting) by virtually all workers in collective and state farms.

3. The expression gave rise to an inevitable anecdote: an American goes up to a queue and asks what is being sold. People tell him, "They're selling (throwing out) boots!" He has a look and says "Yes, in America they throw those out too" (Voinovich 1985, 42).

4. Dollar sales were officially eliminated at the beginning of 1994.

5. Cash is worth up to 20 percent more than the equivalent sum in *beznalichnye*.

6. During 1993 Moscow benefited from the disastrous situation in the Ukraine and Belorussia. The total collapse of these economies and currencies made even the ruble an attractive proposition, and peasants from these countries came to sell their produce at railway stations and roadsides.

7. Banks and money-changing kiosks sprang up during 1993, but ordinary people avoided using them. Not only were deposits taxed, but the state sometimes forbade withdrawals point blank.

8. In March 1993 a single rose at the Orangery nursery in northern Moscow cost 125 rubles; in flower shops the price was around 300; street traders charged 1,000 rubles.

9. This was made up of a man's salary of 33,000, a grown-up daughter's income of 12,000, the wife's pension of 15,000, and two smaller state benefits for a school-age daughter who was in bad health.

10. This was calculated using the minimum of buyable foods estimated necessary for survival for adult men, adult women, the elderly, and children per day. The portions did not represent the actual diet of any studied group of people but theoretical dietary requirements. Added to this were sums for heating, rent, and other expenses and the absolute minimum of products required for sanitation and health. The costs of clothing, furniture, footwear, television, and similar goods were not included, as "unfortunately the situation today is such that it is necessary to make do on existing reserves of these things" (Valiuzhenich 1993, 3).

11. Hansen (1993, 95) notes that over 60 percent of households in the Kola Peninsula kept stockpiles in 1992, and that these included not only food but also medicines, clothing, footwear, and consumable durables. A majority of his respondents said they drew constantly from their stockpiles and expected them sooner or later to be exhausted.

12. As Bukovskii has written (1981, 99), "It is not in the Russian character to economize. 'Eh, the devil!' concludes the husband, 'We've never lived well and now is not the time to start.' Somehow or other it seems they do manage. Our families are maintained by women, and all their economy consists of buying cheap products." This gender difference in consumption is an issue I have not been able to develop in this paper, though it is highly important. With the new emphasis on subsistence production (such as potatoes) even among urban families, the expectations of women are even more burdensome.

13. There is more trust in the sphere of private services for known people. Many of those on low incomes are beginning to develop little sidelines to make ends meet: mending furniture, selling medicinal herbs sent from a relative in Siberia, massage, "consultations," and so forth. The prices for these are subject to bargaining and agreement.

14. A recent study of the "new class" in Ulan-Ude showed that virtually none of them supported the extreme nationalist Vladimir Zhirinovsky in the recent elections, although 60 percent of the rest of the regional population backed him (Osinskii 1994).

15. The ambivalent status of markets (and probably many other financial institutions too) is exacerbated by their quasi-illegality. It is not forbidden to trade, yet it is forbidden to trade at given places (in Ulan-Ude it was banned everywhere in the city in 1991). In practice, this only adds another layer to the labyrinthine connections between financial and other institutions. Because the mayor banned markets in Ulan-Ude, the police were able to take fines from all the people who nevertheless went on selling, fines that went into the police fund; at the same time there appeared numerous "inspectors," empowered to take a sizable "state tax" from the same traders.

16. A study of the "new class" in Ulan-Ude in early 1994 showed that most of its members are aged between twenty-five and thirty, are well educated (though not second-generation intellectuals), and had left jobs like medicine, teaching, engineering, or management. Only 9 percent were from the working class (Osinskii 1994).

4. Traders, "Disorder," and Citizenship Regimes in Provincial Russia

1. Originally published in *Uncertain Transitions: Ethnographies of Change in the Postsocialist World*, ed. Michael Burawoy and Katherine Verdery (Lanham: Rowman and Littlefield, 1999): 19–52.

I am grateful to the History and Economics Centre, King's College, Cambridge, for financial support during the research for this paper. Many thanks to Victoria Bonnell, Roberts Kilis, David Sneath, and the participants in the "Ethnographies of Transition" conference who read earlier drafts of this paper and made valuable comments.

2. During the nineteenth and early twentieth centuries, only two or three trading posts were found along the entire border with China and Mongolia (Khokhlov 1985, 67).

3. Diatlov (1995) writes, for example, that in 1992, 49 percent of the citizens of Irkutsk were personally involved in trading. That figure had declined to 21 percent by late 1994.

4. "The characteristic of Russian business is that it produces almost nothing," writes Gomelev (1995, 2). "The 'New Russians' take legendary profits by re-selling what we succeeded in creating during the years of Soviet power, and their highest goal is selling across the frontier."

5. Each year $10–$12 billion escapes from Russia, a total of around $45 billion during the period 1991–95; state reserves amount to $12 billion, *Moskovskii Komsomolets* (1995): 1.

6. The restrictions on export of strategic goods began in 1993 (Handelman 1994, 114). In eastern Siberia such goods include rails and engineering parts, deer organs, food, KamAZ trucks, glass, antiquities and art objects, medicines, precious metals, and weapons (Gomelev 1995). Several of these items are still exported by local governments with agreement from Moscow.

7. I use the term *province* here for oblasts and republics within the Russian Federation.

8. *Pravda Buriatii* (1996): 1.

9. In the Soviet period state enterprises did not have charters because they were regarded as branches of the state. Collective farms had charters, but they were identical to one another and were not effective as a basis for independent economic activity.

The terminology for current charters, such as the *aktsionernoe obshchestvo,* the *tovar-ishestvo s ogranichestvennoi otvetstvennostiu,* and others, is largely the same as that used in tsarist times; see Owen (1991).

10. I acknowledge the work of David Anderson (1995), who introduced this term in his Ph.D. thesis on Evenki reindeer herding in northern Siberia. The term is intended to be historically neutral, but I recognize that it is not indigenous.

11. *Kommersant* (1995): 8.

12. The cost of a license to trade as a physical person was 400,000 rubles a year in 1996 in Ulan-Ude, about one month's worker's wages.

13. Physical persons were liable for taxes of 12 percent of profits in 1996 in Ulan-Ude.

14. Some estimates are given in Handelman (1994) and Gomelev (1995). In 1994, before the Russian currency was made convertible, a single customs' haul at the Ulan-Ude airport uncovered an attempt to export illegally $18,600,000 (Gomelev 1995).

15. Personal checks are virtually unheard of in the provinces, mainly because people do not trust that they will be honored. Bank transfers have recently become more common in transactions between firms.

16. Security staff are often recruited from former KGB, police, and military personnel.

17. Usually a band of handpicked friends of the director of the bank. They are employed to watch the employees of the bank as much as to protect top managers (Tania Zhimbieva, personal communication).

18. Hiring security guards may be more than a matter of protection. The anthropologist David Sneath suggested to me that the Soviet era generated a model of inclusive institutionalization that reproduced in miniature many of the functions of the state, and that modern corporations may reproduce that model.

19. Dollars are the most valued, and also the most suspect, form of money (Lemon 1996). In eastern Siberia counterfeit dollars are rumored to come from China. Most currency exchanges have special machines to detect counterfeit notes.

20. The cannabis trade is active in southern Siberia, but it seems to be a relatively makeshift affair. In the summer, naked men are said to run through fields where wild hemp is growing, accumulating the pollen on their bodies. The pollen is scraped off with a knife, rolled into a ball, and sold. Local people know this goes on but do not interfere because of threats from the drug-running gangs.

21. In February 1994, the latest date for which exact figures are available, of the 206 collective and state farms in Buriatia about 53 percent (60 collective and 49 state farms) had made no change to their status; 6 state farms had become collective farms; of the 97 farms that "privatized," 60 became associations, 20 became limited companies, 4 became agricultural cooperatives, 5 became joint-stock companies, and 8 became subsidiaries of other enterprises, *Buriatiia* (1994). As the tempo of privatization has slowed since 1994 and several farms have reversed privatization, it can be estimated that even nominal privatization in agriculture is still little over 50 percent.

22. An example from agriculture is the Buriat Unegetei specialized vegetable farm which has remained a state farm (*sovkhoz*) on the old Soviet model. In hard times in 1995, it was helped by an entrepreneurial support scheme of the Buriat government, which

bought Dutch seed potatoes and offered them to the state farm for a return of 15 percent of the profits. The government got its return, but when asked if the farm made a profit, the director replied:

> No. We remained a state farm, that is, government property. We thought of becoming a joint-stock company, but we decided not to because of our difficult financial position. Last year vegetables gave us 800 million rubles income, but our 900 cows gave us 460 million in losses. If I submitted (*podchinil'sia*) to logical reasoning and economic calculation, I would get rid of the cows. But that would mean getting rid of work for our people. I repeat, the vegetables saved us. After all, they cannot import fresh vegetables from the West. But our difficulty is that even here we did not sell our product but made a 'gift' of it to the state. To this day we have not been paid for it. On paper the farm looks good, but in real life—terrible. (Shelkunova 1995)

Note here how the director associates economic dependency with a state-farm type of enterprise and clearly does not take seriously the idea of giving up the cows and sacking part of the workforce.

23. The 1992 presidential edict to this effect was only gradually implemented. The socialist enterprise had controlled the land in both public and private use, as well as the housing stock, central heating, lighting and roads, medical facilities, transport, clubs, kindergartens, and sporting facilities; in the agricultural sector it provided firewood, fodder, fertilizer, young livestock, seed, and use of machinery to its members for their private plots. Some enterprises also constructed their own medical centers, paid teachers, built schools, and provided school buses for their members. By 1996, enterprises varied in the extent to which they had relinquished these responsibilities.

24. As the director of a Buriat collective farm explained:

> In deciding economic matters in the conditions of the wild, and to us very unfamiliar, market, we do everything not to leave people without work, because the principle of collectivism is highest of all for us. So we decided to go in for production that does not cost much but needs a lot of labor—namely, herding horses and increasing our stock of Kazakh white-head cattle for meat. We have given up mechanized cleaning-out, watering, heated fodders, and even electrical lighting, and we have gone back to horse carts for transport. In a word, we have turned backward, to the distant past. And for our own internal use we have decided to keep some sheep, pigs, and foxes for fur. . . . A problem that much concerns us [is] that ten hectares of our best fields were never given back to us by Kyren. And by the gasoline pump at the edge of our land our fields are being trampled by their cattle. The Kyren village administration does not lift a finger to help fence off our fields, and all this is made worse by a twenty-four-hour commercial shop they have set up—night and day their drunken louts attack and steal from our people. When will the district administration decide to get rid of that spreader of moral decay? (Uskeev 1994, 2)

25. Nevertheless, there was some indignation within the firm because the state had not used its 20 percent of shareholding rights to intervene and had not agreed to liquidate the firm's debts (Nikolaev 1994).

26. People active in setting up a *zemliachestvo* told me they experienced initial hostility from the provincial government because the group might provide "parallel power." To gain control of the localism movement, the Buriat government has set up its own local cultural organizations in each district.

27. Attachment to place emerges in local religious cults in Buriatia at sites often placed at the entrances and exits of communities based on enterprises and rural districts.

28. *Argumenty i Fakty* 32 (1996): 14.

29. Gomelev (1995) describes the "shameful" nature of the inward trade goods registered by Irkutsk customs in 1994: 255 tons of food (which should have been produced internally, he implies), 3 tons of calculating and computer equipment, and 2,096 tons of alcohol.

30. In Russian the *Velikii Shmotkovyi Put'*.

31. Government credits are important here, but there are also more symbolic ties. For example, the two firms have offices in government-owned property in the center of town, and Arig Us has a plane called *Buriatia*, often used by government officials, with the firm's logo painted on it.

32. For example, valuable copper is sold to an agent who acknowledges receipt of "metallic waste" and resells it back to the firm (for which service the agent receives a fee). Now officially consisting of metallic waste, the consignment is sold abroad, and customs are bribed to look the other way, or it is simply hoped that no inspection will take place.

33. In Soviet times, visas had been needed to travel to Mongolia and China, and even people with relatives abroad were restricted to one visit per year, whereas most people were unable to travel at all. Everyone knew, however, that these visits to relatives were used to obtain valuable goods for resale.

34. An unprecedented rise in agreements to "cooperate" between Russian and Mongolian collective and state farms, factories, and similar organizations covered the emergence of mass trade. For Russians in Trans-Baikalia, Buriat friends were suddenly in great demand to act as interpreters in Mongolia.

35. Balzhan Zhimbiev, personal communication, referring to Ulan-Ude in 1992.

36. When the collective farms came to terms with the unprofitability of livestock and were also instructed to privatize (around 1992–94), great numbers of animals were sold.

37. Set up in the 1920s, consumer cooperatives originally operated shops locally on the basis of members' fees. Later, the organization became a huge state-supported operation that conducted international trade, operated its own bakeries, and had a monopoly retail position in rural areas.

38. This prejudice of local people is not well-founded: the co-ops I visited did not necessarily sell useful items. Items on sale at a private village shop included three rolls of toilet paper, two German deodorant sprays, one bottle of shampoo, bandages, a few bars of three types of soap, toothpaste, one pair of jeans, a few pairs of children's shoes and socks, a tablecloth, one pair of women's evening shoes, two tins of liver paste, and a few packets of biscuits, tea, soda, and salt. Vodka was also sold but was kept under the counter. This shop was operating at a loss, according to the owner.

39. An example is a Buriat entrepreneur who had a contact in distant Rostov-on-Don, arranged to sell fruit conserves from Rostov in Mongolia, and after several visits to Ulaanbaatar obtained a consignment of Chinese oranges and mandarins in Mongolia just in time to ship them to sell in Buriatia for the new year. This entire operation was conducted through barter. A less successful example is the Mongolian entrepreneur who set up a factory sewing leather coats in Ulaanbaatar. He and his family lived in Russia and stayed in Irkutsk, Bratsk, Angarsk, and Ulan-Ude in search of partners. His best hope was an Angarsk oil company, which he hoped would buy his coats for its workers and would also accept a consignment for resale by their commercial department. In return, he aimed to obtain several cisterns of gasoline to sell in China, which would enable him to bring back a huge consignment of goods to sell in Russia. Nothing came of this plan.

40. A new type of trader is the "dealer" (*diler*), who obtains a concession to sell an international product, such as the magazine *Marie-Claire*, in a local market.

41. A presidential edict of January 1, 1996, gave the state the right to confiscate from a Russian firm the full value of imported goods if the goods do not arrive in Russia within 160 days of the order. The reason for this edict is that Russian firms were fraudulently "ordering" goods abroad, sending payment immediately, and arranging for the payment to be put in a foreign bank account while the goods "failed to turn up." The law states that if the importer does not have the money, the firm's bank will be charged. The edict will hit small firms, since banks will not risk lending them money for foreign orders unless the firms can show at least twice the value of the order on its account books (Alla Kuz'mina, "Dolzhniki otvetyat sobstvennym imushchestvom'," *Moskovskii Komsomolets* 1995 (34–184) Sept. 20, pp 1, 9.

42. *Kavkaztsy* is the politest term by which these people are known locally (*chernozhopye*, black-assed, is another). I put quotation marks around "Kavkaztsy" to show that this is a general appellation by Siberians, who often neither know nor care about the traders' ethnic identity.

43. In 1993, there were apparently 455 criminal groups known to the police in Irkutsk Oblast, of which 30 were "ethnic"; of the 369 groups known in 1994, only 9 were ethnic (Diatlov, Demid, and Paliutina 1995, 8).

44. An interesting article by Diatlov and colleagues (1995) discusses local reactions to the trial of an Azerbaijani vegetable trader accused of raping a local Russian girl. The girl's mother, hearing he was to be allowed out on bail, shot and killed the accused as he emerged from jail. The city of Irkutsk was in an uproar over these events, and hundreds of letters were written to the local papers. The great majority defended the mother. What is significant is that relatively few of those assailing the accused attacked him for his specific ethnicity (Azerbaijani). Rather, they railed at him for being an outsider (*chuzhak*) and a trader: "We are in our own home, so why should we be afraid of foreigners in our own country? They all trade; not one of them works."

45. *Informpolis*, 30 (174) (1996).

46. Diatlov (1995) estimates that 2.5 million Chinese were living in Russia in 1993, of which 1 million were long-term residents. In Irkutsk, according to official figures,

there were 40,000 arrivals during 1994; according to nonofficial estimates there were 72,000 to 110,000 arrivals in that year. These figures seem greatly exaggerated. According to Minakir (1996) there were no more than 50,000 to 80,000 Chinese immigrants in the entire Far Eastern territory of Russia.

47. The mechanism is for the trader to bring in goods, sell them to a Russian contact, and put the money in an underground Chinese bank, receiving a note whereby the sum can be recovered in yuan in China for the next trade trip. The Chinese bank can use the rubles received to purchase real estate or set up a joint venture, but most of the rubles are converted to dollars for illegal export back to China. It is said that ten to fifteen Chinese a day are arrested at the Irkutsk airport as money couriers (Diatlov 1995, 16).

48. *Pravda Buriatii* (1995): 2.

49. In the face of demands for sovereignty and ethnic unification, a presidential decree in the early 1990s made certain "lower" autonomous okrugs equal in status to republics and oblasts of the federation, thus giving them equal representation in Moscow and the opportunity to obtain direct credits from the center. This policy effectively disarmed the rhetoric of ethnic unification, since the okrugs could now operate with the center directly and gained no advantage by joining up with ethnic brethren.

5. Russian Protection Rackets and the Appropriation of Law and Order

1. Originally published in *States and Illegal Practices,* ed. Josiah Heymann (Oxford: Berg, 1999): 199–232.

2. Quotation marks have been placed round "law" when referring to the gangster's *zakon* partly to make the text clear for readers, and partly because the bandits' law did not have the paraphernalia of law as defined by professional lawyers (courts, prosecutors, and established procedures). However, in an anthropological comparative sense this was as much law as any other kind.

3. Thus Konstantinov (1996, 250) writes of what he calls the "cop's syndrome." According to one officer, this has two phases, the first when the cop sees any person as a potential criminal, and the second when bandits and thieves become more understandable, close, and intimate than ordinary law-abiding people. In this second phase the cop begins to feel at home in the world of thieves—and where you feel at home it is easy to change roles, or to take on another role.

4. Andrei Konstantinov, "Nepobedima li 'russkaya mafia,'" *Komsomol'skaia Pravda* (1997): 4.

5. UOP (*Upravlenie po bor'be s Organizovannoi Prestupnost'iu*) is the Directorate for Fighting Organized Crime.

6. Handelman (1994, 25) notes that the early Bolsheviks made a point of recruiting criminals to their cause, and that the harsh discipline, secrecy, and defiance of conventional society of the gangs also characterized the Bolshevik cells and eventually the Communist Party itself.

7. This opposition was strengthened by the waves of antirevolutionaries, dispossessed factory owners, and White sympathizers who joined the bandit ranks after 1919 (Rawlinson 1997, 37).

8. The term "thief" (*vor*) was used metonymically to refer to all types of self-defined criminals.

9. A "person" in criminal slang meant someone who had achieved the highest status category in the camps, that of *vor* (thief). Below this was the status of *muzhik* (peasant), and below that were the *chushki* (piglets) or *obizhennye* (hurt ones). Samoilov notes that within each of the three "castes" the same triple ranking would occur, so that the *chushki* had their own "thieves," "peasants," and "piglets" (Samoilov 1993, 35–37). Kabo (1993) also notes a triple ranking, though with different names.

10. Kabo (1993, 63–64) points to the tightly knit, disciplined, and hierarchical nature of bandit society (similar to that of the Communist Party), the parallel between proceedings against "bitches" and those against "enemies of the people," and the fact that low-ranking bandits were expected to labor honestly and pay an income tax.

11. For example, Koretskii (1996, 182) recounts how a thief in law was planning to hand over his ruling position in a camp but was unable to pass it to the most suitable man, as the latter was disqualified by common knowledge that he had infringed the "law" in the distant past.

12. The crime novel genre has its conventions, and realism is one of them. The wider Russian literary tradition of panoramic inclusiveness and huge casts of characters illustrating every social type is also evident here. Plot structures, hero and villain characteristics, and other features would be an interesting subject for research.

13. In Koretskii's novel *Anti-Killer* (1996, 156) a thief in law is attacked by a more traditional bandit for not respecting the law, and he replies, "I have not broken the law; I have not appropriated the treasury; everyone knows that."

14. Konstantinov (1996, 278). In some cases the gang may take over the running of the income source (garages, casinos, prostitutes) entirely, thus becoming a producer and providing "protection" to its own subsection.

15. The cost of such protection with guards in 1993–94 was 20–30 percent of the profits, and particularly greedy racketeers would demand 40 percent. The guards are not held responsible in cases of car theft, burglary, or physical attacks, and Konstantinov comments that they really only provide protection against drunks and street hooligans (1996, 175).

16. For example, the St. Petersburg Kazantsy were known for their inexplicable cruelty to the businessmen to whom they gave a roof. This surprised the Tambov gangsters, who said, "They are completely 'thawed out'; they squeeze their own clients dry and won't let them expand." But Konstantinov points out (1997, 296–297) that despite their apparent excessive violence, it would be wrong to judge the Kazantsy as lacking in all far-sightedness. It was they of all the gangs who had the strongest position among the law-protection agencies of the city.

17. In 1996, in St. Petersburg alone there were 468 security organizations and 191 bodyguard services officially registered. These firms employed 11,444 licensed agents, with an additional 1,500 other employees (Ivanov 1996).

18. The "thawed-outs" have their linguistic place alongside "cool ones," "laid-back ones" (*zamorozhennye*).

19. Varese also points out rightly that estimating a "sensible," as opposed to a "predatory" level of appropriation enables the supply of funds to continue regularly (1994, 257).

20. The New York State Organized Crime Force Report (1997, 200) makes the interesting observation that Russian émigré crime organization in the United States is different, consisting of "floating structures on an as-needed basis to enable them to carry out particular crimes." The difference may well be explainable by the fact that Russian-Americans do not base their operations on protection rackets but on crimes of deception, counterfeiting, confidence schemes, and insurance fraud (1997, 185–189).

21. In this case, it is forbidden by the thieves' law for other gangs to take over their "spots," although in practice this does happen, as can be understood from the rash of killings when famous bandits are released (Konstantinov 1996, 152).

22. In 1996, the whole of Moscow and its surroundings was "under" some fourteen gangs, and practically all businesses paid money to racketeers (Pogonchenkov 1996, based on police sources).

23. Dunn (1997, 65) thus provides a different picture of Moscow from Pogonchenkov: there are around 150 gangs, of which 20 are relatively large and well-armed and 6 wield real power. The difference arises mainly from the criteria by which "a gang" is defined: for example, Pogonchenkov counts "the Chechens" as one, while Dunn counts them as three gangs.

24. Handelman (1994, 29) writes that in the early 1990s there were around six hundred city-level bosses in Russia. Formally, these were equal, but some thirty senior leaders set general policy for the country's entire criminal class at private councils. Within this group, in the late 1980s and early 1990s there was an even smaller core, the *Bratskii Krug* (Circle of Brothers) consisting of around seven leading thieves in law. This seems like an overly tidy account, given the evidence of turbulence from other sources. Konstantinov declared at the end of 1997 that although organized crime had grown during the 1990s it was in a state of "feudal fragmentation," did not have a pyramidal structure for the country as a whole, and was not in fact as "organized" as people imagined. Andrei Konstantinov, Nepobedima li "russkaya mafia," *Komsomol'skaia Pravda* (9 December 1997): 4.

25. Even some of the currently largest gangs started in late Soviet times with "protection" of gambling and deceitful games of chance, and moved through prostitution and the cooperatives and supply depots of the Gorbachev era, to commercial businesses in the present ("Investitsionnye" 1996, 34).

26. For example, a fatal battle took place in Moscow in 1994 over the Aliens car showroom between a Slav gang and a Chechen gang (Dunn 1997, 68).

27. This can be seen from Hohnen's analysis (1997, 116–117) of the huge Gariunai market. Here only central trading places were judged worth paying for by traders. The racket took from $400 to $2,000 per place, according to the site, but did not bother with distant trading rows where traders made only minuscule profits.

28. The massive Togliatti factory is an example. Bandits have not succeeded in getting places on the board, but they take their toll from all purchasers (one car from each twenty ordered). One man attempted to defy them, the head of the Togliatti finance

department, whose father was highly placed in the local procuracy. The bandits left this man alone but attacked his "roof": the procurator's car was machine-gunned in the main street of the city, and since then payment of the toll has been universal ("Investitsionnye" 1996, 36).

29. This possibility is discussed by Sacco (1995, 111–112), who suggests that mafia codes of honor have this function because members of gangs are hired on the basis of "incomplete contracts": they are chosen for idiosyncratic abilities to perform unforeseeable tasks for uncertain remuneration.

30. In 1990, Kumarin and around seventy of his confederates were arrested, and in 1993, many of the Tambovtsy still free were murdered when it was rumored that Kumarin would shortly be released (Konstantinov 1996, 152–153).

31. These bands may not have defined territories, but they have some notion of common economic resources: for example, it is necessary to pay a redemption fee to leave the group (Koretskii 1996, 8–10).

32. Handelman (1994, 22–23) describes more ritualized initiations—for example, the kissing of a dagger and swearing allegiance before a portrait of the boss in Stavropol, or the respectful visiting of the graves of the elders in Ekaterinburg in 1992.

33. It is used to pay lawyers' fees, bribe officials, and support Chechens serving sentences (Dunn 1997, 66).

34. The bandit "Gorbatyi" ("Hunchback") said on his deathbed to Konstantinov, "A strong criminal world, with harsh discipline and internal laws, is only possible in a strong country. But no one wants a strong Russia these days" (Konstantinov 1996, 87).

35. Commenting that "bad and incomplete" law arouses nihilism and the wish to step beyond it, Konstantinov (1996, 272–274) cites a policeman who said that the meaning of his work was the same as the meaning of life. "And that is the struggle of Good and Evil. This struggle goes on everywhere, including in the soul of each person. I believe in the Good. Evil cannot eternally triumph—life will stop it. In our country much Evil has accumulated. It is difficult to overcome. Difficult, but possible. We must not give in."

36. "Welcome to the New World of Private Security," *The Economist* (19 April 1997): 25–26.

37. "Why should I pay all these taxes for pensions?" said one bandit. "Just give me three *babushki* (old women). I'll look after them. Then let me get on with my own life."

6. Rethinking Bribery in Contemporary Russia

1. Originally published in *Bribery and Blat in Russia: Negotiating Reciprocity from the Middle Ages to the 1990s*, ed. Steven Lovell, Alena Ledeneva, and Andrei Rogachevskii (New York: St. Martin's Press, 2000): 216–241.

2. As Noonan (1984) points out, the secrecy of bribery means that it is always impossible to document how much of it exists.

3. Another way to put this is that bonds of loyalty to close relations outweigh those to organizations, the state, or the social system itself (Reisman 1979, 136).

4. The contemporary English connotations of bribery may have changed historically from a form closer to the Russian, since the Middle English *briben*, to purloin or to steal, derives from the Old French *briber*, *brimbert*, to beg.

5. Hohnen (1997) describes how in contemporary Lithuania selling at the open market at Gariunai is regarded as shameful and traders hide from friends and relatives if they see them coming. People say, "The ones who trade are those without influential aunts and uncles." Bribery similarly is something done only if no other avenue is available.

6. It is more "easeful to the soul" (*spokoino na dushe*) to pay an open "fee" than to worry about how much to give undercover, one woman said to me.

7. See the distinction made by Firlit and Chlopecki (1992, 97–100), referring to Poland in the late 1980s–early 1990s, between "theft," which was highly stigmatized because it was conceived as an action against an individual, and "lifting" from one's place of work, which was regarded as morally tolerable because the bearer of the loss was abstract and unknown.

8. Pawlik (1992, 80) describes a similar ethic for Poland. Quoting a mechanic, Pawlik writes, "If you can't steal, then you can take bribes. Even the director who doesn't trouble himself with production, steals; he 'arranges' something for someone, 'takes' from him in return, and this is really stealing from him. Maybe that is really a worse crime than stealing from society, since society as a whole gets robbed [by the communist state]. But that director robs an individual."

9. In this period (1991–95) the smuggling out of unsanctioned strategic raw materials was counted as an administrative rather than a criminal offence, and therefore the KGB was not involved in following up cases. Until 1993, furthermore, there was no external frontier between Russia and the Baltic states, so for one and a half years between 1991 and 1993 Russian firms experienced a "golden period" of export during which they had to breach only one border (that of the former USSR). The smugglers were inadvertently aided by the activities of "Soviet nationalists," who burned down the first customs posts established with the Baltic countries (Konstantinov 1997, 307–308).

10. Lena's stamp was accredited to the wrong department, which was noticed by the customs official but not by Artem, the smuggler (Konstantinov 1997, 310).

11. In one of his speeches Gorbachev deplored the practice of *blat* and said that the government must improve the situation in the country so that *blat*, along with the verb *dostavat'* (to procure, obtain something with difficulty or through manipulation) would disappear from the Russian language (Corten 1992, 30).

12. The study found that in Russia birthdays are celebrated much more widely and frequently (a person often has several birthday parties) and at far greater cost than in Helsinki (Lonkila 1997, 6.4–6.5).

13. The intense desire for Western goods has been counteracted by a retroactive condemnation of them which goes together with a new positive discourse about Russian goods as "familiar," "pure," and "solid" (Humphrey 1995).

14. In her recent study of seven large businesses, Hertz (1997) demonstrates that Russian firms do rely above all on personal relations, often those established over many years and set up in Soviet times. Only two of the seven firms were beginning to look for new suppliers on the basis of price and quality, as opposed to using old links. Contracts are so open-ended that they are subject to endless renegotiation, while debts between

firms are very rarely pursued in the courts. In the frequent cases of nonpayment between companies, "friendly discussion" is preferred over any other option, and the firm owed money may even help the debtor firm sell its goods in order to keep the whole network afloat (1997, 114). In such a business environment, it is evident that shifting mutual indebtedness over rather long periods is the norm, and bribery is not only difficult to prove but may be less common than is generally supposed.

15. As Putnam (1993) noted in his study of civic traditions in different regions of Italy, customary practices and discourses regarding illegality can reach back for centuries.

16. "Everything I have described on the model of one producer should be translated into the scale of the entire country—thousands and thousands of workshops and factories—and then you will get an almost realistic picture of a gigantic organized subterranean business. The goods, geography, technology of production, all may change, but the structure of the crime remains the same—the substitution of costly components by cheap ones or the secret disposal of non-accounted materials, or both at the same time . . . The main problem was how to render discovery impossible, or at least unlikely" (Zemtsov 1976, 24–25).

17. Hertz (1997, 144) writes that in the mid-1990s, one major reason why foreign investors and shareholders in Russian companies tried to oust previous directors and insert their own man was to try to cut out the long-standing practice of selling on the side and distributing the proceeds upward.

18. Ruth Mandel, personal communication.

19. In more official language this is known as *moshchenichestvo* (extortion). In the courts, the distinction between bribery and extortion is often made according to whether the receiver of the payment is an official (bribery) or not (extortion) (Konstantinov 1997, 139), but ordinary Russians admit the idea of extortion by state officials too.

20. For example, see Konstantinov's account of one such case, when a bureaucrat accused of taking a bribe tried to argue that he took the money only because the briber showed him photographs of his children and threatened that they would suffer if he did not comply (1997, 189).

7. Avgai Khad

1. Originally published in *Anthropology Today* 9, no. 2 (1993): 13–16.

8. The Domestic Mode of Production in Post-Soviet Siberia?

1. This chapter grew out of an invitation from Stephen Gudeman and Richard Wilk to take part in a session of the American Anthropological Association's 1997 annual meeting devoted to Marshall Sahlins's classic text, *Stone Age Economics* (1972). It was originally published in *Anthropology Today* 14, 3 (1998): 3–7.

2. Chaianov's work (1966) inspired Sahlins and, as it concerns Russian peasant households, relates more closely to my own materials than to the tribal economies for which Sahlins adapted the model. Disapproved of in Soviet times, Chaianov has more recently been taken up by certain Russian academics, but his work has had little impact on policy makers.

3. The view that sees Russia as "Eurasia" emphasizes the Byzantine Orthodox religious tradition and the Mongol-Tatar idea of the state as an authoritarian, hierarchical organization (Suptelo 1997).

4. Urbanaeva writes about the thirteenth-century Mongols: "The understanding of *ulus*, which originally meant 'people-domain' or appanage, specifically 'people,' expresses the traditional mechanism by which the nomads established statehood. First, the *uluses* were gathered into a collectivity; second, however, not all collectivities were called *ulus*, but only those in which the 'people-domain' was organized as a dependency, as part of the vassal system. Thus, the Taichiiut, looked at as a series of kin-related clans, was seen as an *irgen* (a tribe of lineages). But the very same Taichiiut, or even just part of them, when united for example under the protection of Targutai-Kiriltukha, was an *ulus*, the 'people-domain' of a named khan. Subsequently, *ulus* came to mean the 'people-state' or the 'people forming a state domain.' Third, the 'collected' *ulus* was organized administratively, and had special civil servants who led its affairs and were rewarded by their 'share' (*khubi*) of the total wealth" (Urbanaeva 1995, 204).

5. This direct mapping occurs when a section of a clan dominates a section of a collective. It is almost never the case that a single clan dominates a whole collective, which is a large entity of 300–700 families.

6. In Siberian conditions and with the species kept by Buriats, only horses can live throughout the year with nothing more than hay as a winter supplement to grass grazing. Sheep, cattle, and pigs all require other, more concentrated fodders.

7. Buriats regard bread, noodles, and dumplings as core parts of their diet, though they do not eat as many flour products as Russians (Tulokhonov and Manzanova 1996, 146).

8. In 1992–93, some 15 percent of households indicated that they would like to separate off and set up as private farmers, according to a social survey in Buriatia. By 1996, the proportion had shrunk to 3 percent. The many complex reasons for this are discussed in Manzanova (1997) and Humphrey (1998).

9. Land spirit masters are called in Mongolian *gazaryn ezed* (sing. *ezen*), a word applied in daily life to the "master of the household" (*geriin ezen*). Buriats often use the Russian term *khoziain* (master), again both for spirit masters of the land and for political masters such as Stalin.

10. Whether to allow the buying and selling of land is still a matter of agonized debate at the highest levels—it is being called a "hellish mechanism" in the State Duma. The Russian President has withdrawn advocacy of land sales and now is struggling to persuade people of the usefulness of land mortgaging, the point being to enable farmers (collective or otherwise) to obtain credit without going through the corrupt state bureaucracy (Nikolai Kharitonov and Aleksandr Kotenkov, "Zemlya: prodavat'- ne Prodavat'." *Argumenty i Fakty* 42 (1997): 5.

11. Some collectives have not even gone this far, but operate entirely as in the late Soviet period, by work orders to members who earn wages.

12. Žižek (1997, 29–30) writes, "Each hegemonic universality has to incorporate *at least two* particular contents, the authentic popular content as well as its distortion by the

relations of domination and exploitation. . . . However, in order to be able to achieve this distortion of authentic longing, it has first to incorporate it. . . . Etienne Balibar was fully justified in reversing Marx's classic formula: the ruling ideas are precisely *not* directly the ideas of those who rule."

13. In Buriat regions prerevolutionary local communities were clan-based taxpaying units which allocated hay land and carried out certain collective works (irrigation, fencing, common moves to summer/winter pastures).

14. A Buriat philosopher has written that the worship of the ancestors is the essential act in which the individual gets his "face," his place in the social categorization of the world. In this context, one's *khubi* (share, destiny) is both inevitable and relative (to others), and it is immediate (specific in time). At another time, as one's place in the shifting web of relations changes, the share will be different (Morokhoeva 1992, 97).

15. In some West Buriat areas, the meat is chopped up so as to eliminate the symbolic differences between the parts of the animal in the shares (Sanzheev 1980, 115). This is not done elsewhere, and the symbolic significance of different parts of the carcass is used to mark social status.

16. Among Western Buriats earlier in the twentieth century, the meat trays were set out before a row of birch branches in a line, one branch for each family, using the common Mongolian denotation of seniority from west (senior) to east (junior) (Sanzheev 1980, 107).

17. Mongolia has privatized more thoroughly than Russia, and by 1997, few livestock were state or collectively owned.

18. Buriat writers contrast this with their understanding of the type of power exercised by the *khagan* (e.g., Chinggis Khan), which was essentially organizational rather than repressive. It was the moral fault of deception that was punished severely. Disobeying orders was a lesser matter punishable by fines. Imprisonment was hardly used at all by the Mongol state, for the political culture valued a kind of organized freedom (Urbanaeva 1995, 228). Nevertheless, other Buriats write of the likeness between the Soviet state, especially under Stalin, and "eastern despotism." "Therefore, the harsh unitary right (*edinonachalie*) of the ruler did not traumatize the ordinary Buriat in the way that it would have traumatized, for example, the Englishman spoilt by democracy" (Morokhoeva 1994, 172).

19. These should be paid for at reduced rates, well below market prices, but in fact the people usually cannot pay for them and remain in debt to the collective.

20. Anger is not a tight-lipped, polite kind of anger but a deeply insulting, annihilating fury which is frightening to behold (which one does very rarely, as it is hidden from foreigners).

21. Jagchid and Heyer (1979, 306–308) describe the Mongols' tributary relations with the Chinese emperor in terms of power-swayed trade, but Sahlins (1994) and Hevia (1994) provide a more culturally nuanced account of the way in which such rituals of tribute and obeisance defined the status of the subjects within the empire.

22. "Power resides in the office, in an organized acquiescence to chiefly privileges and organized means of upholding them. Included is a specific control over the goods and

services of the underlying population. The people owe in advance their labor and their products." (Sahlins 1972, 139).

23. It is virtually obligatory for heads of sectors and chairmen of collectives to have higher degrees in agricultural sciences.

9. The Villas of the "New Russians"

1. Originally published in *Focaal* 30–31 (1998): 85–106.
   I am very grateful to Viktor Buchli, Catherine Merridale, and the editors of *Focaal* for comments on an earlier draft of this paper, and to Catherine Cook, Baiar Gomboev, Sergei Panarin, and Balzhan Zhimbiev for helpful discussions and materials.

2. This chapter is based on research in Moscow and eastern Siberia in 1996–97. I talked with and visited some people who were described as New Russians, but had greater opportunity to discover other people's views of them from outside. I hope to do further research on this subject, which is why I call this chapter a sketch.

3. *Blat* refers to the practice of seeking personalized favors and backdoor transactions, which was omnipresent in the Soviet period.

4. New Russians prefer a range of English-derived terms for themselves—*professionaly* (professionals), *delovye liudi* (business people), *dilery* (dealers), *menadzhery* (managers) and so forth. The Russian *predprinimateli* (entrepreneurs) is used in reference, and *gospoda* (gentlemen) is often used in address—for example, in advertisements.

5. Alternatively, people may talk of New Buriats, New Kazakhs, and so forth.

6. This is a generalization; gender representations changed in interesting ways during Soviet history, though never portraying women as passive or dependent. See Bonnell (1991, 1993).

7. Unlike former state enterprises, which are often dependent on government subsidies, New Russians' businesses are relatively autonomous, and tax avoidance is endemic to the Russian economy. Former state enterprises often deal with the situation simply by not having any money, while the New Russians have invented a myriad of ways of secreting their millions from the tax authorities.

8. This example is given in the excellent analysis of nonpayment of wages in Russia by Clarke, Ashwin, and Borisov (1997, 5).

9. According to a World Bank study conducted in 1996, 64 percent of households had a total income per head below the official subsistence minimum of $66 per month. Half the households had only one-third of the amount they estimated they needed to live normally, 83 percent had less than two-thirds of that amount, and only 7 percent had what they considered a normal income (Clarke, Ashwin, and Borisov 1997, 10–11).

10. Preliminary analyses of the rich in terms of class are very contradictory. However, there is some agreement on the approximate numbers involved, although all observers note the difficulty in making such calculations when virtually everyone underreports their earnings to avoid taxes. Varoli (1996, 7), quoting Soviet sociological sources from 1994, writes that 1.6 percent of the population can afford to purchase nearly all of its desires, a figure that translates into 2.3 million people. He also mentions more recent American research which estimated that some 60,000 people earn

more than $1 million a year, while the ultrarich, around 1,000 individuals, earn tens of millions a year.

11. My own observations and the comments of well-informed Russians suggest that New Russians are little represented among the managers of the privatized industries, but newly set-up firms, banks, and stock exchanges are usually run by well-educated young people from a variety of backgrounds. Parts of government, too, are staffed by highly trained young technocrats: in an abrupt reversal of Soviet life, the old Party higher training schools have become schools of management studies and breeding grounds of potential New Russians. Many entrepreneurs made fortunes at the beginning of privatization, particularly in trading spin-offs from the oil and energy industries. Some of these diversified their firms and created subsidiaries, so, for example, someone who started by selling tires might now head a conglomerate including oil sales, garages, secondhand cars, timber trade, supermarket retailing, and so forth. The climate for starting new businesses worsened in the mid-1990s, making it difficult to move from trading into production. This is one reason why entrepreneurs have so frequently been accused of being "speculators" (Nelson and Kuzes 1995, 123; Humphrey 1996). However, the firms that flourished in the early 1990s are now established in the economy; tied in with local government and the banks (they may even set up their own banks), they are courted as "sponsors" by poverty-stricken organizations of all kinds. Another source of the New Russians are the protection-racket groups. These have increasingly taken hold of the privatized and retail sectors as the state's ability to enforce law weakened. A 1994 study showed that at least 70 percent of privatized enterprises and commercial banks in Russia had connections with organized crime (Nelson and Kuzes 1995, 131), and more recently Russians simply say that it is impossible these days to start a business without a "roof," meaning in this context a protector to whom illicit payments are made.

12. *Nomenklatura* refers to the lists of trusted officials who were placed in positions of responsibility in Soviet times. About nine-tenths of the *nomenklatura* directors of privatized enterprises remained in their positions at the end of voucher privatization (Nelson and Kuzes 1995, 129).

13. According to Eyal, Szelenyi, and Townsley (1997) the *nomenklatura* retains power in Russia, unlike the situation in Central Europe where a managerially skilled business elite is dominant. In Russia, power is used to amass personal wealth, especially in real estate, to a much greater extent than in Central Europe.

14. In parts of the CIS like Kazakhstan, the new rich may be radically differently constituted from those in Russia—relatives and clients of the President rather than heterogeneous and independent entrepreneurs.

15. It is important to remember that in the mid-1990s, many people were still in prison who had been charged with "private entrepreneurial activity" (Nelson and Kuzes 1995, 124).

16. Konstantinov (1997, 180) writes, "If we do not indulge in self-deception we must acknowledge that over 90 percent of the private business sector in Russia is linked one way or another with the world of bandits or thieves in law [racketeers]," and he re-

marks (1997, 175), "Protection rackets take 20–30 percent in cash of the monthly profits. It should be remembered that if another gang attacks, the racketeers will not protect the business and its owner, for whom they do not give a fig, but their own interests, their 20–30 percent."

17. Kryshtanovskaia's article (1997) describes a day in the life of a New Russian from the provinces. This was an 18.5-hour day of hectic activity, filled with eight important meetings, over six hours spent in shuttling between offices, fourteen contracts made over the phone, a total expenditure of $1,812, and only fifty minutes spent with his family.

18. The social currency of stereotypical jokes about New Russians is that they operate "in the opposite way from everyone else." For example: two New Russians meet on the street in Paris. One says to the other,

"That is a very splendid tie you are wearing. How much did you pay for it?"

"One thousand francs."

"Oh, you fool. I saw one round the corner for two thousand francs."

19. An essentialist understanding of identity would see it as the solidarity or allegiance naturally arising on the basis of recognition of the common origin or social characteristics of a group.

20. This could also be described as a failure of "hybridization" or "creolization," the process of recontextualization whereby foreign goods are assigned indigenous meanings and uses by the culture of reception (Howes 1996, 5–8).

21. Even large transactions are still normally made in cash (Ruble 1995, 70); mortgages, planned payments, and similar arrangements are still little known in Russia.

22. Leaders are also allotted luxurious country houses, known as *gosdachi* (state dachas).

23. Rykovtseva (1996) reports that, apart from the representatives of "the people," only Egor Gaidar and Pavel Grachev of the top leaders seemed to live fulltime in this block, which is nevertheless surrounded by numerous security guards and continuously supplied by couriers with food and other goods.

24. The first such plots were usually 800 square meters (8 *sotok*) in size, and later ones were 600 and 400 square meters. They were given to women with more than three children, veterans, and deserving invalids, among others.

25. A *sotka* (gen. pl. *sotok*) is 100 square meters.

26. Even by mid-1992, the Leningrad Region had established a zone, extending up to 70 kilometers round the city, in which 250,000 building sites were allocated for detached dwellings (Ruble 1995, 123).

27. In the summer of 1996 in Ulan-Ude, a wooden house cost 1.6 million rubles per square meter to build, whereas a brick house cost 3 to 4 million rubles per square meter (interview with P. G. Zilberman, head architect of the city of Ulan-Ude).

28. In 1990, around 15 percent of city dwellers in the Russian Federation lived in log houses (Ruble 1995, 68), which were "private property," although the land they stood on was the property of the state. Such houses are commonly without running water, drainage, or central heating, though they usually have electricity. They are considered inferior to apartments and Russians normally move out of them when they can, so in effect they remain the habitations of the disadvantaged.

29. This unusually well-built development of large private houses included some much smaller houses for the victims of a recent flood. One can imagine that the city had aimed to cover the costs of the flood relief housing by selling the villas. Some flood victims were living in their houses, but the villas were unfinished.

30. The General Plan of Ulan-Ude is in force until 2005 and the city architect was awaiting the arrival of the new one, 2005–20. These plans are still designed in St. Petersburg, but with the consultation of local planners.

31. "Have you any idea how many bits of paper must be collected to build that villa? . . . In the kingdom of the magnificent palaces there will necessarily be one small hut with a flag on its roof—the local administration. Though your house may be your castle, whatever you want to do (let's say, to move a doorway) you'll have to go to the administrator on your knees. And the 'people's control' over there love collecting your donations for themselves" (Sivkova 1997, 2).

32. Individuals may request a land committee for a site, and the committee then offers them a plot on one of the areas it has acquired for villa development. Alternatively, the land committee may allocate land to an institution or firm, which then builds the villas and advertises them for sale.

33. It is almost as though firms use new types of heating systems and so forth in order to eliminate the native workman. "The plumber with a cluster of packing fiber hanging out of his pocket has been banished to the ranks of comedy films" (*Business in Russia* 1995, xxv).

34. This arouses much dismay among architects and is regarded as a continuation of the subdued war between the profession and the Ministry of Construction of Soviet times (interview with the head of the State Committee for Architecture of Buriatia, July 1997). Architects' struggles to be included in the design and decision-making process for important projects have sharpened since the state-run Buriat Civic Project was privatized as a joint-stock construction company. In Buriatia the economic situation is so serious that there is little work for the company; however, it has remained as a *kollektiv* and makes ends meet by trading in wood, fertilizer, and other products.

35. Such an album of designs for individual houses was produced by architects of Buriatia in 1996. The plans include houses in wood and brick, with many interesting native and vernacular features, but none of them has been built.

36. These include the Church of the Kazan Mother of God on Red Square, the Cathedral of Christ the Savior in place of the open swimming baths in the center of Moscow, the Red Porch of the Great Kremlin Palace, and the palace of the Russian President.

37. See Luzhkov (1996). The foreword starts, "In Moscow it is not only the power which has changed, it is the whole concept of what power is. We shall implement a mechanism of government which is founded on the idea of service, not command. We shall establish an administration in which power is no longer an instrument of forcing people to reach targets set from above but is part of the capital's service system to improve the capital's economy."

10. Shamans in the City

1. Originally published in *Anthropology Today* 15, 3 (1999): 3–10.
2. See, however, Kuczynski (1988) on African marabouts in Paris.
3. Hoppal means by this phrase shamanism that has survived modernity. He distinguishes the continuous traditions of places like Korea from the revived traditions of Siberian regions like Sakha or Tyva, and both of these from "neo-shamanism," the reinvention of shamanism in Europe, America, and parts of Russia where shamanic practices were almost obliterated.
4. One of the numerous cultic groups at large in Russia in the mid-1990s. The government has since tried to limit the activities of such groups.
5. Agniezska Halemba, private communication.
6. Stefan Krist, private communication.
7. Terms for spiritual energies in Buddhist idiom

BIBLIOGRAPHY

Alexander, P. 1992. "What's in a Price?" In *Contesting Markets: Analyses of Ideology, Discourse, and Practice*. Edited by Roy Dilley, 79–96. Edinburgh: Edinburgh University Press.

Anderson, David. 2000. *Identity and Ecology in Arctic Siberia: The Number One Reindeer Brigade*. Oxford: Oxford University Press.

——. 1995. "National Identity and Belonging in Arctic Siberia: An Ethnography of Evenkis and Dolgans at Khantaiskoe Ozero in the Taimyr Autonomous District." Ph.D. Dissertation, University of Cambridge.

Appadurai, Arjun. 1996. *Modernity at Large*. Minneapolis: Minnesota University Press.

——. 1991. "Global Ethnoscapes: Notes and Queries for a Transnational Anthropology." In *Recapturing Anthropology: Working in the Present*. Edited by Richard Fox, 191–210. Santa Fe, N.M.: School of American Research.

——. 1986. *The Social Life of Things*. Cambridge: Cambridge University Press.

——. 1981. "The Past as a Scarce Resource." *Man* 16, 2: 201–219.

Bachelard, Gaston. 1994 [1958]. *The Poetics of Space*. Boston: Beacon Press.

Baiduzhii, Andrei. 1993. "Tat'iana Regent: Rossiia ne mozhet vypolnit' svoi obiazatel'stva v otnoshenii bezhentsev" [Tat'iana Regent: Russia cannot fulfill her obligations with regard to refugees]. *Nezavisimaia gazeta* (23 April): 6.

Baldaev, D. S. 1989. Unpublished drawings of prisoners' tattoos. Some of Baldaev's drawings of life in the camps are published in the Hungarian journal *Beszélő* (August 31, 1991).

Balzer, Marjorie Mandelstam. 1999. *The Tenacity of Ethnicity: A Siberian Saga in Global Perspective*. Princeton, N.J.: Princeton University Press.

——. 1993. "Two Urban Shamans." In *Perilous States: Conversations amid Uncertain Transitions*. Edited by G. Marcus, 131–164. Chicago: University of Chicago Press.

Barthes, Roland. 1985 [1982]. *The Responsibility of Forms*. Translated by Richard Howard. Oxford: Basil Blackwell.

——. 1979. *The Eiffel Tower and Other Mythologies*. Translated by Richard Howard. New York: The Noonday Press.

———. 1957. *Mythologies*. Paris: Editions du Seuil.

Bataille, Georges. 1998. *The Accursed Share: An Essay on General Economy*. New York: Zone.

Bauman, Richard, and Charles L. Briggs. 1990. "Poetics and Performance as Critical Perspectives on Language and Social Life." *Annual Reviews of Anthropology* (19): 59–88.

Berkutov, Viktor. 1996. *Krysha: russkie razborki*. Moscow: Martin Polina.

Bloch, Maurice. 1995. *Interpreting Archaeology: Finding Meaning in the Past*. London: Routledge.

———. 1989. "The Past and the Present in the Present." In *Ritual, History, and Power: Selected Papers in Anthropology*. London: Athlone Press.

Bonet, Pilar. 1992. Figures in a Red Landscape. Translated by N. T. di Giovanni and S. Ashe. Washington, D.C.: Woodrow Wilson Center Press and Baltimore: Johns Hopkins University Press.

Bonnell, Victoria E. 1993. "The Peasant Woman in Stalinist Political Art." *American Historical Review* 98 (1): 55–82.

———. 1991. "The Representation of Women in Early Soviet Political Art." *Russian Review* 50: 267–288.

Boym, Svetlana. 1994. *Common Places: Mythologies of Everyday Life in Russia*. Cambridge, Mass.: Harvard University Press.

Bredin, Marian. 1996. "Transforming Images: Communication Technologies and Cultural Identity in Nishnawbe-Aski." In *Cross-Cultural Consumption: Global Markets, Local Realities*. Edited by David Howes. London: Routledge.

Brubaker, W. Rogers. 1992. "Citizenship Struggles in the Soviet Successor States." *International Migration Review* 26 (2): 269–291.

Brumfield, William Craft. 1993. "Redesigning the Russian House, 1895 to 1917." In *Russian Housing in the Modern Age: Design and Social History*. Edited by W. C. Brumfield and B. A. Ruble. Woodrow Wilson Center Series. Cambridge: Cambridge University Press.

Bruno, Marta. 1997. "Women and the Culture of Entrepreneurship." In *Post-Soviet Women: From the Baltic to Central Asia*. Edited by Mary Buckley. Cambridge: Cambridge University Press.

Bukovskii, V. 1981. *Pis'ma russkogo puteshestvennika* [Letters of a Russian traveler]. New York: Chalidze Publications.

Burawoy, Michael, and Pavel Krotov. 1993. "The Economic Basics of Russia's Political Crisis." *New Left Review* 198: 49–69.

Bushnell, John. 1990. *Moscow Graffiti: Language and Subculture*. Boston: Unwin Hyman.

Butler, W. E. 1991. *The Customs Code of the USSR and the Law on the Customs Tariff of the USSR*. Introduced and Translated by W. E. Butler. London: Interlist.

Carrier, James, ed. 1997. *Meanings of the Market: The Free Market in Western Culture*. Oxford: Berg.

Carsten, Janet and Hugh-Jones, Stephen. 1996. "About the House, Lévi-Strauss and Beyond." *Architectural Design*, profile no. 24, Special Issue on Architecture and Anthropology: 66–67.

Chaianov, A. V. 1966 [1925]. *The Theory of Peasant Economy*. Edited by Daniel Thorner, Basile Kerblay, and R. G. F. Smith with a foreword by Teodor Shanin. Manchester: Manchester University Press.

Chalidze, Valerii. 1977. *Criminal Russia: A Study of Crime in the Soviet Union*. Translated by R. Falla. New York: Random House.

Cheremisov, K. M. 1973. *Buryaad-Orod slovar', Buriatsko-russkii slovar'*. Moscow: Izdatel''stvo Sovetskaia Entsiklopediia.

Chock, P. P. 1991. " 'Illegal Aliens' and 'Opportunity'—Myth-making in Congressional Testimony." *American Ethnologist* 18 (2): 279–295.

Clarke, Simon. 1992. "Privatization and the Development of Capitalism in Russia." *New Left Review* 196: 3–27.

Clarke, Simon, Sarah Ashwin, and Vadim Borisov. 1997. "The non-payment of wages in Russia." Unpublished ms.

Colloredo-Mansfield, Rudolf. 1994. "Architectural Conspicuous Consumption and Economic Change in the Andes." *American Anthropologist* 96 (4): 848–865.

Condee, Nancy, and Vladimir Padunov. 1995. "The ABC of Russian Consumer Culture." In *Soviet Hieroglyphics: Visual Culture in Late Twentieth-Century Russia*. Edited by Nancy Condee, 130–172. Bloomington: Indiana University Press.

Corten, Irina. 1992. *Vocabulary of Soviet Society and Culture*. Durham, N.C.: Duke University Press.

Diatlov, V. 1995. " 'Torgovye men'shinstva" sovremennogo Irkutska: problema stabil'nosti i konflikta v rossiiskoi provintsii." Unpublished ms.

Diatlov, V., D. Demid, and E. Palyutina. 1995. " 'Kavkaztsy' v rossiiskoi provintsii: kriminal'nyi episod kak indikator urovnia mezhetnicheskoi naprayzhennosti." *Acta Eurasica* [Moscow] 1 (1): 46–63.

Dilley, Roy, ed. 1992. *Contesting Markets: Analyses of Ideology, Discourse, and Practice*. Edinburgh: Edinburgh University Press.

Douglas, Mary. 1967. "Primitive Rationing." In *Themes in Economic Anthropology*. Edited by Raymond Firth, 119–148. London: Tavistock.

Dunn, Guy. 1997. "Major Mafia Gangs in Russia." In *Russian Organized Crime: A New Threat?* Edited by Phil Williams, 63–87. London: Frank Cass.

Eyal, Gil, Ivan Szelenyi, and Eleanor Townsley. 1997. "The Theory of Post-Communist Managerialism." *New Left Review* 222: 60–92.

Fedin, E. 1995. "Chto godit'sia po granitse podoidet i TEKu." Business *Moskovskie Novosti* (20 September): 1.

Field, Daniel. 1989 [1976]. *Rebels in the Name of the Tsar*. Boston: Unwin Hyman.

Figes, Orlando. 1989. *Peasant Russia, Civil War: The Volga Countryside in Revolution 1917–1921*. Oxford: Clarendon Press.

Firlit, Elzbieta, and Jerzy Chlopecky. 1992. "When Theft Is Not Theft." In *The Unplanned Society: Poland during and after Socialism*. Edited by Janine Wedel, 95–109. New York: Columbia University Press.

Friedman, J. 1990. "Being in the World: Globalization and Localization." In *Global Culture: Nationalism, Globalization and Modernity*. Edited by M. Featherstone, 311–328. London: Sage Publications.

Gal, Susan. 1991. "Bartok's Funeral: Representations of Europe in Hungarian Political Rhetoric." *American Ethnologist* 18 (3): 440–458.

———. 1989. "Language and Political Economy." *Annual Reviews in Anthropology* 18: 345–367.

Garros, Véronique. 1992. "Dans l'ex-URSS: de la difficulté d'écrire l'histoire." *Cahiers des Annales* 47: 989–1002.

Gates, Hill. 1996. *China's Motor: A Thousand Years of Petty Capitalism*. Ithaca, N.Y.: Cornell University Press.

Gellner, Ernest. 1994. *Conditions of Liberty: Civil Society and Its Rivals*. London: The Penguin Press.

———. 1981. *Muslim Society*. Cambridge: Cambridge University Press.

Gomelev, L. 1995. "Za derzhavu obidno." *Pravda Buriatii* (Ulan-Ude) (17 March): 2.

Goriacheva, I. 1993. "Stoimost' produktov s nachala goda vyrosla na 70 protsentov." *Izvestiia* (24 March).

Grant, Bruce. 1995. *In the Soviet House of Culture: A Century of Perestroikas*. Princeton, N.J.: Princeton University Press.

———. 1993. "Siberia Hot and Cold." In *Between Heaven and Hell: The Myth of Siberia in Russian Culture*. Edited by Galya Diment and Yuri Slezkine, 227–253. New York: St. Martin's Press.

Groys, Boris. 1993. "Stalinism as Aesthetic Phenomenon." In *Tekstura: Russian Essays on Visual Culture*. Edited by A. Efimova and L. Manovich, 115–126. Chicago: University of Chicago Press.

———. 1992. *The Total Art of Stalinism: Avant-Garde, Aesthetic Dictatorship, and Beyond*. Translated by C. Rougle. Princeton, N.J.: Princeton University Press.

Hall, Stuart. 1996. "Introduction: Who Needs Identity?" In *Questions of Cultural Identity*. Edited by Stuart Hall and Paul du Gay, 1–11. London: Sage Publications.

Haltod, Mattai, John Gombojab Hangin, and Ferdinand Lessing. 1982. *Mongolian-English Dictionary*. Bloomington, Ind.: The Mongolia Society.

Handelman, Stephen. 1995. *Comrade Criminal: Russia's New Mafiya*. Updated edition. New Haven: Yale University Press.

———. 1994. *Comrade Criminal: The Theft of the Second Russian Revolution*. London: Michael Joseph.

Hansen, E. 1993. "Living Conditions on the Kola Peninsula." FAFO-SOTECO Report no. 155. Oslo: FAFO-SOTECO.

Hertz, Noreena. 1997. *Russian Business Relationships in the Wake of Reform*. London: Macmillan Press.

Herzfeld, Michael. 1991. *A Place in History: Social and Monumental Time in a Cretan Town*. Princeton, N.J.: Princeton University Press.

———. 1987. *Anthropology Through the Looking-Glass: Critical Ethnography in the Margins of Europe*. Cambridge: Cambridge University Press.

——. 1986. "Of Definitions and Boundaries: The Status of Culture in the Culture of the State." In *Discourse and the Social Life of Meaning*. Edited by P.P. Chock and J.R. Wyman, 75–93. Washington, D.C.: Smithsonian Institution Press.

——. 1985. "Lévi-Strauss in the Nation-State." *Journal of American Folklore* 98: 191–208.

Hevia, James. 1994. "Sovereignty and Subject: Constituting Relations of Power in Qing Guest Ritual." In *Body, Subject and Power in China*. Edited by A. Zito and T. Barlow, 181–200. Chicago: University of Chicago Press.

Hohnen, Pernille. 1997. "A Market Out of Place? Remaking Economic, Social, and Symbolic Boundaries in Post-Communist Lithuania." Ph.D. dissertation. Institute of Anthropology, University of Copenhagen.

Hoppal, Mihaly. 1996. "Shamanism in Postmodern Age." In *Tsentral'no-Aziatskii Shamanizm: Simpozium iiunia 1996*, 108–110. Ulan-Ude: Russian Academy of Sciences.

Howes, David. 1996. "Introduction: Commodities and Cultural Borders." In *Cross-Cultural Consumption*. Edited by D. Howes, 1–18. London: Routledge.

Humphrey, Caroline. 2000. "An Anthropological View of Barter in Russia" and "How is Barter Done? The Social Relations of Barter in Provincial Russia." In *The Vanishing Rouble: Barter Networks and Non-Monetary Transactions in Post-Socialist Societies*. Edited by Paul Seabright, 71–92 and 259–297. Cambridge: Cambridge University Press.

——. 1999. "Russian Protection Rackets and the Appropriation of Law and Order. In *States and Illegal Practices*. Edited by J. Heyman. Oxford: Berg.

——. 1998. *Marx Went Away, But Karl Stayed Behind* (updated edition of *Karl Marx Collective*), University of Michigan Press.

——. 1997. "Myth-making, Narratives, and the Dispossessed in Russia." *Cambridge Anthropology* 19 (2): 70–92.

——. 1995. "Creating a Culture of Disillusionment: Consumption in Moscow in 1993, a Chronicle of Changing Times." In *Worlds Apart*. Edited by Daniel Miller. London: Routledge.

——. 1991. " 'Icebergs,' Barter, and the Mafia in Provincial Russia." *Anthropology Today* 7 (2): 8–13.

——. 1989. "Janus-faced Signs: The Language of Politics of an Ethnic Minority in the Soviet Union." In *Social Anthropology and the Politics of Language*, Sociological Review Monograph 36. Edited by R. Grillo, 145–175. London and New York: Routledge.

——. 1985. "Barter and Economic Disintegration" *Man* (March).

——. 1983. *Karl Marx Collective: Economy, Society and Religion in a Siberian Collective Farm*. Cambridge: Cambridge University Press.

Humphrey, Caroline, and David Sneath. 1999. *The End of Nomadism? Society, State, and the Environment in Inner Asia*. Durham, N.C.: Duke University Press.

"Investitsionnye proekty rossiiskikh banditov." 1996. *Kommersant Daily* (27 August): 34–36.

Ivanov, Andrei. 1996. "Chastnye okhranniki: svoi sredi chuzhikh, chuzhie sredi svoikh." *AiF-Peterburg* 51 (174): 5.

Jagchid, Sechin, and Paul Hyer. 1979. *Mongolia's Culture and Society*. Boulder, Colo.: Westview Press.

Kabo, V. R. 1993. "The Structure of the Camps and Archetypes of Consciousness." *Anthropology and Archaeology of Eurasia* 32 (3): 59–69.

Karaulov, Andrei. 1993. *Vokrug Kremlia*, Volume 2. Moscow: Izdatel'stvo Slovo.

———. 1990. *Vokrug Kremlia: kniga politicheskikh dialogov*. Moscow: Novosti.

Kavelin, K. 1989. *Nash Umstuenny Stroi*. Moscow: Pravda.

Kelly, Aileen. 1987. "Self-Censorship and the Russian Intelligentsia, 1905–1914." *Slavic Review* 46 (2): 193–213.

Kendall, Laurel. 1996. "Korean Shamans and the Spirits of Capitalism." *American Anthropologist* 98 (3): 502–527.

Khagaev, V. V. 1998. *Shamanizm i mirovye religii*. Irkutsk: Izdanie GP.

Khaldurova, N. 1993. "Sultanki, Generaly, Chankaishisty, i drugie." Unpublished ms. Later published as "Molodezh Ulan-Ude: 'Sultanki,' 'generaly,' 'chankaishisty' i drugie," *Acta Eurasia, Vestnik Evrazii*, no. 1 (Moscow 1995): 167–172.

Khamgushkeev, L. M. 1997. "Sviashchennye korni moi." *Doklady i tezisy mezhdunarodnogo simpoziuma "Buriat-Mongoly nakanune III tysiacheletiia: opyt kochevoi tsivilizatsii, Rossiia-Vostok-Zapad v sud'be narod,"* 148–149. Ulan-Ude: Russian Academy of Sciences.

Khangalov, M. N. 1958. *Sobranie sochinenii*, 1. Ulan-Ude: Buriatskoe Knizhnoe Izdatel'stvo.

Khapeva, Dina, and Nikolai Kopossov. 1992. "Les démi-dieux de la mythologie soviétique." Étude sur les représentations collectives de l'histoire. *Cahiers des Annales* 47 (4–5): 963–988.

Kharkhordin, Oleg. 1999. *The Collective and the Individual in Russia: A Study of Practices*. Berkeley: University of California Press.

Khokhlov, A. N. 1985. "The Kiakhta Trade and Its Effect on Russian and Chinese Policy in the Eighteenth and Nineteenth Centuries." In *Chapters from the History of Russo-Chinese Relations: Seventeenth to Nineteenth Centuries*. Edited by S. L. Tikhvinskii, 214–256. Moscow: Progress Publishers.

Konstantinov, Andrei. 1996. *Banditskii Peterburg*. St. Petersburg: Folio Press.

Konstantinov, Andrei, et. al. 1997. *Korrumpirovannyi Peterburg*. St. Petersburg: Folio-Press.

Konstantinov, Iulian. 1997. "Memory of Lenin, Ltd.: Reindeer-herding Collectives on the Kola Peninsula." *Anthropology Today* 13 (3): 14–19.

Kordonskii, Simon. 2000. *Rynki vlasti: Administrativnye rynki SSSR i Rossii*. Moscow: OGI.

Koretskii, Daniil. 1996. *Anti-Killer*. Moscow: Eksmo.

Korotkova, Elena. 1999. "Tropa dukhov: puteshestvie s shamankoi v potustoronnii mir." *Pravda Buriatii* (29 May, 1999): 6.

Krom, Yelena. 1996. "Profi—eto khorosho trenirovannyi zombi." *Chas Pik* 217 (722) (18 December): 10.

Kryshtanovskaia, O. 1997. "Odin den' iz zhizni 'novogo russkogo.'" *Argumenty i Fakty* no. 19: 7.

Kuczynski, Liliane. 1988. "Return of Love: Everyday Life and African Divination in Paris." *Anthropology Today* 4 (3): 6–9.

Kurochkin, V. 1995. "Nesbyvshiesia nadezhdy." *Pravda Buriatii* [Ulan-Ude] (17 March): 2.

Lacaze, Gaelle. 1996. "Thoughts about the Effectiveness of the Shamanism Speech: Preliminary Data to the Study of Today's Uses of Maledictions by the Darxad of the Xovsgol." In *Tsentral'no-aziatskii shamanizm: simpozium iiunia 1996*. Ulan-Ude: Russian Academy of Sciences, pp. 149–150.

Ledeneva, Alena. 1998. *Russia's Economy of Favors: Blat, Networking and Informal Exchange*. Cambridge: Cambridge University Press.

———. 1996. "Formal Institutions and Informal Networks in Russia: A Study of Blat." Ph.D. dissertation, University of Cambridge.

Lemon, Alaina. 1997. "Talking Transit and Transition: The Moscow Metro." In *Ethnographies of Transition in East Central Europe and Russia*. Edited by M. Lampland, M. Bunzl, and D. Berdahl, 14–39. Oxford: Berg Press.

———. 1996. "Indic Diaspora, Soviet History, Russian Home: Political Performances and Sincere Ironies in Romani Cultures." Ph.D. Dissertation. University of Chicago.

Leonhardt, Manuela. 1998. "Report about fieldwork in Derbent, Daghestan." November. Unpublished ms.

Lonkila, M. 1997. "Informal Exchange Relations in Post-Soviet Russia: A Comparative Perspective." *Sociological Research Online* 2 (2). (http://www.socresonline.org.uk/socresonline/2/2/9.html.)

Luzhkov, Iurii. 1996. *My deti tvoi, Moskva*. Moscow: Vagrius.

Maksimova, Vera. 1997. "Spor mezhdu novymi i vechnymi russkimi." *Izvestiia* (5 June): 6.

Manzanova, G. B. 1997. "Trudovye motivatsii zhiteli natsional'nykh grupp v period krizisa sel'skoi obshchnosti." Unpublished ms.

Marchenko, Anatolii. 1989. *To Live Like Everyone*. London: I.B. Tauris and Co., Ltd.

Marzeeva, Svetlana. 1996. "Reket zhil, reket zhiv, reket budet zhit." *Izvestiia* 130 (17 July): 5.

Miller, Daniel. 1994a. *Modernity, An Ethnographic Approach: Dualism and Mass Consumption in Trinidad*. Oxford: Berg.

———. 1994b. "Artefacts and the Meaning of Things." In *Companion Encyclopedia of Anthropology*. Edited by T. Ingold. London: Routledge.

———. 1987. *Material Culture and Mass Consumption*. Oxford: Blackwell.

Minakir, P. A. 1996. "Kitaiskaia immigratsiia na rossiiskom dal'nem vostoke: regional'nye, natsional'nye, and mezhdunarodnye aspekty problemy." Unpublished paper given at the International Conference on Migration in Post-Soviet Space, Minsk.

Morokhoeva, Z. P. 1994. *Lichnost' v kul'turakh Vostoka i Zapada*. Novosibirsk: Nauka.

———. 1992. "Problema individual'nogo v traditsionnoi Buriatskoi kul'ture." In Filosofiia i istoriia kul'tury: natsional'nyi aspekt. Edited by Z. P. Morokhoeva, 89–114. Ulan-Ude: Russian Academy of Sciences.

Nelson, Lynn D., and Irina Y. Kuzes. 1995. "Privatization and the New Business Class." In *Russia in Transition: Politics, Privatization, and Inequality*. Edited by David Lane, 119–141. London: Longman.

New York State Organized Crime Force. 1997. "An Analysis of Russian Emigré Crime in the Tri-State Region." In *Russian Organized Crime: A New Threat?* Edited by Phil Williams, 177–226. Frank Cass: London.

Nikitina, E. 1996. " 'Chelnoki' tonut v more poshlin." *Argumenty i Fakty* (32): 7.

Nikolaev, V. 1994. "Onokhoiskii peredel 1. Kombinat zakryt. Vsekh ushli . . . po iagodu, 2. Mama, mama, chto my budem delat' . . . " *Pravda Buriatii* [Ulan-Ude] (8 and 9 September): 2.

Nikol'skii, Sergei. 1993a. "Agrarnaia reforma i krest'ianskii fundamentalizm." *Krest'ianskie vedomosti* no. 2 (22–29 March).

———. 1993b. "V Rossii krest'iane lishnye liudi?" *Moskovskie novosti* (4 April).

Noonan, John T., Jr. 1984. *Bribes.* New York: Macmillan.

Obeev, S. 1992. "Sem'ia—tema vechnaia." *Buriatiia* (28 October): 2.

Omel'chenko, Elena. 1996. "Young Women in Provincial Gang Culture: A Case Study of Ul'ianovsk." In *Gender, Generation and Identity in Contemporary Russia.* Edited by Hilary Pilkington, 216–235. London: Routledge.

Osinskii, P. 1994. " 'Novyi klass' v zerkale sotsiologii." *Buriatiia* (14 January).

Oushakine, Sergei. 2000. "The Quantity of Style: Imaginary Consumption in the New Russia." *Theory, Culture and Society* 17 (5): 98–120.

Owen, Thomas C. 1991. *The Corporation under Russian Law, 1800–1917: A Study in Tsarist Economic Policy.* Cambridge: Cambridge University Press.

———. 1981. *Capitalism and Politics in Russia: A Social History of the Moscow Merchants, 1855–1905.* Cambridge: Cambridge University Press.

Panarin, Sergei. 1993. "Tadzhiki-bezhentsy v gorodakh sibiri." Unpublished ms. Later published under the same title in *Acta Eurasica Vestnik Azii* 2, no. 1 (1996): 154–165.

Parry, J. 1989. "On the Moral Perils of Exchange." In *Money and the Morality of Exchange.* Edited by J. Parry and M. Bloch, 64–93. Cambridge: Cambridge University Press.

Pawlik, Wojciech. 1992. "Intimate Commerce." In *The Unplanned Society: Poland during and after Socialism.* Edited by Janine Wedel, 78–94. New York: Columbia University Press.

Pejovich, Svetozar. 1997. "The Transition Process in an Arbitrary State: The Case for the Mafia." *International Business Review* 1: 1.

Perevalova, T. 1994. "Zima, avtobus, i . . . proza zhizni." *Buriatiia* (20 December): 4.

Pesmen, Dale. 2000. *Russia and Soul: An Exploration.* Ithaca, N.Y.: Cornell University Press.

Pilkington, Hilary. 1994. *Russia's Youth and Its Culture: A Nation's Constructors and Constructed.* London: Routledge.

Pipes, R. 1974. *Russia under the Old Regime.* London: Penguin Books.

Pluzhnikov, N. V. 1996. " 'Lichnyi mif' v shamanskoi praktike narodov Sibirii." In *Tsentral'no-aziatskii shamanizm: simpozium iiunia 1996,* 146–147. Ulan-Ude: Russian Academy of Sciences.

Pogonchenkov, Aleksandr. 1996. "Anatomiia kriminal'nogo mira." *Moskovskii Komsomolets* (12 August): 3.

Polukeev, O. 1995. "Bandity ubivaiut, GAIshniki otbiraiut." *Business Moskovskie novosti* (20 September): 4.

Putnam, Robert D. 1993. *Making Democracy Work: Civic Traditions in Modern Italy.* Princeton, N.J.: Princeton University Press.

Rawlinson, Patricia. 1997. "Russian Organized Crime: A Brief History." In *Russian Organized Crime: A New Threat?* Edited by Phil Williams, 28–52. London: Frank Cass.

'Razborki v Irkutske: Irkutskaia Mafiia svodit schety s gruzinskoi gruppirovki." 1996. *Informpolis* (Irkutsk) 174, 30 (25 July).

Reisman, W. Michael. 1979. *Folded Lies: Bribery, Crusades and Reforms.* New York: The Free Press.

Revzin, Gennadi. 1993. "Paper Architecture in the Age of the French Revolution." In *Tekstura: Russian Essays on Visual Culture.* Edited by A. Efimova and L. Manovich, 219–231. Chicago: University of Chicago Press.

Ries, Nancy. Forthcoming. "'Honest Bandits' and 'Warped People': Russian Narratives about Money, Corruption, and Moral Decay." In *Ethnography in Unstable Places.* Edited by Carol Greenhouse, Kay Warren, and Elizabeth Mertz. Durham: Duke University Press.

———. 1997. *Russian Talk: Culture and Conversation during Perestroika.* Ithaca, N.Y.: Cornell University Press.

Ruble, Blair A. 1995. *Money Sings: The Changing Politics of Urban Space in Post-Soviet Iaroslavl.* Cambridge: Cambridge University Press.

Rykovtseva, E. 1996. "Nash dom—Osennaia, 4." *Moskovskie novosti* no. 26: 27.

Sacco, Pier Luigi. 1995. "Discussion." In *The Economics of Organized Crime.* Edited by Gianluca Fiorentini and Sam Peltzman, 109–115. Cambridge: Cambridge University Press.

Sahlins, Marshall. 1994. "Cosmologies of Capitalism: The Trans-Pacific Sector of 'The World System.'" In *Culture/Power/History: A Reader in Contemporary Social Theory.* Edited by N. Dirks, G. Eley and S. Ortner, 412–456. Princeton, N.J.: Princeton University Press.

———. 1972. *Stone Age Economics.* London: Tavistock Publications.

Samoilov, Lev. 1993. "Ethnography of the Camp." *Anthropology and Archaeology of Eurasia* 32 (3): 32–58.

Sanzheev, G. D. 1980. "Tailgan Buriatskikh kuznetsov." In *Byt Buriatov v nastoiashchem i proshlom.* Edited by K. D. Basaeva, 100–120. Ulan-Ude: AN SSSR BFION.

Scott, James. 1990. *Domination and the Arts of Resistance: Hidden Transcripts.* New Haven: Yale University Press.

Seabright, Paul, ed. 2000. *The Vanishing Rouble: Barter Networks and Non-Monetary Transactions in Post-Soviet Societies.* Cambridge: Cambridge University Press.

Shchepanskaia, T. 1996. "The Body Encoded: Notes on the Folklore of Pregnancy." In *Gender, Generation and Identity in Contemporary Russia.* Edited by H. Pilkington, 264–281. London: Routledge.

Shelkunova, L. 1995. "Shturman v stikhii rynka." *Pravda Buriatii* (Ulan-Ude) (31 May): 2.

Shelley, Louise. 1997. "Post-Soviet Organized Crime: A New Form of Authoritarianism." In *Russian Organized Crime: A New Threat?* Edited by Phil Williams, 122–138. London: Frank Cass.

——. 1996. *Policing Soviet Society: the Evolution of State Control.* London: Routledge.

Shevelev, Mikhail. 1996. "Vstrecha dachi s kottedzhom." *Moskovskie novosti* no. 26: 26.

Shvidkovskii, Dmitrii. 1997. "Moscow Architecture in 1997: Trade, Power, and the 'New Russians.'" *Architectural Association Files* 33 (Summer): 3–12.

——. 1996. *The Empress and the Architect: British Architecture and Gardens at the Court of Catherine the Great.* New Haven: Yale University Press.

Simmel, Georg. 1978 [1907]. *The Philosophy of Money.* Translated by Tom Bottomore and David Frisby. London: Routledge and Kegan Paul.

Sivkova, Veronika. 1997. "Narodnyi kontrol'." *Argumenty i Fakty* no. 25: 2.

Smart, Alan. 1988. "The Informal Regulation of Illegal Economic Activities: Comparisons between the Squatter Property Market and Organized Crime." *International Journal of the Sociology of Law* 16: 91–101.

Sneath, David. 1996. "Mastery and Property: Land, Indigenous Understanding, and the Conceptual Basis of Development Policy in Pastoral Mongolia." Unpublished manuscript.

Solomon, Peter H., Jr. 1996. *Soviet Criminal Justice under Stalin.* Cambridge: Cambridge University Press.

Strathern, Marilyn. 1988. *The Gender of the Gift.* Berkeley: University of California Press.

"Struktura potrebitel'skikh raskhodov rabochikh i sluzhashchikh na chlena sem'i." 1993. *Argumenty i Fakty*, no. 12 (649).

Subbotin, A. 1990. *Pravda Buriatii* (7 October): 2.

Suptelo, A. V. 1997. "Teorii gosudarstvennoi vlasti v otsenke evraziitsev." In *Rossiia i Vostok: istoriia i kul'tura. Materialy IV Mezhdunarodnoi nauchnoi konferentsii, Institut Vostokovedeniia.* Edited by N. A. Tomilov. Omsk: Russian Academy of Sciences.

Szynkiewicz, Slawoj. 1990. "Mythologized Representations in Soviet Thinking on the Nationalities Problem." *Anthropology Today* 6 (2).

Taussig, Michael. 1993. *Mimesis and Alterity: a Particular History of the Senses.* New York: Routledge.

Tsing, Anna Lowenhaupt. 1993. *In the Realm of the Diamond Queen: Marginality in an Out-of-the-Way Place.* Princeton, N.J.: Princeton University Press.

Tulokhonov, A. K., and G.V. Manzanova. 1996. "The Introduction of New Forms of Economy in the Buriat National Region." In *Culture and Environment in Inner Asia.* Volume 1. Edited by Caroline Humphrey and David Sneath, 141–160. Cambridge: White Horse Press.

Turner, Terence. 1992. " 'We Are Parrots, Twins Are Birds' ": Play of Tropes as Operational Structure." In *Beyond Metaphor: The Theory of Tropes in Anthropology.* Edited by James W. Fernandez, 121–158. Stanford, Calif.: Stanford University Press.

Urbanaeva, I. S. 1995. *Chelovek u Baikala i mir Tsentral'noi Azii: filosofiia istorii.* Ulan-Ude: Russian Academy of Sciences, Siberian Branch.

Uskeev, B. 1994. "Ne do zhiru, no . . . zhivem." *Pravda Buriatii* (Ulan-Ude) (22 July): 2.

Vaksberg, Arkadii. 1991. *The Soviet Mafia*. London: Weidenfeld and Nicholson.

Valiuzhenich, G. 1993. "Porog vyzhivaemosti." *Argumenty i Fakty* no. 4: 3.

Varese, Frederico. 1994. "Is Sicily the Future of Russia? Private Protection and the Rise of the Russian Mafia." *European Journal of Sociology* 35: 224–258.

———. 1998. "The Society of the *Vory-v-Zakone*, 1930s–1950s." *Cahiers du Monde Russe* 39 (4): 1–24.

Varoli, John D. 1996. "There Are More 'New Poor' and 'New Russians.'" *Transition* 4 (October): 6–11.

Vengerov, A. B. 1990. *Dialog* (2): 58.

Verdery, Katherine. 1996. *What Was Socialism and What Comes Next?* Princeton, N.J.: Princeton University Press.

———. 1992. *The Transition from Socialism: Anthropology and Eastern Europe*. Lewis Henry Morgan Lectures. University of Rochester. Cambridge: Cambridge University Press.

———. 1991. "Theorizing Socialism: A Prologue to the 'Transition.'" *American Anthropologist* 18 (3): 419–439.

Viatkin, A. R. 1993. "Bezhentsy v Krymu: tadzhikistanskie koreitzy v avangarde agrarnykh preobrazovanii." Unpublished ms.

Visens, E. 1992. "Bezhentsy." *Nezavisimaia gazeta* (1 December).

Voinovich, Vladimir. 1985. *Antisovetskii sovetskii soiuz* [The Anti-Soviet Soviet Union]. Ann Arbor: Ardis.

Volkov, Vadim. 1998. "The monopoly of legitimate violence: diffusion and reconstruction of the Russian state, 1987–2001." Unpublished ms.

Voloshinov, V. N. 1973. *Marxism and the Philosophy of Language*. Translated by Vladislav Matejka and I. R. Titunik. New York: Seminar Press.

Vysokovskii, Aleksandr. 1993. "Will Domesticity Return?" In *Russian Housing in the Modern Age: Design and Social History*. Edited by W. C. Brumfield and B. A. Ruble, 271–308. Cambridge: Cambridge University Press.

Wedel, Janine. 1992. "Introduction." In *The Unplanned Society: Poland during and after Socialism*. Edited by Janine Wedel, 1–20. New York: Columbia University Press.

Weiss, Brad. 1996. *The Making and Unmaking of the Haya Lived World: Consumption, Commoditization and Everyday Practice*. Durham, N.C.: Duke University Press.

Williams, R. 1973. *The Country and the City*. London: Hogarth Press.

Womack, Helen. 1993. "Moscow Expels Traders." *The Times* (13 October): 7.

Woodruff, David. 1999. "Barter of the Bankrupt: The Politics of Demonetization in Russia's Federal State." In *Uncertain Transition: Ethnographies of Change in the Postsocialist World*. Edited by Michael Burawoy and Katherine Verdery, 83–124. Lanham, Md.: Rowman and Littlefield.

Zelizer, Viviana. 1997. *The Social Meaning of Money: Pin Money, Paychecks, Poor Relief, and Other Currencies*. Princeton, N.J.: Princeton University Press.

Zemtsov, Il'ia. 1991. *Encyclopedia of Soviet Life*. New Brunswick and London: Transaction Publishers.

———. 1976. *Partiia ili MaWia: razvorovannaia respublika.* Paris: Les Editeurs Réunis.

Zhukovskaia, N. L. 1997. "The Shaman Is the Context of Rural History and Mythology (Tory Village, Tunka District, Buriat Republic)." *Inner Asia* 2 (1): 90–107.

———. 1996. "Drugaia zhizn' sela Tory." *Rossiiskaia Provintsiia,* 3 (16): 140–144.

———. 1992. "Buddhism and Problems of National and Cultural Resurrection of the Buriat Nation." *Central Asian Survey* 11 (2): 27–41.

Žižek, Slavoj. 1997. "Multinationalism: A new Racism?" *New Left Review* 225: 28–51.

INDEX

collectives and, 22–28
definition of, 21–24
examples of, 33–39
gangs and, 29–31
mythmaking of, 31–33
Domains, 21–39
Domestic Mode of Production, 164–174
leadership and, 174
Dostoevsky, 26, 178
Dry law. *See* Tyva
Dushanbe, 33–39, 47

Eej khad. See Avgai Khad
Entitlements, 26–27
Entrepreneurs, 48–50, 89–90
Estonia, 113

Farming. *See* Collectives
Federal Migration Service, 21, 25, 36, 47
Firms. *See* Corporations; Protection rackets
Firsanovka, 193
Food cards, 7–8
Fraternity. *See* Bratva
Frontiers, 82–85

Gahaichin. See Shuttlers
GAI, 84–85, 144
Gangland, 31
Gangs
bandit gangs, 99–126
Caucasus gangs, 117
and children, 118–119
implosion and expansion of, 117
as protection, 91–92
representations of, 118–121
suzerainties and, 18–19
in Ulan-Ude, 30–31
Gender
Homo Sovieticus and, 178–181
New Russians and, 178–179
Thieves' World and, 105

tributes and, 144
Generaly, 30–31
Georgians
as dispossessed, 37
in gangs, 91–92, 102–103
as New Russians, 177
as traders, 50
Germany, 54–55, 106
Glasnost, 36, 218
Goods Customs Declaration, 134
Gorbachev, 11, 17, 41
Gorbachev period, 29–30, 58. *See also*
Perestroika
Government Customs Committee, 77
Grazhdanskoe Edinstvo, 74
Great Trash Road, 85
Gusinoozersk, 189
Gypsies, 34–37, 177–178

Helsinki, 138
Hierarchical shareholding, 165–170
Homes, 175–201
Homo Sovieticus, 178–181
Household budgets, 50–52
Hunghudze, 30

Icebergs. *See* Suzerainties
Iconography, 194–198
Identity, 175–176, 182–185
Income tax, 47
Irkutsk, 34, 73, 81, 90–93, 102–103
Ivanovno province, 37
Ivolga, 210
Izmailovo Park, 44

KGB, 20, 100
Kalinin Oblast, 76
Kalmyk, 9, 74
Kaluga province, 38
Karategin, 33–34
Karl Marx Collective Farm, 10–12, 19–20

United States, 125–126

Urals, 81

Value-in-life, 57–58

Villas, 175–201. *See also Kottedzh*
  aesthetics of, 194–198
  architecture of, 195–196
  dachas and, 185–189
  expense of, 189–190
  interior design of, 196–198
  locality and, 190–194
  sabotage of, 176
  security and, 192–193

Vlast´, 28–29, 39

Vor, 116. *See also* Gangs; Thieves in law

Voronezh, 37

Vory v zakone. See Thieves in law

Vyborg, 134–137

Vykolachivat´dan´, 143

Vziatka. See Bribery

War of the Bitches, 106–107

"Western" goods, 54–56

Window displays, 45

Work collective. *See* Collectives

Yakutia, 10

Yaroslavl, 189

Yeltsin, 22, 39, 55, 72, 165, 185, 196

Zafimaniry, 199

Zemliachestvo (regional association), 83

Zhirinovsky, Vladimir, 93

Zurich, 43